The Mourning for Diana

Edited by

Tony Walter

Oxford • New York

First published in 1999 by
Berg
Editorial offices:
150 Cowley Road, Oxford, OX4 1JJ, UK
70 Washington Square South, New York, NY 10012, USA

Berg is an imprint of Oxford International Publishers Ltd.

Library of Congress Cataloging-in-Publication Data
A catalog record for this book is available from the Library of Congress.

British Library Cataloguing-in-Publication Data
A catalogue record for this book is available from the British Library.

ISBN   1 85973 233 X (Cloth)
       1 85973 238 0 (Paper)

Typeset by JS Typesetting, Wellingborough, Northants.
Printed and bound in Great Britain by Biddles Ltd, Guildford and King's Lynn

Contents

Contents

List of Illustrations

Notes on Contributors

Marion Bowman is a folklorist and course director of the MA in Contemporary Religions at Bath Spa University College. Her research interests include pilgrimage, vernacular religion, contemporary spiritualities and spiritual aspects of the contemporary Celtic revival.

Jennifer Chandler is a writer specializing in myth and legend, is Books Editor of the Folklore Society, and teaches courses in traditional narrative and popular religion for Extra-Mural Studies, at the University of East Anglia. As Jennifer Westwood, she is author of *Albion: a guide to legendary Britain* (Granada 1985) and *Sacred Journeys: paths for the new pilgrim* (Gaia 1997).

Grace Davie is Senior Lecturer in Sociology at the University of Exeter. Among her books are *Religion in Britain Since 1945* (Blackwell 1994) and *European Religion: a memory mutates* (Oxford University Press, forthcoming).

Christie Davies is Professor of Sociology at the University of Reading and has been a visiting lecturer in India, Poland and the United States. His main research interests are in the sociology of morality and the sociology of humour, his latest books being (with Mark Neal) *The Corporation Under Siege* (Social Affairs Unit 1998) and *Jokes and their Relation to Society* (Mouton de Gruyter 1998).

Douglas Davies is Professor of Theology and Principal of the College of St Hild and St Bede at the University of Durham. His publications include *Death, Ritual and Belief* (Cassell 1997), and he is currently working on Mormonism and on the relation between anthropology and theology.

Mark Davies is senior lecturer in psychology at Nottingham Trent University, following posts at Nottingham University and University College London. His research interests include experimental psychology, fine-grain video analysis of behaviour, and evolutionary processes.

Dell Davis is the social sciences librarian at the M.D. Anderson Library, University of Houston. She specializes in Internet information management and retrieval, and has assisted in the publication of other works in the field of death, dying and bereavement.

Doris Francis is a Visiting Professor and Principal Research Officer at The Centre for Environmental and Social Studies in Ageing, University of North London. She is an anthropologist, holds a diploma in horticulture from the Royal Botanic Gardens, Kew, and is presently engaged in comparative research on mourning behaviour in American cemeteries for a forthcoming volume *Cemetery as Garden*.

Wendy Griffin, Associate Professor of Women's Studies, California State University, Long Beach, is researching the social construction of gender, and is the editor of *Daughters of Gaia: healing and identity in goddess spirituality* (Altamira 1999). In addition to her academic work, she is a community activist, published novelist and performance artist.

C. Allen Haney is a Professor of Sociology on the Central Campus of the University of Houston. His teaching and research are in medical sociology, the sociology of ageing, and the sociology of death, dying and bereavement. He is currently researching the sociology of health and human performance, in particular athletic injuries in the sport of rodeo.

Chris Harris teaches sociology at the University of Wales, Swansea. His previous publications have been in the area of family sociology, economic sociology and the sociology of religion. He is the joint author of a study entitled *The Church in Wales* (University of Wales Press 1999).

Jenny Hockey is a social anthropologist in the School of Comparative and Applied Social Sciences at the University of Hull. She is author of *Experiences of Death* (Edinburgh University Press 1990) and co-editor of *Death, Gender and Ethnicity* (Routledge 1996).

Allison James is Reader in Applied Anthropology in the School of Comparative and Applied Social Sciences at the University of Hull. She is author of *Childhood Identities* (Edinburgh University Press 1993) and co-author of *Theorising Childhood* (Polity Press 1998).

Bethan Jones is doing a PhD in the Sociology Dept at the University of Reading. She is researching afterlife beliefs in modern Britain.

Leonie Kellaher is Director of The Centre for Environmental and Social Studies in Ageing at the University of North London.

Jenny Kitzinger works at the Media Research Unit at Glasgow University. She is co-author of *The Mass Media and Power in Modern Britain* (Oxford University Press 1997) and *The Circuit of Mass Communication* (Sage 1998).

Tom Laidlaw recently retired as a Commander in the Metropolitan Police, where much of his career was concerned primarily with public order policing. He now acts as a consultant and has recently completed a MSc in Risk, Crisis and Disaster Management at the Scarman Centre for the Study of Public Order at the University of Leicester.

David Martin is Emeritus Professor of Sociology at the London School of Economics and Honorary Professor in the Department of Religious Studies, University of Lancaster. His most recent books are *Does Christianity Cause War?* (Oxford University Press 1997) and (with Bernice Martin) *Betterment From On High: the life worlds of Pentecostals in Brazil and Chile* (Oxford University Press 1999).

Georgina Neophytou conducted the study of Greek Orthodox Cemeteries for the University of North London 'Landscape as Garden' project. She is a doctoral candidate in Sociology at the London School of Economics.

Tina Ramkalawan works in the Department of Primary Care and Population Sciences at the Royal Free and UCL Medical School, London, having previously lectured in psychology at Nottingham Trent University. Her research interests include health and the development of cognitive processes.

Anne Rowbottom is Lecturer at the Centre for Human Communication at Manchester Metropolitan University, and researches popular royalism.

Mark Shevlin completed his D.Phil. at the University of Ulster at Jordanstown. After lecturing in psychology at Nottingham Trent University, he now lectures at Magee College, University of Ulster. His research interests include the application of structural equation modelling, psychometrics and individual differences.

P.A.J. Waddington is Professor of Political Sociology at the University of Reading. He has written and researched extensively on policing, especially public order issues. His books include *Liberty and Order: Public Order*

Policing in a Capital City (UCL Press 1994) and *Policing Citizens* (UCL Press 1999).

Stephanie Walker lectures at Nottingham Trent University. Her research interests include experimental psychology, the cognitive processes involved in face recognition, and neural network modelling.

Tony Walter is Reader in Sociology and director of the MA in Death and Society at the University of Reading. He has written *Funerals and How to Improve Them* (Hodder 1990), *The Revival of Death* (Routledge 1994), *The Eclipse of Eternity* (Macmillan 1996) and *On Bereavement* (Open University Press, forthcoming), and edited (with Ian Reader) *Pilgrimage in Popular Culture* (Macmillan 1993).

John Wolffe is Senior Lecturer and Head of the Department of Religious Studies at the Open University. He is the author of *The Protestant Crusade in Great Britain 1829–1860* (Oxford, 1991) and *God and Greater Britain: Religion and National Life in Britain and Ireland, 1843–1945* (London 1994). He is currently writing a book on responses to prominent deaths in Victorian and Edwardian Britain.

Preface

Many books have been written about both the life and the death of Diana, Princess of Wales, including a rapidly increasing number of scholarly works. This book documents the public response in the week following her death. A number of the contributors share my own research interests in death and religion, and the reader will find more on these topics than on the media or politics. Apart from Chapter 4, which expands an earlier article, none of the chapters has been published before.

Though the response to Diana's death was hailed by many as unique and unprecedented, it was not; it was rather the latest episode of a centuries-long ever-evolving folk response to the news of tragic death, a response increasingly influenced by the mass media. But since such episodes occur infrequently, popular memory of the last episode may be weak, leading to the impression of *this* response being unprecedented. In order to understand this evolving tradition, it is important that each new episode be accurately recorded and intelligently discussed. That is what this book sets out to do, using the tools of the social sciences, in particular those of ethnography, anthropology, sociology, history, folklore, psychology, religious studies, media studies and gender studies. Several contributors make sense of events by placing them in an appropriate social or historical context, re-presenting as normal and comprehensible what at the time seemed abnormal and incomprehensible.

Death typically shatters the social fabric, which has to be repaired – through ritual, through conversation, through negotiating new roles. Death therefore provides a natural experiment in how a society constructs order in the face of disorder and anomie. This was particularly so with the death of Diana. Its unexpectedness and the ambiguity of her social position created for a few days an unusual situation: a vacuum in which the normal power-brokers were taken off guard and temporarily disabled, leaving a free space for popular action to flex its muscles, something more than normal post-mortem liminality. Several chapters show how – through the media, through acts of popular devotion, through policing, through irreverent joking – the social order was rapidly put together again. The final chapter asks whether what was put back was any different from what existed before.

Part 1

Introduction

1

The Week of Mourning

Douglas Davies

Diana, Princess of Wales, died in the early hours of Sunday, 31 August 1997. Sixteen years previously, she had fulfilled the romantic ideal of youthful bride when she married the heir to the British throne, Charles, Prince of Wales; she became the most photographed of all celebrities, and her marital troubles and eventual divorce were conducted in ablaze of media publicity. Many anticipated a new marriage because Diana spent part of the summer with Dodi Al Fayed, whose controversial Egyptian father, Mohammed, owned London's famous Harrods store but remained largely unaccepted by the British establishment. On the fateful night, Diana and Dodi dined at the Paris Ritz, itself a Fayed hotel, and then left at speed trying to avoid press photographers who pursued on motorcycles. Tragically, the chauffeur driven Mercedes sped through the city and, for whatever reason, crashed into a pillar in an underpass. Diana, Dodi and the driver were killed. The bodyguard alone survived.

Diana's death led, throughout the United Kingdom, to a most extensive and dramatic public response, with acts of tribute and memorial throughout the following week until, and indeed continuing after, the public funeral service at Westminster Abbey and a private interment on Saturday, 6 September. Not only did hundreds of thousands visit Kensington Palace in London to place flowers and sign books of remembrance, but so did many hundreds of thousands more throughout the British Isles and in embassies abroad. Diana's death led to more newsprint, and her funeral to a bigger global television audience, than had any previous event. This introductory chapter[1] sets the public response to Diana's death (which collectively I term 'the Diana event') into an appropriate social scientific classification of social action, describes crucial elements in the public events surrounding the death and funeral and, finally, suggests some theoretical approaches for its analysis.

---

1. An early draft of this chapter was delivered at a day seminar 'Dodens Dager og Dodens Steder' at the Diakonhjemmets Hogskolesenter, Oslo on 31 October 1997.

Framework and Classification

The Diana event is not unique, at least not in type even though maybe in extent. It belongs to a distinctive type of human activity. The family resemblance of popular responses constituting this type involves extremely large numbers of people acting in an unexpected and unrehearsed fashion in relation to a triggering event – focused in tragedy and resulting in death – which touches the depth of human sentiment and social morality and which may involve a perceived inadequacy of official action on behalf of public authorities.

The category of events into which the Diana event may be placed include the death in childbirth of Princess Charlotte and her baby in 1817 (second and third in line to the throne respectively, see Chapter 3); the sinking of the *Titanic* (1912); the unveiling of the Cenotaph in Whitehall on Armistice Day 1920 (Cannadine 1981: 223–4); the assassination of President John F. Kennedy (1963); the explosion of the Challenger space shuttle live on television, killing all its crew including a teacher who, like Diana, was in her thirties and a mother of two (1986); the Hillsborough soccer stadium disaster (1989); and the Estonia ferry disaster in Sweden (1994). Slightly less obvious are the White March in Belgium of 1996, and the pop-music Live Aid Concert organized by Bob Geldof in 1984.

To summarize some of the more recent of these events. At the Hillsborough soccer stadium, ninety-six Liverpool supporters were crushed to death while the match (a semi-final) was being televised live. The following day thousands came to visit the team's home stadium at Anfield and it is reckoned that by the end of a week a million people had passed through the football ground. Additional religious services took place alongside mass tributes of flowers, scarves and other objects left by fans (Walter 1991). The Estonia disaster, in which a ferry sank with the loss of over 900 lives, touched very many Swedish communities and prompted a popular reaction involving informal and more formal events in which Swedes lit candles and engaged in acts of commemoration. With conventional media and political discourse failing, Swedish Church leaders were much involved. The White March in Belgium involved many thousands of individuals gathering together in mass response to a series of paedophile murders and an apparent high-level political cover-up.

For the moment I want to highlight the *Titanic* and its sinking. In that pre-television era, it fell to newspapers to report it, and they did so in stories of bravery and unity, as rich and poor stood side by side as the ship went down. *The Times* (20 April 1912, p. 9) tells how 'men of all classes stood shoulder to shoulder in the hour of their supreme agony.' The Lord Mayor of London opened an appeal and money poured in. We are also told that 'the pity of all people was poured out in another way – in prayer and solemn memorial services for those who were lost.' A memorial service for the sinking of the *Titanic* took place at St Paul's Cathedral, London on 19 April 1912; many thousands were unable to get into the church. *The Times* reports that

> the great doors were closed an hour before the service. The cathedral was full and many were left outside. It was a vast, black multitude . . . People of rank and wealth, these city clerks and shop-keepers, and slum dwellers had come together into the quiet sanctuary, not in any formal spirit, but in a comradeship of grief, greater than the small conventions of life.

There were many people weeping during the playing of the 'Dead March' from Saul. The music of the drums was awe-inspiring. There were soldiers and sailors who had heard it play for dead comrades, 'and they, too, stood erect, with tears streaming down their faces, not ashamed of tears. It may be said in all sincerity that the hearts of all these people were stirred to their uttermost depths by thoughts deeper than may be put into words.' A similar great service was held in the Catholic Westminster Cathedral. We are even told that the figure of Nelson in Trafalgar Square looked down on 'those who knelt below his monument' (Gibbs, no date: 26–8).

The Diana event was therefore one of a type, and yet – like each of its predecessors – had its own distinctiveness. The response to her death is the latest episode of an evolving folk tradition, partly Western, partly Anglophone, partly British, and the prime purpose of this book is to document this episode: to record the ways in which the Diana event participated in this folk tradition, to identify the ways in which it was innovative. What is needed is an intelligent record and interpretation of what happened, so that at the next death of this kind commentators can know what is new, and what is the same, compared with Diana's death back in 1997 and compared with other such events. Only thus can this particular category of social action be understood.

The Diana Event

The Diana event was, primarily, a media event – but with a difference. The difference consisted of two elements: the active and practical participation of millions of people on the one hand, and the idea that the media were, perhaps, responsible for the death on the other. Theirs was an unusual dual role, reporting on something for which many thought them responsible, at least to some degree. Theirs was a process of self-analysis alongside their normal activity of reporting. One aspect of this ambiguous position, one that perhaps made their situation easier, lay in the constant use of interviews with and comments from the public.

As far as many amongst the British public were concerned the event began as a media story before becoming part of their own behaviour in a group sense. In the early hours of the Sunday morning there was a news item that Diana had been in a car crash in Paris, this rapidly passing into news that she was dead. The story was intrinsically connected with the idea of a car chase in which the word 'paparazzi' rapidly, for the first time, became part of everyday English. These were the bad men, the freelance photographers who sell their pictures to the press, who had caused the accident and killed Diana. The moral argument seemed clear; there was a focus of blame. Already her media life was explicit.

At breakfast time on the television the recently elected Labour Prime Minister, Tony Blair, was interviewed on his way to church as part of his own Sunday morning activity in the North of England. The interview was solemn and emotional, and could readily be accepted as personal and not political, except in the sense that he was speaking for the nation, and spoke words of astonishment and of shock. His use in this interview of the phrase 'the people's princess' (borrowed from writer Julie Burchill) was prophetic of events to come in the week ahead.

In another Sunday morning journey to church the spotlight fell upon the Royal Family. They were going to church by car whilst on holiday at their Balmoral estate in Scotland. This rural area is very far removed from London geographically and, in terms of social geography too, is not in the mainstream of social life as far as urban Britons are concerned. To the astonishment of some, Diana's children, William (15) and Harry (13), went to church with the rest of the family. It was reported that there were no special prayers for Diana or any recognition of her death at that ordinary Sunday morning service. By contrast, in practically every other British church that day special mention was made of the death and of the family's bereavement.

There now existed a strange lack of focus. Diana was dead in France, the Royal Family was in Scotland, while the British people focused their attention on what we might call empty buildings in London, and on two palaces in particular. One was Kensington Palace, where Diana lived and the other Buckingham Palace, the Queen's London residence. On the same day (Sunday) Charles, Prince of Wales along with his ex-wife's two sisters went to France to bring the body home. That was televised. In a highly and oddly symbolic way the plane returned while a special service from St Paul's Cathedral was being broadcast (see Chapter 12). The television producer can hardly ever have been as alert as when pictures of the arrival of the coffin were merged with the sound of the service playing behind it. It could not have been better arranged if it had taken months to plan.

This sense of immediacy added an authenticity to the medium of television at that moment. Meanwhile other television and radio commentary moved from one mode to another. Early in the day reporters spoke like ordinary people. They too were shocked, their words unscripted. Unusually they were dealing with an unexpected event of considerable magnitude. But, as the day proceeded an increasing, though slight, degree of journalistic observation emerged, even though comment continued to be restricted. Old television footage of Diana was replayed, especially that which portrayed the compassionate dimensions of her complex character; a documentary about her campaign against landmines was shown on the Sunday evening, viewed by many who had shown no particular interest in its first showing earlier in the year. People were being constantly interviewed, largely in London. That the death occurred early on a Sunday meant that most people were off work, able to watch the television all day; the death came too late for the Sunday papers. Consequently, television rather than print media set the agenda for the days to come, and people were most likely to share the news and their immediate reactions with family rather than with friends or workmates. In North America, where the news broke on the Saturday evening, it was very differently mediated.[2]

People were now beginning to place tributes at Kensington Palace. Over the next few days these grew to an immense flow of people with flowers and gifts at increasingly large sites, not only in London but across the country. Town halls and other municipal buildings, cathedrals, churches, war memorials and supermarkets were the most common locations. A distinctive feature was the use of books of remembrance (see Chapter 13). One was opened at St James's Palace in London and was followed by many in other parts of the country. At St James's and Kensington Palaces, the queues to sign the books stretched for hours, and eventually the number of books was expanded considerably. The actual number of books nationwide and worldwide is unknown. Some were bound and sent to Althorp in Northamptonshire, Diana's ancestral family home; others remained in their town of origin. This being the age of the Internet, condolences were also sent via cyberspace, many from North America. In the first two weeks, the Royal Web Site alone received 600,000 condolences, and 35 million visits (*Diana – the Week the World Stood Still*, 31 December 1997, ITV), a considerable

---

2. Compare the death of John Kennedy during the day on a Friday, leading to a weekend dominated by television; the funeral was on the Monday. For those who heard the news at work, radio was more important in the first instance (Greenberg & Parker 1964).

increase on the 150,000 plus condolence messages posted in the first two weeks to friends and family following the disappearance in 1996 of TWA Flight 800 (Sofka 1997).

But it was the use of flowers that emerged as the key feature in the British response (see Chapters 8, 9 and 10). Millions of people across the country brought and placed them along with very personal messages written on attached cards (Figures 1.1, 1.2, 1.3). Some resembled ordinary funeral wreaths, others expressed sadness or personal sympathy, most remained in their wrappers. A single flower with a message laid in London by the Monday read 'Beautiful Lady, Rest in Peace, With love, Sam (A homeless friend).' Some linked Diana with Dodi Al Fayed, her current companion and host in the fateful car journey, saying things like, 'now you are together for ever'. The media again and again referred to an 'outpouring of grief' from 'the people'.

As the week progressed comment on Diana and the Royal Family became central, as did news about a possible drunken driver. Blame for the accident now sat less easily on the paparazzi. Strong feelings were expressed in the newspapers that the Royal Family was still in its Scottish hideaway and not in London. It was no secret that Charles's ex-wife had not got on well with her in-laws, who for several days kept well out of camera's way. Calls were made in the tabloid press for the Queen to come to London and 'lead the nation's grief' and to 'show us you care'. In fact the Queen then came to London a day earlier than planned and walked around amongst the crowds. She also gave an unprecedented live television message to the nation, which was reported as doing much to placate the increasingly hostile (but always royalist) populace.

One highly symbolic event concerned Buckingham Palace and the flying of a flag. By tradition the Royal Standard flies above the palace when the Monarch is in residence; when she is not in residence, no flag flies. The Royal Standard is not taken down at the death of a monarch, or even flown at half-mast, for the next monarch lives. By mid-week, the tabloids reported that the crowds were calling for the Palace to abandon its 'stuffy' protocol and fly the Union Jack, and at half-mast. The requested flag was subsequently seen flying above the palace and was actually lowered to half-mast on the Saturday as the funeral cortege passed the Palace. Here, in fact, was the invention of a new tradition, a public way of the people visibly seeing the Royal Family acknowledge both the Princess and public opinion.

Figure 1.1 Kensington Palace Main Gate, Tuesday, 2 September. *Doris Francis*

Figure 1.2 Kensington Palace Main Gate, Saturday, 6 September. *Doris Francis*

Figure 1.3 Kensington Palace Main Gate, Thursday, 11 September. By week 2, there were more tourists than pilgrims. *Tony Walter*

The Funeral

The funeral service followed on the Saturday (Chapter 12). As announced on the Thursday by the Dean of Westminster Abbey at a press conference, it consisted of three parts: 1) the procession in the street for the public; 2) the service in the Abbey for a royal personage, and technically a combined funeral and memorial service; 3) the private burial at Althorp, the Spencer family estate, for the family. Hence, each of these three groups 'owned' different parts of the funeral.

The Abbey service was traditionally Anglican in form, with fine singing by the Abbey choir, yet was also extraordinary in several respects. Representatives of the charities Diana sponsored were there, also film stars, but relatively few politicians. Her sisters read items of poetry, the Prime Minister read 1 Corinthians Chapter 13 and Elton John sang 'Candle in the Wind', originally composed about Marilyn Monroe (who also died aged thirty-six) and now adapted for Diana. In some respects, though, the service was not a novelty. Many British funerals and memorial services now include some secular or popular music and readings, a choice of the family or the favourite of the dead person, and a eulogy in place of a sermon.

Then when her brother, Earl Spencer gave his speech he spoke largely in the second person singular as though talking to Diana. She was made to be present. He ended by speaking about her and to the world at large. He spoke against the media, he spoke of the blood-family and not of the Royal Family. He spoke of the importance of tradition but of the need for the boy princes to experience more of the world at large. The speech was brilliantly written and delivered. As it ended the masses of people in Hyde Park and outside the Abbey, who were watching the service on screens, began to applaud. That applause then flowed into the Abbey where the congregation too applauded. The sound of clapping united those inside and those outside the Abbey. There is some evidence to suggest that this particular applause was, significantly, enhanced in a moment when those sitting outside were shown a picture – on the big screen – of themselves as a crowd. At which point very many stood and increased the volume of applause significantly; applause that was then heard and echoed within the Abbey. This reflexive appreciation indicates something of the presence and role of the television on that day (Chapter 4).

After the service the coffin was taken on its long drive through the London suburbs and out into the country. Unusually for a funeral, there were no following cars, just a police motorcycle escort; the family travelled to Althorp by train. The car carrying the coffin was met by further applause from the crowds lined for miles along the way, even standing (unprecedentedly) on

Figure 1.4 The funeral cortège passes Junction 9 on the M1 motorway on its way north to Althorp. Crowds move onto the northbound carriageway to watch and clap; cars park on the fast lane on the southbound carriageway, their occupants getting out to watch. *Gavin Fuller*

the slow lane of the empty M1 motorway (Figures 1.4, 1.5). The police presence was minimal, and there was a sense that this was 'the people' escorting 'their' princess to her burial. And another tradition was born, for now flowers were thrown in front of the car and, after some apparently landed accidentally on the hearse, people increasingly aimed their floral tributes to land on the car. At one point the driver had to stop to clear the windscreen to see where he was going.

And so she was taken to the family estates and buried on a small island in a lake quite outside the gaze of public view. There were no cameras, just as in the Abbey there was no showing of the Royal Family. For a Princess haunted by publicity, her final public appearance ended in the most profoundly symbolic privacy of an island on a private estate.

In many cities, towns and villages services were held. Religious and civic leaders, along with representatives of charities, united to express their sadness and to affirm aspects of Diana's life which are morally applauded, not least her charity work for children, for AIDS, leprosy and landmine victims. Shared emotions continued and were reinforced through these events. Huge numbers of people, having watched the funeral on television on the Saturday, went to the royal palaces in London the next day (both days enjoying exceptionally fine weather), and for the next two weeks crowds – including many tourists – continued to visit the royal sites to view the flowers. During this period, the massed flowers outside Kensington Palace became the country's biggest tourist attraction (Figure 1.3).

Theoretical Analysis

In the remainder of this chapter we begin to interpret these varied events by means of three anthropological perspectives drawn from Victor Turner, Maurice Bloch and Emile Durkheim. These have been selected from among other possible social scientific theories because they allow sharp focus to fall, respectively, on the crucial phenomena of monarchy and the people, of the dynamic energy generated by a funeral, and of the wider sense of society as a moral community. Such a strong commitment to the social significance of ritual events also demands firm acknowledgement of the particular historical flow of a culture into which the new events surge.

With that in mind we agree, for example, with the historian David Cannadine (1983) in stressing the importance of interpreting royal ceremonial in Britain against the background of social life. The death of Diana is no exception. Amongst the most important of those backgrounds was the 1997 General Election in which the long-standing Conservative Government was removed by an extremely large majority of socialists (though not, given the British 'first past the post' voting system, a majority of the voters). Key phrases accompanying the election included 'the people' and 'the voice of the people'. The new and young Prime Minister symbolized this dramatic change and, as already mentioned, he played the first major public visual role on the day of Diana's death as he was interviewed on his way to church for an ordinary Sunday service, speaking of 'the people's princess'. He spoke in an emotional way more as a person than as Prime Minister, reappearing to read the lesson at the Funeral Service.

So it was that the phrase 'the people' came into extensive use throughout the funeral week. It was 'the people' who wanted the Queen to appear, and so on. The British started talking about themselves as a collectivity just as so many also acted in a uniform way. Crowds and massed action visibly portrayed 'the people'. Those who did not wish to join in the national mourning felt that they had better, for this week at least, put up and shut up. The British habit of forming a queue also came into its own as people made very long queues over many hours to sign books of remembrance. It was a kind of sacralizing of queuing.

Status and Equality in Emotion

These crowds and queues allow us to raise a theoretical issue, drawn from the anthropology of Victor Turner (1977), concerning hierarchy, liminality, and communitas. In Turner's view, rituals – especially rites of passage – entail a liminal (or in-between) period in which everyday order is reversed, social hierarchy is abandoned, and ritual participants bound together in a temporary common experience which he terms 'communitas'. Diana's death clearly triggered a kind of liminal period, beginning with the death and ending with the funeral (or rather, the day after the funeral, given the numbers who spent that Sunday revisiting the funeral route). In addition, there was a liminality of the media (Couldry 1999). Their normal structure, function and planning had been thrown at just the time when the emotional response of many people was strong yet open for direction.

We might, perhaps, interpret the people's sense of communitas as being contradicted by the Royal Family which remained in its state of hierarchy. It was reported through the media that many felt that the immediate Royal Family were maintaining themselves aloof from the nation, not only in expression of sentiment but also in the geographical fact of their remaining at their Scottish estate of Balmoral. Here we could interpret the evidence in terms of a clear dissonance between the popular masses and their sense of communitas and the retained hierarchy of the Royals. Symbolically speaking, it was only when the Royal Family returned to London, earlier than originally planned, and walked about amongst the crowds and before the media cameras, that a sense of the propriety of the circumstance emerged and a sense of sympathy grew. The Queen even gave a special message on the television. Contextually this, too, is interesting in that the only other recognized time when she does this is at another liminal occasion: Christmas. And that Christmas Message of the Queen is, itself, traditionally set in the more communal and less hierarchical frame of domestic Christmas festivities.

But, returning to that phrase, 'outpouring of grief' as a media and popular description, what does it say about the sense of grief, or 'new grief' as some called it? For the most part I think the emotional response can be seen as an aspect of communitas in relation to a negative social sentiment. It is reminiscent of the Live Aid Concert of 1984 in which millions united in sympathy for the drought victims of the world. Bob Geldof's autobiography (1986) spoke of the total sense of unity and emotionality at that time when millions around the world were united through the televising of the concert from Wembley Arena. That was a positive emotion, the opposite of the Diana scenario.

Death's Conquest

Another possible theoretical perspective can be drawn from the anthropology of Maurice Bloch (1992) and his idea of rebounding vitality. Bloch's disarmingly powerful thesis is that nature begins with life and ends in death, but culture begins with death and turns it into a life-affirming event. I have explored and developed his ideas elsewhere (Davies 1997): a negative experience is transformed into a positive life-affirming value, often through rituals of initiation, including death rites.

There are signs of this in the Diana event. The idea of new grief was, in some ways, associated with the hope that people would adopt a new attitude of care towards others as a reflection of Diana's charitable work. The media might, perhaps, become more responsible, reducing the market for photographs produced by a predatory paparazzi. Perhaps the Royal Family would become less set-apart and more united with the people. Perhaps her work for landmine removal would gain an added impetus. In other words the negative feature of death would yield a positive result, and the popular ritual of being a crowd, of queuing and placing memorials would be part of that transformation.

The morally positive features of her life were strongly reinforced by the death, the day before Diana's funeral, of Mother Teresa of Calcutta, widely acclaimed for her saintly life. Through media images these events were linked. The two women had met, both had interests in suffering people, and each added some value to the other by a kind of mutual exchange of attributes. The *Express and Star* announced on Saturday 6 September, 'Mother Teresa is dead, it's lovely to think she's with Diana.'

The death of Mother Teresa made it symbolically possible for the positive values of care and concern for the poor and underprivileged to be still further accentuated in Diana's life, already begun with television coverage the day of Diana's death. Similarly the high level of emotional arousal at Diana's death furnished a frame for Mother Teresa. Both had high-profile funerals that were symbolically odd. That of the Princess of Wales was not, officially and technically, an event of national mourning, despite her status as mother of princes, while the poor and childless nun was accorded a state funeral. In India, there were reports of popular religious responses investing the Princess with a degree of divine status.

But it is in the figure of the two young Princes that the rebounding conquest element might be most clear. The fact that William looks so much like his mother might even be significant here. The more negative emotion engendered by Diana's death will, on this theory, rebound to the advance of her son when he becomes king. Her funeral rebounds in his coronation. In this sense the popular feeling of the Diana event will serve as a social force in validating and empowering her offspring. On this reading Prince Charles becomes a problematic figure, perhaps even a caretaker monarch, certainly one whose status has been dramatically changed through Diana's death.

At a different level there exists another symbolic expression of rebounding vitality. The millions of flowers placed in memorial were not thrown away. As symbols they were so powerful they could not simply be discarded. Flowers placed in London were eventually composted, turned into fertiliser to be used in a new garden of remembrance. Similarly at the Althorp Estate. In other words flowers that marked a death would become the basis for life. Other flowers were given to hospitals or old people's homes. We may compare some of the Anfield flowers which were ritually thrown into the River Mersey (Walter 1991). Rather like the symbolic elements of bread and wine remaining after the Christian Eucharist, these flowers of mourning were too invested with symbolic significance to be merely thrown away, and had to be ritually consumed.

Both communitas and rebounding conquest motifs raise existential issues within sociology. And it is these existential issues involved with social values that characterize the category of events into which Diana's death needs to be placed. This category, mentioned at the outset, draws fundamentally from a Durkheimian analysis of society as a moral body (Durkheim 1915). The death of what can be regarded a social symbol involves a challenge to society; it is what I have called the death of a microcosm (Davies 1997: 11). There is a sense in which the paedophilic murders in Belgium triggered the mass social response of the White March precisely because of the belief that persons in positions of authority, those who should be the guardians of morality, had failed, and had, perhaps, even been implicated. By contrast, it was the death of millions, brought to focus by Bob Geldof in his Live Aid Concert of 1984 which united human action focused in a sentiment of sympathy with the victims of starvation in Ethiopia (Ignatieff 1985), an event also involving a degree of antagonism towards and a public altercation with the then Prime Minister, Mrs Thatcher. Interpreted through the notion of communitas, it marked the drop in the sense of hierarchy and distinctions between people and the emergence of a sense of unity of purpose and feeling. Geldof (1986) emphasized the oneness of the performers with the world at large. Whether the long-term implications of Diana's death will, in fact, prove so positive, is discussed in the final chapter.

Displaying the Moral Sentiment

The Diana event prompted existential responses to challenges of the established and current social order. Within the Durkheimian tradition they may be seen as mass moral movements in response to a cause which, if left untreated, might be anomic. The degree of response matches the extent of the triggering cause and the degree to which moral issues are revealed. The sinking of the *Titanic* marked the demise of a symbol of British engineering and industrial supremacy. Claims of empire might also have been involved, and certainly there was a degree of star quality to many of the first-class voyagers.

The central element in all these cases involves the loss of a highly charged symbol of social meaning. In Victor Turner's grammar of symbolism, Diana was a condensed symbol of love, divorce, fragmented families, stardom and failure, beauty and eating disorders, also of marginalized groups of AIDS, leprosy, and landmine victims. She also had the charisma that only certain royals have: an undoubted regality that sets apart, along with the ability to connect with ordinary people through touch and look. Through her, the ordinary subject could connect symbolically to society itself. Those who actually met and touched her, could connect physically.

This may have been particularly important in the period when the British premier, Margaret Thatcher, stated that 'there is no such thing as society' and when social and economic policy was made on precisely this negative premise. In so far as Thatcherism spread to many other countries in this period, it forms a global as much as a national context to Diana's life and death (Walter 1998). The popular designation of a royal personage as a symbolic connection with society at precisely the time when the nature of that society was in doubt prompts comparison with Belgium's King Baudouin. His Diana-like charisma was important at a time when the two halves of Belgium were threatening to split apart; like Diana, his unexpected death in 1993 prompted massive public grief. The political implications of Diana's life and good works will remain contentious, but what is clear is that her sixteen years as Princess coincided closely with the eighteen years of Conservative government of Margaret Thatcher and her successor John Major, and her death – and the response to it – occurred in the year that his government was voted out of power. Diana was inextricably bound up with the changing symbolic fortunes of the individual and the collectivity in that period.[3]

---

3. For further discussion of this, see *New Formations*, special issue on 'Diana and Democracy', 1999.

Bibliography

Bloch, M. (1992) *Prey into Hunter*, Cambridge: Cambridge University Press.

Cannadine, D. (1981) 'War and Death, Grief and Mourning in Modern Britain', in J. Whaley (ed.), *Mirrors of Mortality: Studies in the Social History of Death*, London: Europa.

—— (1983) 'The Context, Performance and Meaning of Ritual: the British Monarchy and the "Invention of Tradition"' in E. Hobsbawm & T. Ranger (eds), *The Invention of Tradition*, Cambridge: Cambridge University Press.

Couldry, N. (1999) 'The Geography of Celebrity and the Politics of Lack', *New Formations*.

Davies, D. (1997) *Death, Ritual and Belief*, London: Cassell.

Durkheim, E. (1915) *The Elementary Forms of the Religious Life*, London: Unwin.

Geldof, B. (1986) *Is That It?*, London: Sidgwick & Jackson.

Gibbs, P. (no date) *The Deathless Story of the Titanic*, reprint of Lloyd's Weekly News.

Greenberg, B.S. & Parker, E.B. (eds) (1964) *The Kennedy Assassination and the American Public: Social Communication in Crisis*, Stanford: Stanford University Press.

Ignatieff, M. (1985) 'Is Nothing Sacred? the ethics of television', *Daedalus* 114(4): 57–78.

Sofka, C.J. (1997) 'Social Support "Internetworks", Caskets for Sale, and More: thanatology and the information superhighway', *Death Studies*, 21(6): 553–74.

Turner, V. (1977) *The Ritual Process*, Ithaca: Cornell University Press.

Walter, T. (1991) 'The Mourning after Hillsborough', *Sociological Review*, 39(3): 599–625.

—— (1998) 'Diana, Queen of Hearts: Mourning and Social Solidarity' in C. Sugden (ed.), *Death of a Princess: making sense of a nation's grief*, London: Silver Fish Publishing.

2

The Questions People Asked

Tony Walter

Early September 1997 was one of those rare occasions when lay people and social scientists pondered the same questions. Even my mother, who had hitherto never understood what sociology was about, began – at the age of eighty-six – asking the same questions that scholars were asking: had the British suddenly changed their character? why such grief for someone relatively few had actually met? was it crowd hysteria, or media manipulation? what on earth was going on? The everyday world had been rendered strange, not only for social scientists who regularly use this as a device to aid research, but for every man and woman. People we thought we knew were acting strangely, and everyone – including those who were acting strangely – wanted to know why.

In this chapter, I discuss some of the questions lay people and commentators were asking, before sketching the responses of academics. In so doing, I indicate the ways in this present book contributes to the debate and to scholarship.[1]

People power or media manipulation?

In a perceptive article published in the immediate aftermath of Diana's death, Michael Ignatieff (1997) argued that it caught everyone by surprise, leaving major institutions without a game plan. Throughout the twentieth century there have been detailed contingency plans for the funerals of all leading members of the Royal Family (Bland 1986), but the recent exit of Diana from that family and her ambiguous status meant that no such plan existed for her untimely demise (see for example Chapter 11). Three great families –

1. I am grateful to Nick Couldry, Jude Davies and Deborah Steinberg for providing material at short notice, and to Rosalind Brunt, Sally Macintyre and Gordon Riches for their comments while preparing this chapter. None of these, of course, are in any way responsible for the analysis that follows.

the Windsors, the Spencers and the Fayeds – duelled with each other for ownership of her remains and of her memory. Both the monarchy and the press found themselves under intense criticism. Into this vacuum of power stepped 'the people' who, for a few days, sensed that 'they – and not the families and the institutions – would shape the rituals of their princess's passing'. Such moments make revolutions, and certainly it was the only time in my lifetime that I could *feel* how revolutions happen. A revolution did not occur, and had there been one it would have been a feudal 'Out with the Windsors! In with the Spencers!' in which one aristocratic house takes over the throne from another. Nevertheless 'the people' sensed that it was they, and they alone, who forced the royals to come down to London a day early, they who made it necessary for the Queen to make her speech, they who made the funeral a people's event. Whether or not it was a proto-revolutionary crowd, it was certainly a grieving crowd 'restoring itself in a process of mourning what it perceives to be a real loss' (Grace 1997: 2), and its power to determine how it would do this was evident. Even dissidents recognized the power of the people, objecting to the 'feeling fascism' that forced into silence those whose response to Diana's death was not that of 'the people'.

On the other hand, critics have suggested that 'the people' were crudely manipulated by the media, notably by television and the tabloids. The tabloids, immediately attacked for causing Diana's death, needed to rehabilitate themselves. They did this in a number of ways. First, they ran the story that the driver was drunk, thus absolving the paparazzi of significant responsibility. Second, as the week progressed, the main news story became not the Princess's death but the public response to her death, which was thereby amplified as more and more people decided to join in the mourning portrayed in the media pictures that saturated the week. Third, this enabled the press to point the finger at the Royal Family, holed up in Balmoral Castle, for being out of touch with 'the people' (unlike the Princess, who had clearly been very much in touch with them). By Wednesday and Thursday, it was the royals, not the press, who had become the villains. Thus let off the hook, the press were willing to rehabilitate the Royal Family once they had come to London, mingled with the crowds, and shown that they 'cared'. Meanwhile, the BBC was one of the few institutions that actually had contingency plans for covering Diana's accidental death (Ghosh 1997); BBC television coverage on the day of the death was particularly influential in creating the idealized image of Diana the caring humanitarian. Some commentators, for example Merrin (1999), have argued an even stronger thesis: Diana was herself no more than a media image, and the mourning and the funeral were likewise no more than a media event (cf. Dayan and Katz 1985, 1992).

So which was it? Did the British people, still constitutionally the Queen's subjects, turn themselves into citizens to whom the Monarch became – for a few days – responsible? Or did 'the people' in September 1997 simply become the media's subjects, subjected by the media into feeling compassion and anger in the directions chosen by the media in their own self-interest?

There certainly is evidence that the media influenced people's reactions. Television programmes on the day she died portrayed her in flattering terms, focusing in particular on her charitable work, her involvement in the campaign against landmines, her role as a mother and her common touch with 'the people'. The satirical magazine *Private Eye* compared the at best ambivalent, at worst downright hostile, reporting of Diana in newspapers appearing that weekend but printed before her death with the same newspapers on Monday eulogising her. The thousands who subsequently paid respect to, as one floral message at Kensington put it, 'Diana, the patron saint of love' (Figure 9.6), may well have picked up this kind of positive image from the Sunday television and subsequent newspaper eulogies.

The kind of things ordinary people said about Diana when interviewed by the media largely reflected the other things other people had been reported saying about her. There was little in the way of personally recollected memories of her, because the majority of mourners had never actually met her, and only knew her through the media. 'The people's' memories of Diana were therefore largely other people's memories, recycled through interview after interview (Brunt 1997).

Whether this is media manipulation, however, is debatable. It is, of course, a widely held norm that, at least in the immediate aftermath of a death, one should not speak ill of the dead, and idealization of the dead is common. As Shakespeare put it: 'He's good, being dead.' The media may have idealized her because that is what is typically done after a death. Or, even had there been no mass media, millions of people might have idealized her by the Monday anyway, as a typical reaction to loss.

There is plenty of evidence that the media were reporting, as much as forming, public opinion. Vox pop interviews were used not to illustrate a story whose important parameters had already been defined by journalists, as is normally the case, but to provide the raw material for the story (Brunt 1997). The people spoke and the media reported; and the people felt considerable exhilaration in this reversal of the normal course of events (Couldry 1999). Many journalists have said that the crowds in London were demanding the Queen came to town *before* this became headline news, and radio phone-ins included many such demands before this was picked up by the tabloids (Geraghty 1998: 72). Further, some of the mourning behaviour was barely mentioned by the media, so could not have been media-generated. A significant minority of messages attached to flowers, around a fifth at the sites I visited and many more at Harrods, were addressed to Di *and* Dodi, even though Dodi scarcely featured in media coverage that week. Writers of condolence messages referred to Di and Dodi together in heaven, their inter-faith solidarity sometimes augmented by the presence of Mother Theresa, images by no means adopted from the media (Chapter 13).

Nor does the argument stand up that Diana was simply a creation of the media, like Hollywood stars and soap opera characters. Diana's royal status existed prior to her 'Hollywoodization', and indeed without this status she would never have entered the world of stardom (Billig 1992; Watson 1997). In adding charisma and media-nouce to a public office that existed indep-endent of the media, Diana was more like John F. Kennedy than the stars of cinema and television who are nothing without these media. Evidence is also available of mass grieving before the age of television. The public mourning for the victims of the *Titanic* occurred in the age of newsprint (Chapter 1), while that for Princess Charlotte (Chapter 3) occurred before even the invention of the telegraph, with the news taking days to reach the far corners of the country. Yet the mourning then seems to have been similar in scale and intensity to Diana's, with contemporaries marvelling at it. This is not to say that the media of communication are not important: these earlier griefs did certainly entail the media of newspapers and word of mouth. But it does indicate that the mourning for Diana cannot be accounted for *simply* as a televisual event.

The relation between the media and the people was in fact more subtle. I think Silverstone (1998) has it right. People identified with Diana in all kinds of ways, and acted upon their sense of loss by creating public rituals, which really were their own. It was a performance that was appropriated, encour-aged and sustained by the mass media, but that cannot take away from the tangible, real-time, flower-smelling reality of the performance. There was also subterranean resistance to media manipulation. Chapter 17 argues that 'sick' Diana jokes were a way of opposing the media dominance that week, which indicates not only the power of the media, but also that their power could be seen through and resisted.

Whenever people find themselves in a state of chronic uncertainty, they look to others for cues as to how to behave. The adolescent, proudly pro-claiming his independence and individuality, looks to his peers for cues as to how independent teenagers behave and dress at this most anxious phase of the life cycle; their communal uncertainty causes them to end up as the most conformist of age-groups. A similar social psychology operates with bereavement in a society that has few, or rather conflicting, rules for grief (Walter 1997), and this is *a fortiori* true when the death is tragic and unexpected. Those sitting down to write in the books of condolence often did so with no clear idea what to write; they would scan the previous few entries, and write their own variation of that page's emerging theme (Chapter 13). At Buckingham Palace on the first Sunday, one could observe people wandering about wondering what to do. They watched other people – laying flowers, shrieking, quietly contemplating, hugging their partner – and thus learnt what was acceptable. This was behaviour that people constructed together, by watching each other, learning from each other: it was genuinely *social* behaviour. Within a few hours, they were also learning from mourners appearing on the television screen. The media clearly played an important role in this process of social learning, but not necessarily an initiating or defining role. The media were not the only means by which people learned from each other.

This brings us to one of the major reasons for sociological interest in the mourning for Diana, and to a major theme of this book. Everyone was shocked, nobody knew what to do or what would happen next; Ignatieff is right that there was a sociological and political vacuum. It is rare – at least in ordered, controlled, peaceful western societies – for there to be no social rules. This is not quite the same as ritual liminality, where – though hierarchy is in abeyance – there are clear rules for how ritual participants should behave (Turner 1977). The mourning for Diana provides a natural experiment in how a society creates rules when previous rules collapse. How do people take control when they find themselves, for a few hours or days, no longer controlled by formal social institutions? How do they use words, images, symbols and objects to reconstitute a world gone awry back into one that feels safe and orderly?

Have the British changed their character?

'A quiet madness, a quiet hysteria' was how one self-confessed cynic, a professional photographer who had been to Rwanda and other troubled regions, described what he witnessed in London that week (*The Shrine*, BBC2, 30 December 1997). Some heard the hushed quietness of huge crowds, saw the orderly queuing, and thought it all very British. Others saw the madness, and thought it hysterical. A number of academics from both the Right (O'Hear 1998) and Left (Fitzpatrick 1997; New Formations 1999; Ryan 1997; Wheatcroft 1997; Wilson 1997) went into print with serious worries about a mindless emotionalism threatening the very heart of a democratic, rational society. None of these critics claimed to be against emotion as such, only against a contentless, mindless emotion. Both those of the old left (e.g.

Wilson) and the new right (O'Hear) linked this populist emotion for Diana with the populism of the Blair government, a government which purportedly considers focus groups revealing how people feel as important as old-style surveys revealing their opinions. For O'Hear, Diana epitomized a 'culture of sentimentality'. 'Sometimes in the history of a people there is a defining moment: a moment in which a nation discovers what it has become. In such a moment, it decides what it wants to be.' (O'Hear 1998: 183) Diana's funeral, he laments, was such a moment.

From the perspective of the psychology of grief, such fears are extreme, not to say unfounded. Studies of bereavement clearly indicate that grieving people do not act rationally. Like falling in love and giving birth, grief temporarily makes people say and do daft things. It's special, it's wonderful and/or terrifying, and it will pass. Multiply this individual reaction by a few million and you get something looking like hysteria, but it's nothing to worry about. Just as bereavement books and bereavement counsellors seek to assure anxious grievers that they are not going mad, so these social critics needed to be reassured that the public's daftness was only temporary, that these strange feelings of love, devotion, grief and anger were real, but – for the vast majority of people, and as a cultural formation – would pass.

The anthropology of rites of passage is similarly reassuring. No anthropologist witnessing the strange behaviour that constitutes the mourning for a tribe's leader would jump to the conclusion that the tribe's culture had suddenly and permanently shifted. No, the anthropologist would take great interest in this liminal period in which social structure is temporarily reversed (Turner 1977). Communal mourning behaviour has to be seen as liminal, on the border of everyday life, existing in temporary tension with mainline culture and social structure. For Turner, liminality typically functions to legitimate the social order, not to overthrow it. From such periods of liminality, of time out of time, the culture can, sometimes, be shifted – the solidarity generated by the Second World War, for example, arguably lasted for the rest of the 1940s, thus enabling the welfare state to be legislated into existence. It is likewise possible, as Douglas Davies argued in Chapter 1 in his discussion of rebounding vitality, that the mourning for Diana may have kick-started certain cultural changes, or at least given a big boost to changes already on their way. But to jump to the conclusion that liminal behaviour is prima facie evidence for a long-term cultural shift indicates anthropological ignorance. If anybody became hysterical, it was certain ill-informed critics.

That said, I have argued elsewhere (Walter 1999) that there is a cultural battle going on between those who believe that personal problems should be coped with by the stiff upper lip and those who believe they should be coped with by talking about them. The battle lines are drawn up partly by gender – expressive females have gained more confidence to challenge repressive, and upper-class, male dominance; and partly by age – those formed by the experiences of two world wars and the inter-war depression learned to cope by gritting their teeth and getting on with it, while those formed by post 1950s affluence and peace have the leisure to explore their personal problems. As Barcan (1997) put it, 'Diana's death triggered a sudden and overwhelming irruption of the "popular feminine" into a masculinized public sphere.' It was certainly overwhelming, but it was not so sudden. There are good reasons why expressivism should be on the ascendant, given the dying off of the older generation and the new voice being found by many women. The mourning for Diana seems to indicate that expressivism has now spread beyond the caring and artistic professions which in 1981 Bernice Martin considered its base (Biddle and Walter 1998). On the other hand, Williamson (1998) asks whether emoting for those we don't know rather than for those we do may indicate not a more emotional, but an ongoingly repressed, people.

We must also beware of being misled by the media that September 1997 revealed a peculiarly emotional populace. Those actually present spoke not of a hysterical, Mediterranean crowd of keeners, but of a haunting silence, punctuated by sobs. The weeping was noticeable only because it stood out from the silence. (Compare 'the extraordinary stillness and tranquillity of the people' that was so marked at Elizabeth's coronation: Shils and Young 1953: 72.) But the 1997 media cameras, for some years focused on the new emotional male (notably soccer stars in tears after missing a penalty), were on the lookout for emotion. In September 1997 they would film the tears and hugs of a young couple, then pan away to the crowd, giving the impression the whole crowd was in tears (Chapter 4). Viewers at home could be forgiven for believing that everyone out there was crying and hugging – except perhaps themselves, which may be how so many were made to feel so odd. Academics and publishers, like many intellectuals feeling distant from the whole thing, were bemused to find e-mails arriving from the USA commiserating with 'you and all the British people on your great loss'. It would seem that Americans, devouring televised images of a Britain in mourning, concluded that all Britons shared the grief. It was, therefore, a remarkable achievement that the television coverage of the funeral itself managed to convey an awesome silence (Chapter 4), itself a liminal contrast to the images of weeping and speaking that had dominated the screens for the previous six days.

Why the grief?

Many people were puzzled why so many, including sometimes themselves, were affected by the death of a woman they had never met, and why even those who had not themselves been Diana fans found themselves shocked and moved. The following exchange on an electronic discussion list (cited in Sofoulis 1997: 14) illuminates this question: The cynic complains that 'Personal is when my grandmother dies, not when some play of light and shadow disappears.' To which the mourner responds, 'Diana told "me" (and many others) of her dreams and disappointments – and despair; my grandmother never did. So for whom should I really mourn?' Why this woman touched so many people has to be answered, in part, by looking at her life and what it meant to people (see for example Richards et al 1999), which is not the topic of this book. Here I simply sketch some possibilities.

Diana meant many things to many people. She was that most potent of symbols, a person or object that means many things to many people. She has to be understood therefore not as a sign with one clear meaning, but in terms of complexity, change and ambiguity. As Silverstone writes (1998: 84), there were many connections: 'women identifying with the woman, children identifying with the child, parents identifying with the parent, lovers with the lovers' (see also Braidotti 1997). Because of her support for AIDS work and her own identification with 'the constituency of the rejected', gays and ethnic minorities felt she was on their side.

More than this, her skilled use of her body, especially her eyes and hands, when communicating with people enabled millions to sense she was a conduit between royalty and commoner, society and the individual, even perhaps between the divine and the human. In an era of constitutional monarchy, to be effective in welding individual subjects into the body social, every royal personage must appear both royal and yet ordinary, almost divine yet almost human (Billig 1992: chs 3,4; Nairn 1994; Williamson 1986). It is a difficult combination that comes naturally to few, and few have mastered it. The Queen Mother, walking with her shy husband in the ruins of blitzed London, did; King Baudouin of Belgium, holding the stumped limbs of lepers, belly-laughing at something said by a face in the crowd, going walkabout hand in hand with a little girl, did; and Diana, Princess of Wales did. Such royal personages become the representative Briton, Belgian, or woman; they inspire not (like other royals) respect, but awe, love and devotion; and their premature deaths are felt by many as a catastrophe.

But the mourning was prompted not only by the nature of her life but also by the nature of her death. Though Diana was more than a soap opera character, she appeared like soap characters almost daily in the tabloid newspapers and in magazines such as *Hello!*. This was particularly true in the few weeks before her death, when the popular press were recording her romance with Dodi Al Fayed on a daily basis. When a soap character is to be killed off, warning is given – make sure you watch *Dallas* or *East-enders* next week because something special is going to happen. But no warning was given of Diana's death. This vibrant, colourful young woman had seemed ever present, and immortal. It was impossible to believe she would no longer be there in glossy colour on every newsagent's magazine rack; this was the shocked realization the day she died, yet of course a year later she is still there in glossy colour on every newsagent's magazine rack. Like Marilyn, like Elvis, the tragedy of her death has rendered her immortal.

At the time, it was the shock of her all too real mortality that led both to the moist eyes of sceptics, and perhaps also (Chapter 17) to the sick jokes. Her death seemed both unreal, and at the same time an injection of brutal reality into the mediated world she had inhabited in which image and reality are hopelessly confused. In this Baudrillardian (1983) world in which access to unmediated reality is impossible, the stark reality of death stands out as a shockingly unmediated fact (even if the circumstances surrounding the death were intensely mediated). People may have speculated endlessly about the 'real' Diana, but one thing they knew: yesterday she was alive and today she is dead. The televised funeral, watched by two and a half billion worldwide, was a media event par excellence, yet an event in which image was *not* all. At its heart lay the physical reality of a coffin and a corpse.

Who grieved?

Though millions of Britons mourned the passing of Diana, including people from all walks of life, all ages, and both genders, the mourners were not a representative sample of the British population. Observation at numerous sites (e.g. McKibbin 1997) indicates that women were more involved than men; many more women than men wrote in condolence books (Chapter 13); and Shevlin et al (Chapter 6) indicate that women were more psychologically impacted by Diana's death and funeral than were men (see also Chapter 16, and Braidotti 1997). This is hardly surprising in that the grief of women is in more ordinary circumstances typically more visible and expressive than that of men (Stroebe 1998). Shevlin et al ask whether this means in the case of Diana that men were less distressed, or simply showed their distress less; this is not yet proven, but women showed far more interest in Diana (her marital and eating problems, her clothes, her mothering, etc.) during her life and it therefore seems likely they were more affected by her death. It is also the case that female scholars have gone into print about Diana in disproportionate numbers. Of the eighty-three contributors to Re: Public (1997), Richards et al (1999), Kear and Steinberg (1999) and the present volume, 61 per cent are female, a strikingly high percentage in an academy still dominated by males. Women scholars may or may not have been more distressed than their male colleagues, but they were certainly more interested.

While Shevlin et al found that personal distress correlated with increasing age over a wide age range, those mourning in public seemed disproportionately in the 20–45 age range. It is not surprising if fewer of the elderly struggled with the vagaries of public transport to make their way to Kensington Palace or for the funeral, or even to provincial city centres to sign books of condolence. Moreover, many of the elderly, those of the 'we didn't get through the war by moaning about our sorrows' generation, may not have entirely approved of Diana's style, however much they may have admired her beauty. Teenagers tend toward selfishness, and may not be overindulgent in sympathizing with the sorrows of women their mother's age. Post-feminist teenage girls in particular, now doing better than their male counterparts both at school and in employment, and learning to use rather than be used by boys, may not have identified so readily as did their mothers with the victim image cultivated by Diana. Little children, though highlighted as mourners by the media (Chapter 5), may not have known who Princess Diana was, and were typically brought along to the floral shrines by their mothers, much as they are brought along by parents to tend graves in ordinary cemeteries (Chapter 8/Figure 8.8). If little children were disturbed, it was a secondary result of seeing other family members disturbed, and for some would have been their first awareness of mortality.

If there is one fear that torments parents after the primary fear of a child dying, it is that of the child becoming orphaned. Road traffic accidents are a prime cause of such a tragedy (as was death in childbirth in Princess Charlotte's day, see Chapter 3). Diana appealed particularly to women of childbearing age, and her death must have activated this anxiety in many of them – hence all the messages of vicarious mothering sent to the two Princes (Figure 2.1). What do groups do when threatened by the death of a member? Typically (as evidenced by countless anthropological studies), they ritually symbolize the survival of the group and its values. So, mothers gathered up their kids and got on the train to London, symbolically affirming that OUR family will survive (Figure 1.1). When television journalists attempted to interview children in family groups, the children often didn't know what to say, their mothers speaking for them. At condolence book signings I observed that family groups often took a long time to write their bit, it seemed because the children had little idea what to write. Children were dragooned into rituals

Figure 2.1 Several messages offered to look after the two orphaned princes. Kensington Gardens, week 2. *Tony Walter*

of family solidarity in order to staunch the dread that Di's death had induced in so many mothers. We may compare here Shils and Young's (1953: 73) observation that Elizabeth's coronation crowd consisted of millions of family units, thus creating a ritual that linked nation, family and hope. More prosaicly, Diana week was for some the end of the school holidays, and many mums must have been running out of ideas as to what to do with the kids. For others, it was the first week of term, and a number of teachers arranged class memorials which were laid either at local shrines or on the Internet.

A number of commentators noticed, in London at least, a greater proportion of both gays and people of colour than are normally seen in British crowds. In terms of social class, the lower-middle and upper-working classes – *Daily Mail* readers – appeared to predominate, especially in the city centres where flowers were laid and books signed. Whether the white underclass – trapped by poverty in peripheral housing estates – were uninvolved, or simply were invisible to journalists and social scientists converging on the major 'shrines' remains unclear. London's homeless seemed to feel a particular affinity with the Princess.

So 'the people', Diana's people, were not synonymous with the British people. Her mourners tended to be youngish female adults of social classes III and IV, along with a good number of gays and blacks. But Diana's mourners were at the same time sufficiently diverse to be easily confused with the British people, certainly more diverse than those normally to be found assembled in any one public place, whether football stadium, church, university campus or bingo hall, and more inclusive of marginalized groups than the middle England that voted in the Labour government. In a class-divided and gender-riven Britain, Diana's 'people' were not proportionately representative but were nevertheless remarkably diverse.

Any explanations of the mourning for Diana must account for why it was widespread within Britain, but not universal within the population. Explanations must account for the class, age, gender and ethnic composition of the mourning. And they must account for why, after Britain, the USA grieved the most, and why there was considerable interest in, for example, India and Japan, but relatively little in, for example, Poland, Vietnam (Thomas 1997) or, I gather, Thailand. Theories of national identity or globalization need to be quite sophisticated to account for the variations in Diana's mourning.

Several commentators noted the support for Diana from gays, the homeless and ethnic minorities, and their presence in the crowd of mourners (e.g. Nava 1997). One image of Diana was of her being rejected and marginalized, first as a child witnessing a violent and broken marriage, and then by the family into which she married. She therefore had an intuitive solidarity with the rejected and marginalized or, as her brother Earl Spencer put it in his funeral speech, an affinity with 'the constituency of the rejected'. This resonated with a populist religion of the heart (Woodhead 1999) in which intuition, feeling, mutuality of care and a sense of spiritual connection empower those excluded from book learning and from the establishment. Recent manifestos for this de-hierachised love may be found in Nouwen's (1972) idea of the wounded healer, and in recent writings on health care by Kleinman (1988) and Frank (1995). Diana is a symbol for Frank's postmodern caring professional, one who is not distanced from her patients/subjects but who allows her own pain to generate empathy as one vulnerable human being encounters another. It is not surprising that Diana embraced AIDS charities, the hospice movement and the Leprosy Mission.

The Objectors

It is clear that not everyone mourned. Despite protestations by both mourners (Figure 2.2) and the media, the United Kingdom was by no means entirely united that week. A few were brave enough to say they were glad Diana was dead, but many, many more were simply unmoved by the death of a woman they had never met. They found it hard to say this in public, at least in the first few weeks. Two male engineers, hillwalking on the day of the funeral, commented they felt they really ought to have been watching the funeral 'with the rest of the country', even though they didn't want to. Others said they didn't know a single person who actively mourned, but it was not the done thing to mention such facts. Those who wrote to broadsheet papers such as the *Independent*, *The Times* and most notably the *Guardian* about their non-feelings, about their resentment about being expected to feel and their annoyance at being able to find nothing on the television to watch apart from Dianorama, elicited many letters in support. One complained of 'a kind of floral fascism . . . a country patrolled by the grief police' (Jack 1997: 18). After a few months, it was okay to recognize publicly that many were not mourning. A number of the original complainants were invited to expand their thoughts (Jack 1997). By the time of the anniversary, two television documentaries documented the experience of the non-mourners (*Diana: the mourning after*, Channel 4, 27 August 1998; *The Princess's People*, BBC2, 6 September 1998).

That not every Briton participated in the mourning is an important part of the picture. But non-mourners being required to shut up and keep quiet in the days between the death and the funeral is not evidence of floral, emotional or any other kind of fascism. It is merely what happens after any death. In the immediate aftermath, it is simply not done to say you didn't like Uncle

Figure 2.2 The mourners, as much as the media, portrayed a United Kingdom, but the reality was more complex. Kensington Gardens, week 2. *Tony Walter*

Jim, or that you aren't going to the funeral because you can't stand the vicar, or to write an obituary that denigrates the deceased. Or if you do say such things, that the deceased was a bastard or that the family or the church are hypocritical, you must do so discreetly in private to a well-chosen other. There is a tacit agreement, a social rule, that whatever you personally feel, you do not undermine the prime mourners by publicly saying the deceased is not worth mourning. Later on, with the judicious passage of time, such sentiments may seep out, but not before the deceased is decently buried. Indeed, in many societies, the liminal period when the deceased is dead but not buried entails an abeyance of normal social rules (Turner 1977). Fears that the mourning for Diana might be the tip of a fascist iceberg waiting to sink Blairite Britain indicates a lack of understanding of the most basic, if informal, social rules following a death in this country. This ignorance may be explained in terms of bereavement being seen as a private, rather than a socially regulated, affair. Whereas any Victorian could articulate the rules of mourning appropriate for their social class, the typical late twentieth-century Briton has (thankfully) had rather little experience of death and funerals and looks for guidance to contemporary books and leaflets on grief which present it as a personal experience with little if any social dimension (Walter 1999).

An instructive comparison is the Dunblane shooting of 1996. Though the media portrayed the entire country as grieving the deaths of these children, by no means everyone was in fact caught up in the grief. At the time of writing, two and a half years later, it is still not permissible to say publicly that one was not personally affected by Dunblane (Watson-Brown 1998). It seems that murdered children are deemed by 'the people', or by the press, as a greater offence against the normal order of things than the tragic death of a glamorous princess. The death of Diana was by no means the most extreme case of 'required mourning', and perhaps the strongest evidence for this is that the objectors were, within a relatively short time, able to voice their objections in the mass media.

Another comparison may be made. To the best of my knowledge, there were no objectors to the socially expected mourning and wall-to-wall television coverage in the three days between the death and funeral of John F. Kennedy. At the time of his shooting, Kennedy's popularity was at an all-time low, yet even those who had not voted for him and who thought he was a bad president mourned his loss and remained glued to the TV (Greenberg & Parker 1964). Why should the land of the free have been so monolithically involved in Kennedy's mourning and accepted the right of the media to dominate the period of mourning, whereas the deferential British, thirty-four years later, did not?

I think the answer concerns Diana's ambiguous status. With Kennedy's assassination, it was the institution of the presidency, and perhaps the stability of a world in the icy depths of the Cold War, that were threatened, and these were threatened whatever your personal views of JFK. But, following her divorce from Prince Charles, Diana had lost her official status. Though permitted still to call herself Diana, Princess of Wales and still the mother of and responsible for the upbringing of the heir but one to the throne, she had lost the title Her Royal Highness, was technically no longer royal, and was free now to carve out her own chosen roles in both her private and public life. She was technically a private – though glamorous and charismatic – individual, not a formal symbol of the nation. In this respect, she was more like Marilyn Monroe than JFK. And yet, though technically no longer royal, she was perceived by many as royal, indeed by some as more royal than the real royals. This ambiguity may be part of what got both mourners and objectors into such a mental tangle when they tried to make sense of what was going on.

Was the grief real?

'It was grief with the pain removed, grief-lite.' (Jack 1997: 17) Like beer with little or no alcohol. A number who had recently lost close relatives objected that the grief for Diana was taken more seriously than their own grief, when in reality it had little substance compared to their own. Others (for example, Christie Davies in Chapter 17) considered it offensive that the mass reaction to Diana's death could even be compared to grief at the loss of a close relative.

Apart, of course, from those who were Diana's close friends and relatives, it is clearly true that grief for her was not like grief for someone close.

> When people telephoned each other that Sunday morning, they spoke eagerly – 'have you heard that . . .?' – and not with the dread – 'How can I tell him that . . .?' – familiar to bearers of seriously wounding news, which the hearer may recover from only in months or years or sometimes never at all. (Jack 1997: 17)

I suggest that the grief for Diana was indeed real, but – as with grief at losing any such public figure, or even grief at losing a football match or cricket series – it was short lived. The vast majority of Diana's mourners were not left with an empty bed, with nobody to hold them, with one less at the dinner table or with nobody to bring in the bread, but that does not mean that for a few days they did not grieve. For some, Diana's death may have reactivated previous losses, again a well-known aspect of bereavement.

Chapter 6 presents data gathered two weeks after the funeral which demonstrate that Diana's death and funeral did have a measurable psychological impact on a significant proportion of those questioned. Whether this reflects grief, or rather shock at the sudden death of a seemingly immortal being, or dismay at the behaviour of press and monarch, or any number of other things, is not clear.

It must not be assumed that all those who came to the royal palaces were mourners, even though they were invariably described as such by the media. Some came to witness a historical event which, unusually, they could shape and in which they could participate. It is not often that ordinary people can pin messages to royal railings in the knowledge that others will read them with appreciation and interest; this was a once-in-a-lifetime occasion when the people could speak and everyone would listen (Couldry 1999). Some brought their children, so they could in turn tell their own children that 'they were there'. Some were already in London as tourists, and were drawn to what was undoubtedly a tourist attraction. And some came as mourners. Crucially, many individuals played more than one of these roles. The tourist became strangely moved and became a mourner. The mourner wanted to be part of the historical event and brought her camera along. Such flitting between roles is not unusual at such sites – I have myself experienced the shift from tourist to mourner and back to tourist as my stroll on Washington's mall brought me to the Vietnam Veterans Memorial. I have witnessed it at the Anne Frank House in Amsterdam, where the cameras fall silent and in a small room crammed full of tourists you can hear a pin drop; an hour later they are laughing and drinking beer in a cafe. It may be found at any place of conventional religious pilgrimage: pilgrims bring their cameras, the participants become voyeurs, the voyeurs participants. Seen in this perspective, it is irrelevant to ask whether the grief for Diana was real. Rather, people behaved as is normal at emotionally charged sites to do with the death of heroes.

Many critics asserted that if those seen mourning in public were not personally devastated by the death, then their mourning behaviour was neither 'real' nor 'authentic'. The idea that mourners need to feel the loss personally, however, is a peculiarly twentieth-century and particularly north-west European and North American idea. In many periods in Western history, and in many other societies, people are expected to join in the mourning for the loss of a member of the community, whatever their personal acquaintance or affection had been for the deceased. In early modern England, the local lord of the manor would pay the local paupers to turn up at the funeral, for fear that otherwise nobody would be there (Gittings 1984). In many societies, the purpose of attendance at the funeral is not to assuage the grief of those personally distraught, but to reaffirm the survival of the group (Huntingdon and Metcalf 1979). Even in contemporary Britain we see this: when a fifteen-year-old dies of meningitis, the entire school of a thousand or more pupils is shocked and attends the memorial assembly, even though most did not know the deceased. The death touches personal fears of mortality, and challenges the very raison d'etre of the school (educating kids is pointless if they are going to die), so together the school reaffirms that it will survive. Something similar happened at a national level after the Dunblane shooting of 1996. Modern Britain has little difficulty rediscovering communal mourning rituals when major group values are threatened (Walter 1991).

But for more ordinary deaths, mourning has been privatized. From the latter half of the nineteenth century to the first half of the twentieth, most of those living in Britain chose to reject socially imposed mourning, affirming instead that grief was a personal matter. (I write 'Britain' advisedly. Many in Northern Ireland, along with its southern neighbour, retain a strong sense of the funeral as a community event.) This notion is now firmly entrenched in Britain. Funerals are seen as only for those who had some close kinship or chosen friendship with the deceased, and a clear distinction is made between 'the bereaved' and everyone else whose job it is to 'support' them (Walter 1999). The result of this is that millions of people mourning someone with whom they had no ties of kinship or friendship is seen by non-participants as inauthentic, the grief 'not real'. Early Victorians and many tribal peoples would be baffled by such a charge. My point is simply this: complaints that the grief for Diana was not real do indeed say something about the nature of the grief compared to more everyday family grief, but they say even more about the complainers and the culture that has shaped them.

One final note to conclude this section. Scheff (1977) argues that effective ritual is like theatre in entailing an appropriate amount of distancing of emotion. At the theatre we cry real tears and feel sad, though we know it's just a play. Thus we become participant observers of our own emotions. So too, Scheff argues, in mourning rituals: too little distance and we are engulfed in grief, too much distance and we appear unfeeling. Effective funerals generate the appropriate amount of grief, and we are grateful when this happens. The week that followed Diana's death witnessed under-distancers given high visibility by the media on the one hand, and fed-up and temporarily silenced over-distancers on the other. Most people, however, were probably somewhere in between, where Scheff locates most mourners: placing a flower, writing in a book of condolence, shedding one or two tears but not buckets, observing their own reactions with interest.

This brings us back to the question of manipulation. At the theatre, cinema and in certain other rituals such as Remembrance Sunday, we willingly allow our emotions to be manipulated, knowing this is a ritual, liminal experience and we'll be back to normal afterwards. The question now becomes not 'were people post-Diana manipulated by the media and by the crowd?' but 'why did some not wish to be manipulated?' Why did they not wish to participate in this theatre of grief? This I think can only be answered in terms of the twentieth-century British belief (a belief shared in some, but not all, Western nations) that grief should be personally and privately experienced; for many, to join in the public theatre of grief was simply bad taste.

Was the grief religious?

Diana & Dodi
RIP
May you have as much fun in heaven as you did in St. Tropez

Along with messages such as this, Kensington Gardens displayed pictures of Diana, the long elegant face, the large eyes, the dignified sadness lit by candles flickering in the summer night, altogether reminiscent of Orthodox icons. A television documentary entitled 'The Shrine' (BBC2, 30 December 1997) lingered on groups of pilgrims and candle-lit tree shrines (see Chapters 8, 9 & 10). Before Diana's death, Camille Paglia portrayed Diana as 'a new Catholic Madonna, a modern Mary with a taste for rock and roll, a classical pagan goddess' (*Guardian*, 30 July 1992). Religious imagery was rife in describing both Diana and her mourners (Figures 8.1, 8.8, 9.5, 9.6, 10.3). Even the jokes alluded to the required Diana worship (Chapter 17).

But was the mourning religious, and if so, what kind of religion? These questions prompted considerable debate, inside and outside the churches. They are also reflected in several chapters in this book. Several positions may be identified.

First are those (such as Chandler, in Chapter 9) who happily use the language of shrine, pilgrimage and religious devotion to describe much of the behaviour witnessed the week Diana died. Second, the bishops of the Church of England, meeting in October 1997 to discuss the spiritual significance of her death, saw this folk religious behaviour as evidence of a spiritual hunger, an implicit religiosity lurking beneath the surface of an apparently secular society (*Church Times*, 24 October 1997, p. 1). Third are New Agers who see it as evidence of the spirituality that is dawning as we move into the Age of Aquarius (Voices 1997/8). Fourth is Woodhead's (1999) argument that Diana and her mourners were religious, but this 'religion of the heart' must be distinguished both from the Christianity that the churchmen were seeking evidence for in the populace and from the purely 'self-religion' (Heelas 1996) that characterizes much of the New Age. Rather, Diana's religion *combined* 'Golden Rule' Christianity with New Age love of the self. Fifth are some humanists and Marxists who are truly worried at a folk religion that celebrates victimhood and vulnerability (O'Neill 1997; Ryan 1998). Sixth are fundamentalists who, convinced that the sexually immoral Princess went to hell, are worried – for different reasons – at the emerging cult of Diana.

Others, though, are more circumspect in identifying religion. Harris (Chapter 7) argues that, though the concepts of the sociology of religion are helpful in illuminating much of what happened the week Diana died, this does not mean that the events were themselves religious – unless one adopts so wide a definition of religion that virtually anything can be termed religious. Certainly Diana week was full of collective effervescence, but we should beware before automatically labelling all such effervescence as 'religious'. Cathcart (1997: 503) suggests that much of what went on was a *substitute* for religion: 'Britain is primarily a secular society, and people offered flowers and signatures in books of condolence rather than prayers.' We may also note that – unlike traditional pilgrims – they left their offerings outside, not inside, churches. In Chapter 3, Wolffe shows that religious language was much reduced compared to the great funerals of the nineteenth century, while my own (as yet unpublished) research indicates that in towns and suburbs municipal buildings, war memorials, libraries, hospitals and supermarkets (notably Tesco) together outnumbered churches as locations for condolence books and for the laying of flowers. Only in villages and cathedral cities did the house of prayer dominate over secular locations. At the same time, we must ask exactly what did people write in the condolence books (Chapter 13)? Confident hopes of an afterlife written in a supermarket, or irreligious sentimentalities written in a cathedral make for a complicated picture. What we might be witnessing here may be less a secularization than a de-Christianization, and in particular a de-churchification, of contemporary Britain (Woodhead 1999).

The Questions Academics Asked

Mourning is feminine, weak, ignoble; women are more inclined to it than men, barbarians than Hellenes, commoners more than aristocrats. (Plutarch)

I hate the common people and despise them. (Horace)

Given the predominance of women and social classes III and IV amongst the mourners, it is not surprising that academics (social class I/II, largely male) did not, in general, mourn the Princess. Certainly some were, in Ignatieff's phrase, 'ambushed by their own emotions', especially on the day of her death, but my impression was that as the week progressed many social scientists were appalled and/or intrigued by what they witnessed. A lot of intellectual snobbery was expressed, at least in informal conversation. It was assumed that Diana, having no academic qualifications and with an aversion to making public speeches, must be as thick as two short planks. This assumption, elevating one narrow form of intelligence over others, says more about academics than about Diana, and was in any case – judging by the testimony of those who had met her – almost certainly incorrect. Anyway, the assumption that she was not intelligent meant that she was not worthy of mass grief. Therefore, there must be something wrong with the public, or with the media, or with the contemporary psyche, or with all three.

This then prompted a number of explanations which took the form of a sociology or a psychology of error (long discredited in the philosophy of social science), trying to explain where the people went wrong. The explanations and worries I heard, reflecting those we have already encountered in this chapter, were of the following kinds: 1) crowd hysteria, with the crowd working itself up into a frenzy; 2) media manipulation; 3) populist fascism, entailing the triumph of naked emotion over reason; 4) the rise of a dangerous new religion of victimhood. Strikingly, each of these explanations sees people not as self-determining subjects, but as objects of evil forces. That so many contemporary social scientists should perceive their fellow human beings in this way, simply because they did not like the way they behaved for a few days, is disturbing. A more considered position would be that Diana's mourners, like everyone, were both self-determining agents and operating within a particular social and political context. (Silverstone 1998: 82)

By no means all academics were so dismissive of 'the people'. A number were genuinely concerned to make sense of a world gone all strange, and a number of one-off academic conferences and seminars were held in the months after Diana's death, ranging from internal seminars using the response to her death as a teaching tool for undergraduates to well-attended national day conferences. North American and Australian, as well as British, scholars hosted such events, and as a result books are now steadily rolling off the press. I will make a number of observations and sketch several strands of analysis that emerged in these more serious attempts to comprehend the Diana event.

First, popular royalism was not something that the academy had hitherto taken seriously, an omission observed long ago by Shils and Young (1953:

64) who put it down to intellectuals' distaste for the sacred. Michael Billig (1992) suggests that, since most Britons are not republican, popular royalism has not been seen as a social problem and therefore has not attracted research funding. At the same time, I would suggest that a probably disproportionate number of social scientists *are* republican, but they too had ignored popular royalism, perhaps seeing it as too embarrassing. Only a few intellectuals, such as Billig (1992) and Nairn (1994), had staked reputations on major books on the subject. Two much-cited articles appeared following Elizabeth's coronation (Shils and Young 1953, Birnbaum 1955), and more recently there have been a number of short essays by, for example, Rosalind Coward (1984), Judith Williamson (1986), Camille Paglia (1995), Joan Smith (1996), Anne Rowbottom (1998) and Jude Davies (1998), while *Marxism Today* published a number of articles on Britons' troubling penchant for royalism, but it cannot be said that royalism was a trendy theme in academia. The popular response to Diana's death therefore caused a lot of scholars, the present writer included, to inform themselves in short order about popular royalism.

Second, many intellectuals considered offensive and oppressive Diana's sanctification of suffering and victimhood. A number of socialists, though clearly approving of more egalitarian relationships, for example between doctor and patient or between teacher and child, were so obsessed with the dogma that social class is the irreducible dividing line in British society that they could not believe that the personal neurotic sufferings of a millionairess could possibly compare with the sufferings of her subjects. This was seen as false consciousness implanted by an ideology designed to cover up the huge disparities of wealth in contemporary Britain. Humanists, seeking to discover power from one's own capabilities and potential, also had a problem with Diana's celebration of vulnerability. Combine the two (e.g. O'Neill 1998), and the positive image becomes the women of Greenham Common, protesting in the 1980s against the siting there of American Cruise missiles, a vision of the powerless taking power. Such women are the agents of social change. The image of Diana, a powerful woman renouncing her power, or at least her status, as she held the hand of the leper or visited a homeless shelter at dead of night with no publicity, was believed to be at best illusory, at worst ideological (e.g. Smith 1997). Many on the left (e.g. Billig 1997; Wilson 1997) also despaired that Diana legitimated charitable good works over political solutions to deprivation and inequality. (Evidence is rarely given for this assertion. We simply do not know whether it is correct, or whether the profile Diana gave to several marginalized groups instead accentuated the desire for a fairer society.)

Third, feminist scholars could not but be interested in Diana, the most famous and the most photographed woman in the world, the bimbo who sorted herself out with the help of feminist psychotherapist Susie Orbach. Was she, or was she not, a good thing for contemporary women? And what did the, more female than male, mourning say about the present state of women's consciousness?[2] The arguments rehearsed by feminists echo many discussed above. Several (e.g. Wilson 1997) were concerned that the mass feeling was not a reasoned feeling, that Diana and her mourners reinforced a reactionary gendering of emotion, and that Diana was more emotionally incontinent than emotionally intelligent. Others though (e.g. Barcan 1997: 40), considered that the revolutionary potential of Diana's mourning was that it showed that grief can be rational, that emotion can be political. Feminist scholars frequently referred to articles by their journalist sisters. Among these, there was disagreement between, for example, Joan Smith who was disturbed at the sanctification of suffering, and Suzanne Moore who saw Diana as a model of strength and autonomy in the face of precisely the kind of problems faced by so many women – an uncaring husband, bulimia, depression and divorce. Burchill (1992, 1998) and Campbell (1998) also portrayed Diana as a feminist (and, hard to countenance, republican) hero. Sofoulis (1997: 16) notes that what led women to follow Diana's story with such interest was no desire for an ideal hero, but abiding interests in love, sex, emotions, self-disclosure and personal growth. Holt (1998) provides an account of these debates from the anti position.

Many feminist intellectuals struggled with the idea of Diana as a feminist icon, but an interesting difference emerges between Britons and North Americans. Feminism in the UK has been substantially influenced by socialism, so many British feminists have a problem when women identify across the class or racial divide. Can a poor black woman really be empowered by identifying with a rich white princess? Can the suffering of these two women really unite them more than colour, class and wealth divide them? The idea of false consciousness came up time and again in academic feminist discussion. American feminism, by contrast, has its roots less in socialism than in the struggle for emancipation of the slaves, in a liberal struggle for equal rights (Chapter 16). Many American feminists dream the American dream and are far more able to identify with the rich. In this North American view people are divided more by gender, sexuality and race than by class and wealth. It may be, therefore, that American (e.g. Braidotti 1997) and perhaps Australian (e.g. Knox 1997) are more willing than British feminists (e.g. Wilson 1997) to accept at face value, even celebrate, women's identification with Diana.

2. The *Journal of Gender Studies* plans a special issue on Diana: 7(3), November 1999. For a summary of feminist analyses of Diana prior to her death, see Brunt (1998).

Fourth, most scholarly Dianology (both books and conferences) comes from the arena of cultural studies (e.g. Re: Public 1997; Merck 1998; Davies 1999; New Formations 1999; Kear and Steinberg 1999). *After Diana: irreverent elegies* (Merck 1998) includes some worthwhile pieces (such as those by Segal and Williamson), and usefully brings together several previously published pieces (for example, by McKibbin, Wilson and Nairn), but unfortunately much of it is too polemical and cynical to count as serious scholarship. *Planet Diana: cultural studies and global mourning* (Re: Public 1997) is refreshingly different, avoiding the carping criticism of the media-deluded masses found in some British writings and acknowledging that the grief – though mediated – was real. Emanating from Australia, this collection of short original (and unlike Merck, properly referenced) essays was published impressively quickly, a number of the essays (for example, those by Sofoulis, Nava, and Thomas) offering stimulating interpretations of intriguing data.

Miller (1997) identifies two strands within cultural studies: ethnography, and semiotic decoding – in this instance, identifying and deconstructing the symbol system that was, and is, Diana (e.g. Davies 1999). Writing in the context of shopping, Miller observes that there is a tendency for semioticians to decode the meaning of goods and their purchase without ever encountering real shoppers. When basic ethnographic observation and interviews are conducted, a rather different – or at least more complex and differentiated – set of meanings emerges. In the semiotics of Diana there is a similar danger of providing 'readings' of her life and death with scant regard to the evidence.

Semiotic analyses, including analyses of the narrative forms in which Diana presented herself and through which the public followed her, often deconstruct the Diana sign on the assumption that it has no 'real' content. Diana was postmodern, like Madonna reinventing herself time and again, all story and no substance. This reflects the scholarly, and distinctly non-political, interest in discourse. Now it is illuminating to analyse the Diana narrative – as fairy tale, soap opera, classic narrative, Romeo and Juliet (Geraghty 1998) – but the tendency to deny *any* substance beneath the story derives more from postmodern dogma than from the facts of the case. The many who have actually met Diana, especially in her work for children and the sick, attest to a person who found it hard *to* put on an act. Everyone I know who has met her face-to-face attests to the same characteristics – charisma and transparency, a combination of regality and vulnerability found in few other royals.

Jude Davies (1998) contrasts deconstructionism with a very different approach, namely to identify definite images of a real Diana. Those who claim Diana as a feminist inspiration are engaged in this search. Though I find Bea Campbell's (1998) feminist/republican reading of Diana unconvincing, she at least acknowledges that the *Hello!*-reading public were actually following a real drama occurring within the house of Windsor that had potentially major constitutional implications for the United Kingdom. Diana's life had a reality beyond soap opera, even if its telling typically used the format of soap opera. Though Davies prefers the deconstructionist approach, I take the view that there was a real Diana that a surprisingly large number of people personally encountered *and* that her life has been presented and read in myriad and complex ways. It's both/and, not either/or.

Fifth, if some academics have been less than generous in their analyses of both Diana and those who mourned her, a number of other intellectuals have by contrast attempted to co-opt her to their cause. It has been striking how even those who hitherto had showed little interest leapt, on her death, to embrace her and/or her mourners as exemplifying their own pet theories or chosen ideologies. The biographies by Bea Campbell (1998) and Julie Burchill (1998) (who *had* previously shown admiration for her) claiming her for their feminist and republican causes again stand as examples of this tendency, as does Tom Nairn's claiming her for republicanism (1997). I have already noted that various religious groups have co-opted the response to Diana's death to their own cause, from evangelical Christians claiming it represents an enduring spiritual yearning, to New Agers claiming Diana as a goddess of their very own. Unfortunately, the desire to co-opt Diana and her mourners hinders the cause of scholarship almost as much as does the desire to explain them away as demented or deluded.

The Distinctiveness of this Book

In the light of this not entirely flattering review of academia, this book attempts to complement the more theorized works that are emanating from cultural studies, by engaging in the following enterprise:

Documentation

Contributors were asked to document what happened in the week Diana died, and to base any analysis on evidence. Theory is used primarily to illuminate what happened when Diana died, not the other way around. There are, however, two chapters (5 and 7) in which theory and/or interpretation predominate over data.

The next time a death prompts a response of this magnitude, it is crucial that analysts be able to look back at not only journalistic and academic speculation about Diana week but also at solid documentation. Only then will they know how the next mega death fits within this particular type of popular social action. Previous such studies that combine documentation and analysis – such as Shils and Young's (1953) article on Queen Elizabeth's coronation in 1952, and Greenberg and Parker's (1964) survey of the American public's response to media coverage of President Kennedy's assassination – are invaluable for this reason, and indeed inspired the decision to produce this book.

Contributors have been asked to resist any temptation on the one hand to dismiss mourners' actions as erroneous and dangerous, or on the other hand to co-opt them for their own intellectual or political causes. Any judgements upon the events that followed Diana's death must arise out of the analysis, rather than form the motive for the analysis.

Contextualization

Second, the authors have been asked, where possible, to identify an appropriate context in which to place the mourning for Diana. Historical and comparative analysis is crucial if theories are to be tested. As Christie Davies argues in Chapter 17, the most powerful tool for interpreting the events of September 1997 is to look for comparable social events, and to compare and contrast.

A good example is Chapter 3, in which Wolffe reports on the biggest funerals of the nineteenth century – looking at mass response before the age of television is a powerful tool for assessing theories of the role of television in the response to Diana's death. Chapters 8, 9 and 10 offer three different contexts in which the events at Kensington Gardens may be understood. The account of the policing of the funeral in Chapter 11 is informed by the authors' thorough knowledge of how the Metropolitan Police has policed other large crowds. Chapter 13 compares condolence messages written in books in a local town hall, with those posted on the Internet, and finds significant differences. Chapter 15 on spontaneous memorials to Diana in the USA is written by two researchers who have already published on the phenomenon of spontaneous memorials as it has evolved in the USA over the past few years. Chapter 17 is the most rigorous application of the comparative method. Christie Davies makes sense of Diana jokes by setting out the normality of joking in incongruous and hegemonic situations; thus the jokes become comprehensible to readers who otherwise would dismiss them as sick.

The aims of the book, then, are to document the mourning for Diana, to place it in a number of appropriate contexts, and thus to render it comprehensible.

Bibliography

Barcan, R. (1997) 'Space for the Feminine' pp. 37–44 in Re: Public (ed.), *Planet Diana*.

Baudrillard, J. (1983) *Simulations*, New York: Semiotext(e).

Biddle, L. and Walter, T. (1998) 'The Emotional English and their Queen of Hearts', *Folklore*, 108: 96–9.

Billig, M. (1992) *Talking About the Royal Family*, London: Routledge.

—— (1997) 'The Princess and the Paupers', *The Psychologist*, November, 505–6.

Birnbaum, N. (1955) 'Monarchs and Sociologists: A Reply to Professor Shils and Michael Young', *Sociological Review*, 3: 5–23.

Bland, O. (1986) *The Royal Way of Death*, London: Constable.

Braidotti, R. (1997) 'In the Sign of the Feminine: Reading Diana', *Theory & Event*, 1(4). http: //www.press.jhu.edu/journals/theory_&_event/v001/1.4braidotti.html

Brunt, R. (1997) 'People's Princess and People's Voice: Television Vox Pop Coverage of Diana's Death'. Paper presented at the Annual Conference of the Association of Media, Communication and Cultural Studies, Sheffield, December.

—— (1998) 'Icon', *Screen*, 39(1): 68–70.

Burchill, J. (1992) 'Di Hard: The Pop Princess' pp. 233–45 in *Sex and Sensibility*, London: Grafton.

—— (1998) *Diana*, London: Weidenfeld & Nicolson.

Campbell, B. (1998) *Diana, Princess of Wales: How Sexual Politics Shook the Monarchy*, London: Women's Press.

Cathcart, F. (1997) 'For Whom the Bell Tolls', *The Psychologist*, November: 503–4.

Couldry, N. (1999) 'The Geography of Celebrity and the Politics of Lack', *New Formations*.

Coward, R. (1984) 'The Royals' in *Female Desire*, London: Palladin.

Davies, J. (1998) 'The Media Iconicity of Diana, Princess of Wales', pp 51–64 in J. Arnold, K. Davies and S. Ditchfield (eds), *History and Heritage: Consuming the Past in Contemporary Culture*, Shaftesbury: Donhead.

—— (1999) *Diana in the Eyes of the Nation: Constructing the People's Princess*, Basingstoke: Macmillan.

Dayan, D. & Katz, E. (1985) 'Electronic Ceremonies: Television Performs a Royal Wedding', in M. Blonsky (ed.), *On Signs*, Oxford: Blackwell.

—— (1992) *Media Events*, Cambridge, MA: Harvard University Press.

Durkheim, E. (1915) *The Elementary Forms of the Religious Life*, London: Unwin.

Fitzpatrick, M. (1997) 'Beware the Rampant Id', *Living Marxism*, 104: 5–6.

Frank, A.W. (1995) *The Wounded Storyteller: Body, Illness, and Ethics*, Chicago: Chicago University Press.

Geraghty, C. (1998) 'Story', *Screen*, 39(1): 70–3.

Ghosh, P. (1997) 'Mediate and Immediate Mourning', *London Review of Books*, 16 October.

Gittings, C. (1984) *Death, Burial and the Individual in Early Modern England*, London: Croom Helm.

Grace, H. (1997) 'The Lamenting Crowd' pp. 1–11 in Re: Public (ed.), *Planet Diana*.

Greenberg, B.S. & Parker, E.B. (eds) (1964) *The Kennedy Assassination and the American Public: Social Communication in Crisis*, Stanford: Stanford University Press.

Holt, L. (1998) 'Diana and the Backlash', pp. 183–97 in Merck (ed.), *After Diana*.

Huntingdon, R. and Metcalf, P. (1979) *Celebrations of Death: The Anthropology of Mortuary Ritual*, Cambridge: Cambridge University Press. (2nd edn. 1992).

Ignatieff, M. (1997) 'The Meaning of Diana', *Prospect*, October: 6–7. (German version in *Die Zeit*, 12 September 1997.)

Jack, I. (1997) 'Those Who Felt Differently', *Granta*, 60: 9–35.

Kear, A. and Steinberg, D.L. (eds) (1999) *Mourning Diana*, London: Routledge.

Kleinman, A. (1988) *The Illness Narratives: Suffering, Healing and the Human Condition*, New York: Basic Books.

Knox, S. (1997) 'Coincidence, Or, The Last Days', pp. 117–120 in Re: Public (ed.), *Planet Diana*.

Maitland, S. (1998) 'The Secular Saint', pp 63–74 in Merck (ed.), *After Diana*.

Martin, B. (1981) *A Sociology of Contemporary Cultural Change*, Oxford: Blackwell.

McKibbin, R. (1997) 'Mass Observation in the Mall', *London Review of Books*, 2 October: 3–6.

Merck, M. (ed.) (1998) *After Diana: Irreverent Elegies*, London: Verso.

Merrin, W. (1999) 'Crash, Bang, Wallop! What a Picture! The Death of Diana and the Media', *Mortality*, 4(1): 41–62.

Miller, D. (1997) 'Could Shopping Ever Really Matter?', pp. 31–55 in P. Falk and C. Campbell (eds), *The Shopping Experience*, London: Sage.

Nairn, T. (1994) *The Enchanted Glass: Britain and its Monarchy*, London: Vintage.

—— (1997) 'The Departed Spirit', *London Review of Books*, 30 Oct: 3–6.

Nava, M. (1997) 'Diana, Princess of Others: The Politics and Romance of "Race"', pp. 19–26 in Re: Public (ed.), *Planet Diana*.

New Formations (1999) Special edition on 'Diana and Democracy'.

Nouwen, H. (1972) *The Wounded Healer*, New York: Doubleday.

O'Hear, A. (1998) 'Diana, Queen of Hearts: Sentimentality Exposed and Canonised', pp. 181–90 in D. Anderson & P. Mullen (eds), *Faking It: The Sentimentalisation of Modern Society*, London: Social Affairs Unit.

O'Neill, B. (1998) 'New Religion for Old?' *Living Marxism*, 108: 20–23.

Paglia, C. (1995) *Vamps and Tramps*, London: Penguin.

Re: Public (ed.) (1997) *Planet Diana: Cultural Studies and Global Mourning*, Kingswood, NSW: Research Centre in Intercommunal Studies, University of Western Sydney.

Richards, J., Wilson, S. & Woodhead, L. (eds) (1999) *The Making of Diana*, London: IB Tauris.

Rowbottom, A. (1998) 'The Real Royalists: Folk Performance and Civil Religion at Royal Visits', *Folklore*, 109: 77–88.

Ryan, M. (1997) 'A Tyrannical New Religion', *Living Marxism*, 104: 7–8.

Scheff, T. (1977) 'The Distancing of Emotion in Ritual', *Current Anthropology*, 18(3): 483–505.

Segal, N. (1998) 'The Common Touch', pp. 131–46 in Merck (ed.), *After Diana*.

Shils, E. & Young, M. (1953) 'The Meaning of the Coronation', *Sociological Review*, 1(2): 63–81.

Silverstone, R. (1998) 'Space', *Screen*, 39(1): 81–4.

Smith, J. (1996) 'The Frog Princess' in *Misogynies*, London: Vintage. (First published 1989.)

—— (1997) 'To Di for: the queen of broken hearts' in *Different for Girls: How Culture Creates Women*, London: Chatto & Windus.

Sofoulis, Z. (1997) 'Icon, Referent, Trajectory, World', pp. 13–18 in Re: Public (ed.), *Planet Diana*.

Stroebe, M. (1998) 'New Directions in Bereavement Research: Exploration of Gender Differences', *Palliative Medicine*, 12: 5–12.

Thomas, M. (1997) 'Beautiful Woman Dies: Diana in Vietnam and the Diaspora', pp. 149–54 in Re: Public (ed.), *Planet Diana*.

Turner, V. (1977) *The Ritual Process*, Ithaca: Cornell University Press.

Voices (1997/8) 'Voices on Diana, Princess of Wales', *Kindred Spirit*, 41, Winter: 53–6.

Walter, T. (1991) 'The Mourning after Hillsborough', *Sociological Review*, 39(3): 599–625.

—— (1997) 'Emotional Reserve and the English Way of Grief' in K. Charmaz, G. Howarth & A. Kellehear (eds), *The Unknown Country: Experiences of Death in Australia, Britain and the USA*, Basingstoke: Macmillan, pp. 127–38.

—— (1999) *On Bereavement: The Culture of Grief*, Buckingham: Open University Press.

Watson, C.W. (1997) 'Born a Lady, Became a Princess, Died a Saint: The Reaction to the Death of Diana, Princess of Wales' *Anthropology Today* 13(6), December: 3–7.

Watson-Brown, L. (1998) 'Snowdrops and Angels: A Feminist Analysis of Death and Dunblane', paper given at the 4th International Conference on *The Social Context of Death, Dying and Disposal*, Glasgow.

Wheatcroft, G. (1998) 'Annus Memorabilis', *Prospect*, January: 25–8.

Williamson, J. (1986) 'Royalty and Representation', pp. 75–89 in *Consuming Passions*, London: Marion Boyars.

—— (1998) 'A Glimpse of the Void', pp. 25–8 in Merck (ed.), *After Diana*.

Wilson, E. (1997) 'The Unbearable Lightness of Diana', *New Left Review*, 226, Nov/Dec: 136–45.

Woodhead, L. (1999) 'Diana and the Religion of the Heart' in J. Richards et al (eds), *The Making of Diana*, London: IB Tauris.

Part 2

Contexts and Comments

A variety of methodologies and perspectives are used in this section. In Chapter 3, John Wolff uses the documentary sources available to the historian to analyse the mourning for the major royal funerals of the nineteenth century. He identifies many continuities between nineteenth-century mourning and Diana's mourning. One discontinuity is that in the nineteenth century formal church services around the country played a more important role in disseminating information and ritualizing mourning. In Chapter 7, Chris Harris mounts a theoretical sociological discussion about the appropriateness of describing the mourning for Diana as 'religious'. He advocates a common-sense, and fairly narrow, definition of religion, concluding that the mourning for Diana does not indicate – as many have suggested – a still religious Britain. The two chapters point in the same direction: a more secular Britain, at least as far as official religion is concerned.

Whether or not we call it religious, September 1997 certainly saw a coming together of normally isolated people into a Durkheimian ritual celebration of collectivity. There is a paradox here: the television that normally separates us, at times of disaster helps bring thousands together to lay flowers and to perform other rituals in public places. In Chapter 4, Jenny Kitzinger describes the particular relationship between Diana and the moving image of the television. Chapter 2 mentioned how the week of mourning reversed normal television coverage in that, whereas usually the media speak and we listen, in Diana week mourners spoke and wrote in the knowledge that they would be heard and read. Kitzinger identifies another reversal: usually television and radio newscasts abhor silence, yet at the funeral their dominant tone was silence. In pre-mechanized societies, ritual noise – gongs or cymbals, a tolling bell – marks mourning off from the everyday low level of ambient noise. In mechanized and hence ordinarily noisy societies, the ritual marker of grief is now silence, notably the two minutes silence of remembrance for those who have died in war. That television, itself one of the main generators of everyday noise, should be able to capture and hold this liminal silence was no mean achievement.

Liminality characterized not only the mourning but also, Hockey and James argue in Chapter 5, Diana herself. She herself was liminal, marginal vis-à-vis the family into which she married, and this may be why not only did she appeal to black, gay and other marginal adults in contemporary Britain, but also why she was symbolically associated with children – who are themselves marginal to mainline adult society. Indeed, Diana's life and death were presented in terms of childlike innocence and vulnerability, of the slightly plump child growing up into beautiful woman, and finally, in death, a revivification of the motif of child/compassion/purity. In this way, Hockey and James suggest, a symbolic order was retained.

Royals in a constitutional monarchy must be both special and ordinary, formal and informal – a difficult balance. So was Diana's vulnerability and openness good or bad for the monarchy? Hockey and James, and (in Chapter 18) Walter, suggest that Diana had the potential to restore this balance within the house of Windsor; Harris argues she destroyed the balance.

Chapter 6 is written in a very different methodological vein, that of empirical psychology. It finds that measurable distress was indeed suffered by significant numbers of people, the distress tending to be associated with female gender and increasing age. Whether this distress may be classified as grief, or shock, or a general unsettlement at a world gone awry, we do not know. But it is of interest that the social dis-order characterized by the week of public mourning may correlate with personal dis-order in a significant number of people. Individuals as well as institutions were thrown out of gear.

3

Royalty and Public Grief in Britain: An Historical Perspective 1817–1997

John Wolffe

The death of our departed Princess grows every hour upon the hearts of the community. Time, which effaces common griefs, often adds strength to powerful emotions, and renders them more fixed and painful. The object, however, which we lament most tenderly, is not always that the loss of which reflects upon us the most durable sorrow; since reason sometimes heals the wounded affections by enabling us to calculate and measure more quietly the value of the being whom we deplore. But such is not the influence of reason or reflection on the minds of the people of England at the moment. Those who feel most acutely on the present occasion are they who think most deeply upon the excellence of what we have lost, and of the probable consequences of this great public calamity to the highest interests of the nation.

Thus *The Times* described the public mood a week after the untimely, tragic, and probably avoidable death of a young and much-loved princess, an English rose with a reputation for high spirits and charitable good works, who had seemed to present the best future hope of an unpopular royal family. Little apart from the style betrays the fact that the year was not 1997 but 1817, and the subject not Diana, Princess of Wales, but Princess Charlotte of Wales, only child of the Prince Regent (*The Times*, 15 November 1817).

Much was made during the days succeeding Diana's death of the unprecedented nature of the occasion. Jon Snow, the Channel Four newscaster, reflected on his earlier recollections of major deaths in Britain, those of Sir Winston Churchill in 1965 and of Earl Mountbatten of Burma in 1979. Both events had moved the nation, but in both cases the deceased were old men, and even if the violence and abruptness of Mountbatten's end had some parallels with Diana's, the shocking accidental death of a beautiful woman of thirty-six seemed to Snow to constitute wholly uncharted territory (*Guardian*, 8 September 1997). Nevertheless distant recollections still within the range of living memory, such as the death of George VI in 1952, or the death of his younger brother the Duke of Kent in a plane crash in 1942 might seem relevant. Closer and more revealing parallels can, however, be found in a more remote past and these suggest that if viewed in sufficiently long historical perspective, the events of early September 1997 may reveal much about long-term continuities in the human response to death and in the dynamics of the ambivalent adulation focused on the British Royal Family. It is thus the purpose of this chapter to survey and analyse the public responses to three prominent, unexpected, and untimely royal deaths which occurred during the nineteenth century: those of Princess Charlotte in 1817; of Prince Albert in 1861; and of Prince Albert Victor, Duke of Clarence and Avondale, in 1892. Another aspect of the response to Diana's death will then be set in perspective by examining the aftermath of a fourth royal death in this period, that of Queen Caroline, the estranged wife of George IV, in 1821. The limitation of the present analysis to selected examples of British royalty is dictated by constraints of space, and a corresponding need for a sharpness of focus if any useful conclusions are to be drawn.

Princess Charlotte was aged twenty-one at the time of her death on 6 November 1817 and was second in line (after her father) to the throne still occupied by her aged and mentally incapacitated grandfather George III. In the previous year she had married Prince Leopold of Saxe-Coburg, and her perceived domestic bliss was hailed by press and public with great romantic interest. Charlotte was personally popular and perceived as a morally pure and caring young woman, in contrast to her dissolute and self-indulgent father and uncles. The birth of her child was therefore eagerly awaited, not only because of the human interest focused on the Princess, but also because it would have secured the succession to the throne into a further generation. Tragically, however, Charlotte died a few hours after giving birth to a stillborn boy.

Over the next few days, as awareness of the event diffused across the country, a mood of powerful communal mourning gripped the nation (*The Times*, 11–19 November 1817). In that early nineteenth-century autumn there would have been few flowers with which to express grief, but the mood found expression in the cancellation of public functions and entertainments, in the wearing of black, and in a 'mournful silence' which seemed to descend on every town in England. There was an enormous market for published accounts of the Princess's life and last hours, for poetry about the event, and for assorted memorabilia such as pottery and jewellery (Behrendt 1997). The funeral took place at Windsor on Wednesday 19 November, after dark as was then customary, but the day had been marked by a general suspension of business and commercial activity across the country. The road from London to Windsor was 'crowded in a manner of which there is no precedent', and at Windsor itself there were complaints about overcrowding and lack of access at the lying-in-state and the funeral service (Anon. 1817: 43–4, 51). Elsewhere people expressed their sense of solidarity and participation in the event primarily by attending church services, which were often prompted by popular demand rather than by initiative of the clergy. Numerous sermons preached on the occasion were published and served to give spiritual direction and focus to the public mood.

Feelings were intensified by the sudden swing to despair after the eager anticipation of celebrating a royal birth, and by understandable fears regarding the succession to the throne, as Charlotte had been George III's only legitimate grandchild. Deep concern was expressed for the bereaved widower, although there was a significant absence of public sympathy for the Princess's father. The vicar of Harrow, J.W. Cunningham, wrote that the

> great subject of perplexity is the almost necessary silence on everything which respects the Prince Regent. It is painful to every loyal mind to praise the rest of the family and to pass over the actual ruler of the land . . . The character of the Royal Dukes is the subject of great lamentation. (Chalmers Papers [New College Edinburgh]: CHA 4.6.10–11)

In the event the succession problem was to be resolved by the birth in 1819 of the future Queen Victoria, and in the fullness of time the young Queen was married in 1840 to Prince Albert of Saxe-Coburg, nephew of the bereaved Leopold. During the next seventeen years nine children were born to the royal couple. In late November 1861 Albert became ill with what was initially diagnosed as merely a feverish cold, but his condition steadily worsened and he died at Windsor Castle late in the evening of Saturday, 14 December, from a condition variously identified as typhoid or as cancer, but the seriousness of which had not been appreciated until a few days before his death. He was aged only forty-two. As in Princess Charlotte's case the death was untimely and wholly unexpected, at least from the point of view of the public, and its aftermath was also poignant and worrying, in this case because the deceased left a large and young family and a widow who would in future have to carry the burden of the crown alone. (In December 1861 adverse reaction to the perceived undue prolongation of Victoria's grief of course lay in the future, and the immediate public response was to express intense sympathy and concern for her and the children in their bereavement.) Moreover, Albert, like Diana over a century later, had successfully built a strong independent public profile on the basis of his marriage into the Royal Family and was mourned as a distinguished national figure in his own right. The mourning was arguably intensified by guilt for critical feelings towards him because of his allegedly unconstitutional influence while he was alive.

The electric telegraph had been invented since 1817, and accordingly the news reached most parts of Britain the following day, and, indeed, was broken by many clergy to their stunned congregations at Sunday morning service. As in 1817 popular reactions were profound, and widespread, which is all the more remarkable in an age when few could have known anything of the Prince other than from newspaper reports and prints. For example, a clergyman's wife reported from the North York Moors:

> On Sundays between services I have a class of the farmer's daughters, to read the Bible and settle the weeks charities. The fatal news came just as we assembled. We could not read; but we all knelt down and prayed for the Queen and wept bitterly ... In many parts of the wild moorland ... the poor people have not gone to their days works without wearing some mark of mourning. The churches and schools, in some of the most retired spots have been put in regular mourning at the cost of the Inhabitants. (Royal Archives [Windsor Castle]: R2/112)

On 23 December the funeral was held at St George's Chapel within the walls of Windsor Castle, attended only by invited guests and entirely invisible to the public, in deference to Albert's own wishes and protecting the privacy of the young Prince of Wales and his brother Arthur whose mingled dignity and distress in following their father's coffin moved observers (Bland 1986: 170–2). Nevertheless the day was marked by the closing of shops, a general atmosphere of sombre gloom, and by numerous church services and civic processions across the country. The erection of numerous statues and other memorials to the dead prince during the following years served as lasting testimony to the depth of public feeling.

Thirty years later the Prince of Wales, later Edward VII, was again to be the chief mourner at a funeral on which strong national feelings were concentrated, but this time as father rather than as son of the deceased. The Duke of Clarence was his elder son, who died aged just twenty-eight on 14 January 1892, a victim of an influenza epidemic that claimed many other lives. Had Clarence lived he would eventually have followed his grandmother and father on the throne, and accordingly his death, like that of Princess Charlotte three-quarters of a century before, was seen as highly significant in that it disrupted the sequence of succession. Moreover his death was especially poignant insofar as he had recently become engaged to Princess May of Teck, and a nation that was eagerly preparing for a royal wedding suddenly found itself faced with a funeral instead. Clarence had yet publicly to demonstrate objective personal qualities and achievements, but the nation readily projected on to him an image of idealized young manhood. All age groups could identify with the bereavement: not only was there the romantic tragedy of his fiancée, but also the despair of his aged grandmother, Queen Victoria and of his middle-aged parents – the Princess of Wales was known to be greatly and understandably distressed at her son's death.

The newspaper reports on the public response to Clarence's death suggest an intensity of public feeling which matched or even exceeded that apparent in 1817 and 1861. By the 1890s improvements in medical knowledge and living conditions were making untimely natural deaths a much less frequent occurrence than they had been earlier in the century, and reactions of genuine shock were accordingly widespread. The *Scotsman* newspaper reported that the news gave rise to an 'immense sensation' when it reached Edinburgh and that a clerk at its own offices 'did nothing else the whole forenoon but answer telephonic and telegraphic messages from all parts of the city and country demanding confirmation of the sorrowful tidings.' (15 January 1892) The dominant mood was one of intense sympathy and loyalty to the Royal Family, undergirded by a strong sense of national and indeed imperial solidarity and fellowship in mourning. The public expressed their feelings particularly in the wearing of mourning dress, the drawing of blinds, and congregating at churches and cathedrals, especially on the day of the funeral on 20 January. The Royal Family proved noticeably more responsive to the public mood than on previous occasions: the Prince of Wales wanted to mark his son's funeral with a procession through London, but was dissuaded from doing so because of the health risks that would be consequent on a large crowd standing on the streets for many hours in the depths of winter and in the midst of the continuing epidemic (*The Times*, 18 January 1892). There was, however, a public procession through the streets of Windsor before the service at St George's, and a few days later a dignified message was published in the newspapers on behalf of the Queen: 'The sympathy of millions, which has been so touchingly and visibly expressed, is deeply gratifying at such a time . . .' (*The Times*, 28 January 1892)

Comparison of a contemporary event with others that occurred more than a century ago is unlikely to be conclusive, but the indications are that the three deaths described all induced a public mood which had much in common with the atmosphere in the early days of September 1997. Each set of circumstances was unique, but there are still some specific parallels worth highlighting, including the intensity given to tragedy by prior romantic interest, the gendered attitudes evident in perceptions of women whether as victims or as mourners, and the expression of strong emotions by those who had no personal connection whatsoever with the deceased and whose lives would not be affected in any objective way by the loss. At least in 1817, moreover, it was similarly apparent that the specific circumstances of the death resonated strongly with the population as a whole: the dangers of childbirth were seared as deep in the early nineteenth-century consciousness as those of road accidents are in the late twentieth-century one. It was also evident that such events served to point up and illustrate pre-existing attitudes to the Royal Family: the selective sympathy with the bereaved apparent on Princess Charlotte's death contrasted with the much more generally positive feelings expressed in 1861 and 1892. There was also a similar impression that such raw mass emotion produced a difficult situation for the authorities charged with managing an inevitably hastily arranged ceremonial and official response. They were faced with daily dilemmas in their endeavour to achieve an acceptable balance between sensitivity to private loss and awareness of public interest.

The parallels are further apparent in the feelings of those who expressed a measure of dissent from the dominant public mood. The complaints of the columnist Nigella Lawson regarding the ascendancy of the 'grief police' (*The Times*, 10 September 1997) would presumably have struck a chord with the Edinburgh parish minister in November 1817 who felt it inappropriate to hold a service on the day of Princess Charlotte's funeral and was publicly arraigned by a pamphlet which accused him of having 'insulted a nation's grief' (Lucius 1817: 20). Such questioning of dominant responses was likely to have been under-reported, but their existence was indicated by occasional observations such as that of the newspaper in 1892 that reported that 'Some cynics have deemed it an extravagance of emotion' (*Western Times*, 22 January 1892). Although these were in the short term the exceptions that proved the rule, it is worth pondering the wider application of the shrewd implicit insight of *The Times* leader writer in the extract with which this chapter commenced. The communal aspect of initial expressions of grief for a public figure gave them particular prominence and intensity for a few days and weeks, but the effect largely dissipated as individuals reverted to normal life and became aware that for them personally nothing much had really changed. The indications are that collective grief works itself out in a much shorter timespan than does personal bereavement.

This historical perspective therefore points to the need for considerable caution in attributing salient features of the mourning for Diana, Princess of Wales, to culturally specific characteristics of the 1990s, rather than to more universal aspects of the human response to death. At the same time these very underlying similarities serve to point up the ways in which change had occurred since the nineteenth century. Two trends are worthy of particular discussion.

First, the rise of instantaneous communication and information has significantly affected the way in which people perceive and experience such events. On the day of Princess Charlotte's death in 1817, the social round at Bath continued in ignorance of the disaster, the news of which would not arrive from London until the afternoon (*The Times*, 8 November 1817), whereas at 7 a.m. on 31 August 1997, attending summer school in that very same city, I woke to the news on the radio of Princess Diana's fatal accident just a few hours before in Paris. News of Prince Albert's death did not reach Australia until the end of February 1862, more than two months after his funeral, whereas on the evening of 30 August 1997 friends of mine sitting down to dinner in Vancouver were informed by a tearful waiter of the tragedy nine time zones away from them. Comparison between the nineteenth-century cases shows how the massive increases in the speed of communication between 1817 and 1892 changed the pattern of reactions, in particular by prompting a much stronger sense of 'imagined community' (Cf. Anderson 1983) through more immediate and precise awareness of events passing hundreds of miles away. Nevertheless, even in 1892, no one other than those physically present could hear or see the funeral procession itself, except by means of photographs and written descriptions published on the following day. The late twentieth century imagined community of grief also existed in an essentially different way from that of the late nineteenth century, insofar as its characteristic representatives were individuals and small groups gathered round television sets rather that large gatherings in public places.

Second, although there was a striking continuity in the attraction of churches and cathedrals for those seeking a local physical focus for their grief, the role of official religion was in other respects very different. During the nineteenth century explicitly Christian reference was widespread in the public discourse generated by royal deaths, even in essentially secular documents such as daily newspapers and addresses of sympathy by corporate bodies. For example Leeds Borough Council concluded its address of condolence to Queen Victoria on Prince Albert's death as follows:

> We pray God to bless and keep your Majesty – We pray that your Majesty may have great comfort in those to whom your Majesty will naturally turn for solace in your affliction, and, above all, that your Majesty may have Divine strength and consolation, so that in the midst of the darkness your Majesty may have light and peace. (Minutes [Leeds Civic Hall], 24 December 1861)

Moreover the utterances of the clergy in their funeral and memorial sermons received considerable attention and weight as expressions of the public mood, and were widely reported in the secular press. Something of a change was discernible in 1892: although the churches were thronged on the day of the funeral, a religious writer observed 'the absence, to a very wide extent, in our daily journals of the distinct recognition of the Hand of Divine Love in the hand that "presseth sore"' (Bullock 1892: 30). In the late Victorian period the move was not away from Christianity as such, but rather from traditional theological positions which rationalized the untimely death of a young person in terms of divine judgement and the providential ordering of events. In 1997 on the other hand, although a diffuse spirituality stirred by the mystery of death was evident in many of the messages attached to flowers and written in condolence books, the cultural authority of the church as an institution and of orthodox Christianity as a mode of explaining and interpreting events was much reduced. It is also significant that, whereas in the nineteenth century the primary function of church buildings in public mourning was for holding large congregations joined in the solidarity of worship, in 1997 they became primarily places of individual pilgrimage.

Before concluding, a further nineteenth-century case merits discussion in respect of the parallels it suggests with some other aspects of the response to Princess Diana's death. Queen Caroline of Brunswick, the estranged wife of George IV, became a focus of Whig and radical agitation following the accession of her husband in 1820 and his attempt to humiliate her by an abortive attempt to get Parliament to pass a 'Bill of Pains and Penalties' against her. In July 1821 she was refused admission to the Coronation and a few weeks later on 7 August she died. She had become such a partisan and controversial figure that public grief lacked the universal intensity evident in the other cases discussed, but she was nevertheless very sincerely mourned by her numerous supporters. The King meanwhile was on his post-Coronation tour of Ireland, and it was only with a poor grace that he agreed to observe even conventional decencies. The government, relieved that Caroline's will had specified interment at Brunswick rather than Windsor, sought to have her body removed from the country as quickly as possible. An initial scheme to ship the coffin down the Thames from Hammersmith (where she had died) had to be abandoned as indecent and unsafe so a hasty overland journey to Harwich was organized. The late Queen's household complained in vain at what they characterized as an unseemly rush (Liverpool Papers [British Library], Additional Manuscript 38,289: ff. 313, 328–30, 343–3, 351–2).

Queen Caroline's last journey to Harwich on 14 to 16 August became, however, a striking demonstration of what would later be called 'people power'. The government intended to route the procession around the northern outskirts of London so as to avoid demonstrations of public support on the streets of the capital. At Kensington the procession was delayed by the crowd for two hours, and at Hyde Park the military fired on the crowd causing several fatalities but successfully stopped the procession proceeding down Piccadilly, diverting it northwards towards and along what is now Marylebone Road. At the top of Tottenham Court Road, however, Caroline's supporters erected barricades and successfully diverted the procession south again causing it to proceed along the Strand and through the heart of the City of London. During subsequent overnight stops at Chelmsford and Colchester large crowds were attracted to the churches where the body was laid and some disorder ensued (Anon. 1821).

Beatrix Campbell in her exploration of the significance of Princess Diana's life and death has offered an extensive comparison with the case of Queen Caroline (1998: 15–20, 227–31). The parallel is indeed a striking one, especially in respect of a main strand of Campbell's argument: the manner in which both women served as catalysts for the articulation of powerful but normally subterranean currents in sexual politics. Queen Caroline's death, also like Princess Diana's, further revealed the potentiality of public mourning to become a focus for popular protest and demonstrated the explosive posthumous potential inherent in a figure who had come to be seen simultaneously as both royal and a figurehead for the dispossessed. Nevertheless, some important differences in relation to the aftermaths of their respective deaths should be noted. First, the violent scenes of chaos and conflict at Queen Caroline's funeral were a far cry from the orderly consensus achieved, on the surface at least, at Princess Diana's. Second, the political context was very different: Caroline's radical and Whig supporters were using the Queen's memory as a stick with which to beat an unpopular Tory ministry, quite as much as they were directly attacking the King. Following Diana's death, by contrast, the popular recently-elected Labour government proved to be in a strong position to lead public opinion and marginalize more radical voices. Third, although the funeral procession itself gave rise, as we have seen, to popular demonstrations, wider public mourning for Caroline appears to have been relatively limited when compared not only with Diana, but also with the case of her own daughter Princess Charlotte 1817.

Campbell's implication (1998: 19–20) that the sexual politics of support for Queen Caroline fuelled an extensive republicanism founded in resistance to patriarchy is also hard to sustain. Granted that then, as now, a minority of committed republicans found a natural platform in criticizing the personal failures of the Royal Family, Caroline's quarrel, like Diana's, was not with the institution of monarchy itself, but with the particular individuals and circumstances that had cut her off from its inner circle. Moreover, as Linda Colley has argued (1992: 272), the images of Queen Caroline and Princess Charlotte in the medium term contributed to the striking feminization of the British monarchy initiated by Victoria and sustained by the present Queen, producing an institution characterized quite as much by matriarchy as by patriarchy. Meanwhile the undeniable sufferings of royalty, even at the hands of their spouses or other members of the Royal Family itself, served not to weaken the monarchy but to give it enhanced moral authority and identification with the people as a whole. As a preacher on Queen Caroline's death observed, 'An injured woman, a persecuted queen, certainly merits no ordinary commiseration: and, if we are a loyal and affectionate people, what greater occasion for the display of those sentiments, than a member of the royal family thus unfortunate, and calumniated?' (Berry 1821: 26)

In the aftermath of Princess Diana's death, many of the reactions from members of the public conveyed a sense that they were participating in a 'once in a lifetime' event. Such a state of mind was also apparent in the nineteenth-century cases examined in this chapter, a perception reinforced by the authentication of older people who would say that they had experienced nothing comparable since 1817 or 1861, as the case might be. The indications are, indeed, that instances of such intense public mourning have normally been infrequent, although a full survey of the phenomenon over the last two centuries would need to consider in addition at least the cases of Lord Nelson (killed at Trafalgar, 1805), George III (1820), the Duke of Wellington (1852), Queen Victoria (1901), Edward VII (1910), George V (1935), George VI (1952) and Sir Winston Churchill (1965). This list only includes three non-royal figures, all of whom were male, and two of whom died of natural causes at an advanced age, so without any sense of untimely tragedy. The other cases listed are those of successive monarchs with the significant exceptions of George IV (1830) and William IV (1837), whose passings were not mourned by the public with any real feeling. The public emotions stirred on the deaths of the other sovereigns were of a different texture from those of the cases examined in this chapter. They were not wholly unexpected and untimely, insofar as all were relatively elderly, apart from George VI whose visibly failing health had in some measure prepared public opinion for the worst. On the other hand, the death of the titular head of state had immediate if intangible constitutional implications which were lacking in the death of any other member of the Royal Family, however conspicuous his or her profile. Especially at the end of a long reign or if the new sovereign was of a different gender from the dead one, there were liable to be feelings that an era had ended and that the whole fabric of national life had changed.

The specific conclusion offered here is that strong and widespread public reaction to an untimely royal death is an occurrence which has significant precedents. The very fact that the cases examined are remote by more than a century from that of Princess Diana suggests a fruitful basis for assessing the real implications of changes in culture, national identity, communications and religiosity over that period. Moreover, an historical perspective further indicates that many of the specific crosscurrents apparent in September 1997 – implicit and explicit criticism of the surviving royal family; deeper manifestations of social and cultural protest; subconscious linking of a public event to the scars of previous private bereavements; desire for participation in a larger whole and articulation of a sense of national community – all these have their parallels in the past. The mourning for Diana in many ways revealed remarkable continuities: despite the rapid changes during the twentieth century in many aspects of life, the power of death has remained.

Author's Note

Constraints of space preclude detailed referencing other than for quotations and specific details. Support for other statements will be found in the author's publications listed below. Acknowledgement is made of the gracious permission of Her Majesty The Queen to quote from the Royal Archives, and of the generous support for research given by The British Academy and by The Open University.

Bibliography

Anon (1817) *The Virtuous Life and Lamented Death of HRH The Princess Charlotte*, London.

Anon (1821) *A Faithful Account of the Last Illness and Death of . . . Queen Caroline*, London.

Anderson, B. (1983) *Imagined Communities: Reflections on the Origins and Spread of Nationalism*, London: Verso.

Behrendt, S.C. (1997) *Royal Mourning and Regency Culture*, Basingstoke: Macmillan.

Berry, C. (1821) *A Sermon on the Death of Caroline, Queen of England, delivered at Leicester, August 19th 1821*, London.

Bland, O. (1986) *The Royal Way of Death*, London: Constable.

Bullock, C. (1892) *'Ich Dien: I Serve.' Prince Edward. A Memory*, London.

Campbell, B. (1998) *Diana, Princess of Wales: How Sexual Politics Shook the Monarchy*, London: The Women's Press.

Colley, L. (1992) *Britons: Forging the Nation 1707–1837*, New Haven: Yale University Press.

Darby, E. and Smith, N. (1983) *The Cult of the Prince Consort*, New Haven and London: Yale University Press.

'Lucius' (1817) *A Letter to the Rev. Andrew Thomson on the Respect Due to National Feeling*, Edinburgh.

Schor, E. (1994) *Bearing the Dead. The British Culture of Mourning from the Enlightenment to Victoria*, Princeton, NJ: Princeton University Press.

Wolffe, J. (1996a) 'To Die is Gain? Religion, the Monarchy and National Identity in Britain 1817–1910', in I. Brohed (ed.), *Church and People in Britain and Scandinavia*, Lund: Lund University Press.

Wolffe, J. (1996b) 'Responding to National Grief: Memorial Sermons on the Famous in Britain, 1800–1914', *Mortality*, 1: 283–96.

4

The Moving Power of Moving Images: television constructions of Princess Diana

Jenny Kitzinger

This chapter focuses on the role of television in constructing Princess Diana's life and death.[1] I describe reporting in the week after Diana's death, highlight some of the key themes during this period and demonstrate how the camera, sound and editing effects of television were 'moving' in a way less accessible to radio or press coverage in isolation. Words, I argue, were less important than representations of the embodied Diana: moving, looking, gesturing, touching and being touched. Diana was, I argue, princess of the image, and, most especially, princess of the *moving* image.

The death of Diana, Princess of Wales, unleashed a deluge of media coverage. Diana rapidly became a cathartic object of grief, a symbol of hope, caring, and community, and bearer of many grand themes from personal transformation to 'people power', from woman as 'victim' to woman as 'survivor' (Cameron 1998, Kelly 1998, McCollum 1998, Scanlon 1998). Her life was framed by a series of narratives: from chrysalis to butterfly, from fairy tale wedding through 'crowded marriage' to tragic divorce. Her death was presented in poignant contrasts: loving mother, motherless boys; joy at last discovered, joy cruelly thwarted; famous woman seeking and created by media image, woman fleeing and destroyed by media pursuit (Brunt 1998, Geraghty 1998, Kuhn 1998).

Visual representations were central to the construction of this event. Within days the mass media were representing 'the strength of feeling' and 'national mourning' through capturing gesture and symbolism. Cameras panned the carpets of floral tributes, focusing on the guttering flame of a candle, the

---

1. It is a slightly longer version of an article which originally appeared in *Screen* 1998, 39(1): 73–9, reproduced by permission of Oxford University Press.

poignant message or the gift of a teddy bear. Visible acts of mourning were not only volunteered by 'the common people' but demanded of the Royal Family. In response to 'public demand', the Royal Standard fluttered at half-mast at Buckingham Palace and television cameras focused hungrily on the interaction between Prince Charles and his sons. Physical touch (or its absence) was a central motif. When Prince Harry clutched his father's hand while examining tributes left to his mother outside Balmoral Castle this was used to extrapolate about their relationship. It was this moment which was repeatedly shown on television that day and dominated many of the subsequent front pages under headlines such as: 'The Loving Touch' (*Express*, 5 September 1997), 'Touch of Comfort' (*Mirror*, 5 September 1997) and 'Hand of love . . .' (*Mail*, 5 September 1997).

But among all the visual symbolism the most pervasive image was of Diana herself. The press produced tributes entirely devoted to photographs of her, with titles such as 'Diana: a life in pictures and front pages' (*Sun*, 2 September 1997). The face of the most photographed woman in the world was used by mourners to adorn the gates of the palaces. It was reproduced on commemorative plates, posters and T-shirts. Indeed, as if her image had become burnt upon the retina, some people even witnessed a miraculous vision of the Princess as she had looked in one of her magazine poses.

Diana's image also dominated television coverage. Footage of the Princess interspersed commentary and news reports, and for several days, compilations of scenes from her life rounded off lunchtime and evening news bulletins. We were repeatedly presented with Diana in her wedding dress, in fashionable evening gowns or in casual wear with her boys. We saw Diana garlanded with flowers on a visit abroad, Diana in landmine protection gear, or the blond and glowing princess, clothed entirely in white, embracing a sick black child. On one level these 'photo albums' and 'video-portraits' were reminiscent of fashion shots (with exotic backdrops) or even a Cindy doll catalogue – Cindy in her formal wear, Cindy in her riding gear, Cindy in her sports wear. But these representations were about more than Diana's jet-set lifestyle and fashionable or photogenic qualities. All of these were essential to her fame and her effect, but they became the springboard for other leaps of meaning. Diana was represented 'in memoriam' as having a glittering existence and great beauty, but also as a woman who suffered and a woman who cared.

Often these images were presented using cinematic conventions. Diana appeared in soft focus, the BBC framed scenes from her life with white lilies, shots were played in slow motion, there was seldom any synchronous sound. These conventions signal that this is not live coverage, suggesting flashbacks and dream sequences. They also carry a certain glamour, framing Diana in an angelic, 'not of this world', light.

While Diana's image was repeatedly displayed, her voice was rarely heard. Footage of the Princess was literally muted. In death, Princess Diana, creature of the modern media, became star of the silent screen. Most of the compilation tapes and images were wordless, or included only the most brief and mundane remarks. In one 'Reporting Scotland' bulletin the only comment from the Princess was 'I don't eat breakfast', a response to a cameraman's enquiry (*BBC1*, 18.05, 31 August 1997). The absence of words is partly attributable to the fact that Diana was not an orator in any traditional sense. It is also due to the restrictions under which the media and Diana were operating. (With the exception of the notorious 'Panorama' interview, statements about her own life were largely made public through a form of ventriloquism, as was the case with Andrew Morton's biography). However, the absence of words was also testament to the power of Diana's image on its own.

On the day she died, ITN was unusual in framing scenes from Diana's life with at least a few sentences spoken by the Princess. Shots of her dancing, posing for *Vogue* magazine, and cradling a child in her arms like a latter-day Madonna, were intercut with scenes from a public appearance at which she recited a poem. 'Life is mostly froth and bubble', she read, 'two things stand like stone, kindness in another's trouble, courage in your own' (*ITN*, 13.00, 31 August 1997).

The troubles that Diana endured were vividly revealed across a range of media coverage through close-up shots of her looking tearful and by illustrations of her estrangement from her husband: turning away from Prince Charles's kiss after a Polo match, the couple staring coldly in opposite directions in their car (*ITN*, 13.00, 31 August 1997). One particularly famous scene was repeatedly revisited: the Princess sitting all alone in front of the Taj Mahal. Diana as victim, hunted by the paparazzi, was also a recurring theme. Because of the manner of her death, photographers were themselves literally 'in the frame'. Television coverage showed wide-angle footage of Diana pursued by photographers, dodging and turning her back like a hunted animal to escape the circling cameras (*ITN*, 13.00, 31 August 1997).

Diana's compassion was portrayed through her visits to the sick and the homeless and her laying on of hands. AIDS was the first area in which the significance of Diana's touch emerged – shaking hands ungloved at a time when there was intense fear of casual transmission of HIV, hugging and keeping bedside vigil with those considered social pariahs. Under the cloak of retrospective eulogies it is easy to forget some of the hostility that her actions attracted at the time. The *Sun* dismissed Diana as 'the royal clothes horse' and suggested 'maybe Princes Charles should buy her a stethoscope for Christmas, he might get to play doctors and nurses' (4 December 1989). The *Star* argued that it was 'time her husband put down the royal foot and tell Diana "No more visits to adult AIDS centres"' (1 August 1990). The *Mail on Sunday* asked whether she wanted to 'go down in history as the patron saint of sodomy?' (1 September 1991). However, in the context of profound stigma, ignorance and hostility her actions in this area (and defiance of the royal protocol) were seen by many ordinary people as genuine and undoubtedly made a vital difference to the public profile of AIDS (Kitzinger 1994, Miller et al 1998).

Diana's involvement in AIDS marked the beginning of a transformation of her image. Her *touch* began to have meaning over and above its 'royal stamp'. This was quite explicit in the coverage of her death. Newspaper tributes included pages of photographs gathered under different headings such as 'Diana the mother' or 'Diana the fashion icon'. Among these were pages devoted to her touch with titles such as 'Compassionate Touch' (*News of the World*, 14 September 1997) and 'The caring side that saw Diana embrace the world' (*Daily Mail*, 1 September 1997). The television news repeatedly showed her running to embrace her sons, patting a child's knee, cupping an old woman's face, stroking a cheek and embracing a young boy, lifting him bodily from the ground. Such scenes were often displayed with no indication of the nature of the event, nor of the identity of the object of her touch (e.g. *BBC1*, 18.30, 1 September 1997).

It is often remarked, not least by the media themselves, that 'Diana' was a creation of the modern mass media. She was, according to *USA Today* 'the princess of the MTV generation' and, according to the *Sunday Times*, 'first lady of the global village' (quoted in the *Guardian*, 3 September 1997; *Sunday Times*, 7 September 1997). Communications technology, continuous live news reporting and the expansion of radio and television coverage were central to the public experience of her life and death. The media gave its consumers a sense of intimacy with Diana, of involvement in her story, and for many young women a sense of Diana's life as parallel to their own. The message was that, in spite of her wealth and beauty, scenes from her life could represent scenes from Everywoman's biography. A story told through images rather than words also, of course, allowed for more open interpretations and wider identification. As one writer recalled, many women could relate to Diana's troubles: 'I was overseas when the famous Taj Mahal photo appeared of a lonely princess, and a friend who had just broken up with her fiancé faxed it to me with the message "And I thought I had problems!"' (Lamb 1997: 7).

The obsession with Princess Diana's life mirrored the growth in 'reality television', fly-on-the-wall documentaries and video-internet sites (Crane 1997). Her story operated as a modern fairy tale, soap opera and Oprah Winfrey show rolled into one. In addition, as Bryan Appleyard pointed out, when the final episode came, 'Diana dies everywhere and instantly – on the

Internet, CNN and every television screen in the world, on the radio, in every newspaper, she was the first icon fully to live and die in the global village' (Appleyard, 1997: 6).

However, such analyses ignore important distinctions between different media. Rather than generalizing about the imagery in the media as a whole I want to isolate television and explore the extent to which the *moving* image was essential to producing the Diana mythology and shaping the 'national shock and mourning'.

This analysis is informed by the fact that I do not own a television, and as a result, did not watch any of the television coverage of Diana's death until two weeks after the event. In the meantime I had relied on newspapers and radio for constructions of the event. When I did eventually watch video recordings of the period between her death and her funeral I was struck by the extra dimensions the television portraits added and the power of the moving image. I want to illustrate this by looking more closely at what television imagery was able to do in portraying the living princess, starkly framing her death and constructing a seamless unity of public grief.

At its most basic, television was fully able to capitalize on the power of Diana's image, providing hundreds and hundreds of images – not just the few dozen that could be packed into newspaper tributes. These pictures could be juxtaposed with music, words, text or silence and full use was made of television's capacity for framing, editing and camera movement. Television's ability to capture movement and provide time-frames was able to communicate aspects of the living Diana, less accessible to snapshots.

Part of Diana's appeal was created by gesture and movement. Her famous 'look' could not be fully captured in a still photograph. Its 'flirtatious' effect lay in eye movement, the intense glance followed by the shy look away. Her attraction lay not in 'posing' but in 'spontaneity'. It is no coincidence that standard formal paintings of her were said to appear insipid. In this sense Princess Diana was not 'attractive' nor even simply photogenic, she was, above all, 'telegenic'.

The oft repeated theme of 'touch' was also better illustrated by television which provides a time-frame for action. Television could show the *prolonged* stroking of a child's knee, the clasping of hands for *several seconds*, the intense and *maintained* gaze into the eyes of a sick child and Diana kneeling quietly beside a young blind man as he slowly and meticulously felt her face to construct a portrait of her in his mind ('Princess of the People', *ITV*, 21.30–22.00, 5 September 1997). Such scenes showed not only 'the caring touch' but the extent to which Diana was open to the touch of others. In inviting, as well as receiving touch, she also breached royal protocol (remember the outcry when the Australian Prime Minister placed his hand on the Queen's

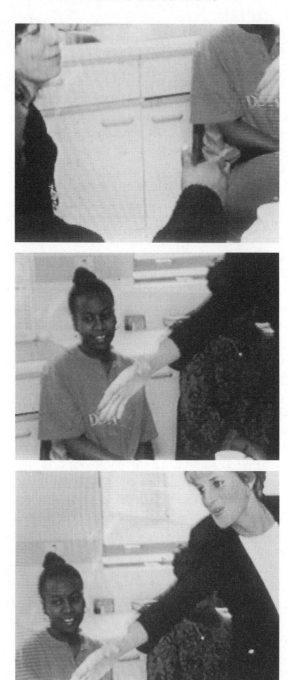

Figure 4.1–3 Television re-films still photographs in order to create an image of Diana in motion: greeting a resident of a battered women's refuge. ITV.

back). By dwelling on Diana's 'touchy-feely' qualities the media were also throwing down the gauntlet to the Royal Family. As one *Guardian* editorial declared: 'Diana's death froze in stark relief the contrast between her openness, their closedness; her warmth, their coldness; her naturalness, their stiffness; her modernity, their tradition; her spontaneity, their protocol; her approachability, their remoteness . . .' (*Guardian*, 8 September 1997: 6)

The television camera not only captured movement, but also provided it. Several news bulletins showed snapshots from private visits where no television cameras were present. The absence of television cameras was used to signal Diana's genuine commitment. But lest we miss their significance, the photographs were scanned minutely. In one photograph of Diana having her hand kissed by a young man, our gaze was directed from the man's lips, along Diana's arm to her face. Another snap-shot (Figures 4.1–3) was filmed to draw the viewer's eye to the Princess's enthusiastic physical contact with others, focusing first on a resident in a battered women's refuge, still seated, holding out her hand, then scanning the image to reveal Diana herself, out of her chair, almost lunging across the table, as she stretched across to reach out to the other woman ('Princess of the People', ITV 5 September 1997). In a tele-visual age, even as a frozen image, the newspaper snapshot takes at least part of its resonance from the television footage, providing an aide memoir and a momentary capturing of the moving image so familiar to audiences from the screen.

Moving camera work was thus used with particular effect to communicate Diana's warmth. Above all it presented her as vibrantly alive. It was this which made it the ideal medium for communicating the drama of her death. The power of television footage is underlined by the fact that film and video recordings have a particular place in Western culture. The dead are immobile and silent, the living speak and move. Technology which reproduces the 'living' voice or moving image is a more startling conjuring up of the dead than other records of existence. Film and video recordings are more lifelike, and we have learned to see them as closer simulations to 'the real thing'. We are acclimatized (relatively) to the dead leaving behind letters and photographs. The contrast between such 'frozen in time' records of life and the facts of death are a little less stark (at least for those who have no personal relationship with the dead). New technologies confront us with new manifestations of the departed. As answer-phones became widespread, people encountered the shock of recorded messages replayed after the speaker had suffered sudden death. Western culture is still getting used to video technology recordings of family members, now deceased.

In Diana's case, of course, most people only ever knew her through her tele-visual portraits. How could her death be absorbed when she 'lived on'

Figure 4.4 Diana's face superimposed on a bird's-eye view from high in the roof of Westminster Abbey during the minute's silence at the end of the funeral. BBC TV.

as television viewers had always known her? How could we not be shocked by the contrast between the intellectual knowledge that she had died, and the visual representation (even if in slow motion) of Diana, 'so full of life'. The use of security camera video, leaving the Ritz moments before her death, added an extra edge to such coverage.

Further drama was provided by the raw immediacy of live television reporting. News reports of Diana's death displayed all the rough edges of live coverage: the clips from CNN, TV anchorman Peter Sissons assigning the wrong name and gender to the BBC's correspondent in Paris, newscasters turning to blank screens where location shots were meant to appear. From the start this marked out these bulletins from their routine counterparts, branding the event with the status of a major disaster, worthy of instantaneous news flashes around the world. The emotional tempo was raised by the way in which journalists and newscasters expressed their own shock. Media professionals traditionally scorn emotional displays (Kitzinger 1998). However, in this case several media professionals publicly stated that they were close to tears. Mingling with the crowds of mourners and even working with the raw footage itself seemed to disturb both those in front of and behind the screen. As one news presenter commented:

> I have never sat at the isolation of a video editing machine and had to give pause for the tears of my video editor. She was not out on the ground, but insulated by the video medium from the event. Normally that's enough to let you look upon the reporting of death and grief, and get on relatively unencumbered by your own reaction. Not with Diana's death. (Snow, 1997: 7)

The intensity of the raw footage was increased for viewers by the editing process and by mobile cameras exploiting the dramatic potential of events. Both ITN and BBC news bulletins treated viewers to a car trip down the tunnel in which Diana was killed. As the camera shot down the tunnel in the front seat of the car we were informed that 'this was the route' of her last journey. While the BBC took a straight line through the tunnel and out the other side, ITN allowed the camera to swerve slightly towards the pillars of the tunnel and the sequence was cut before we emerged once more into the light (*BBC1*, 18.00, 1 September 1997; *BBC2*, 22.30, 1 September 1997; *ITN*, 13.00, 31 August 1997).

Such camera work was combined with dramatic juxtapositions. Bulletin after bulletin showed images of the Princess, closely followed by the mangled wreckage of the car. Pat Kane, writing in the *Herald*, described his own experience of watching such reports. Every time he saw a television clip of Diana, he was disturbed:

> For a second, stunned by her tele-presence, you think: is she still alive then? But almost instantly, the TV report will then transmit that image which is almost becoming a fetishistic object, a necessary visual punctuation . . . the S-class Merc, a knot of painted black metal, squished flat like a cheap toy car . . . If sex, death, and technology were ever compacted into one object, this would be it. (Kane 1997: 17)

Such repeated juxtapositions led him to suggest that the only person with anything 'original to say about this century-defining event' must be 'J G Ballard, controversial author of *Crash*' (a book/film featuring a couple who find car crashes erotically exciting).

The final theme in Diana's post-mortem emerged in representations of public reaction to her death. While the 'nation in mourning' was represented in all the media coverage, it was the *television* images which most insistently presented a 'seamless unity in grief'. BBC news bulletins used a compilation tape, called 'Diana Reflections', self-consciously employing the double meaning of contemplation and imagery. The tape showed familiar scenes from her life, intercut with a singing choirboy, and brief sound bites from representatives of diverse charities. It concluded by cutting between these different interviewees as each spoke, as if with one voice, a consecutive line from a prayer (5 September 1997). The television cameras routinely displayed close-up shots of weeping faces, often then pulling back to show a massive crowd. The impression was that everyone was united in grief and that everyone was in tears.

It was not only the television viewer's gaze which was guided in particular ways. Images of Diana's face were often intercut with scenes of mourning. Giant portraits of the Princess dominated studio discussions ('Princess of Wales: a tribute', *BBC1*, 20.00, 31 August 1997). News bulletin footage panned from close-ups of the Princess's picture, to the writers in books of condolences ('Reporting Scotland', *BBC1*, 18.05, 31 August 1997; *BBC1* Scotland, 21.30, 5 September 1997). In BBC coverage of the funeral, Diana's face was superimposed on a bird's eye view from high in the roof of Westminster Abbey during the minute's silence (Figure 4.4). Her downcast and compassionate gaze appeared to fall on the scene below (6 September 1997).

Unusually, television coverage also made dramatic use of silence. The Channel 5 news on the day of Diana's death simply opened with a picture of the Princess, with no caption. This image was held for a few seconds of silence before the written words appeared: Diana, Princess of Wales, 1961-1997 ('Channel 5 News', 12.50, 31 August 1997). Silence was even more marked in the broadcast of the funeral which was dominated by the clipclop of horses' hooves as they pulled Diana's coffin through the still streets of London. Here, silence was not created by editorial muting of the ambient sound, silence *was* the sound. As Anthony Troon of the *Scotsman* commented, television

> is supposed to be the medium which abhors an audio vacuum, where every unforgiving minute has to be filled with prattle. But at times on Saturday, it seemed that the leaden quiet of the London millions had presented the medium with an unexpected challenge. They were going to have to record hush. Their commentators were going to have to shut up. Hush was the story. (Troon 1997: 26)

To conclude, in a multi-media world momentous events and famous people are created though many forms: television, radio, newspapers, magazines and often also the Internet. But television still has a special role. Of all the multitude of media through which 'Diana' was created, television was the most important. Princesses feature in many stories, and powerful narratives which pre-date television inform the Diana myth. A troubled and troublesome princess, a young life cut short, two motherless princes, are events with their own narrative force which would have entered the repertoire of myths without the aid of television. But the Diana icon that we know depends on images, and especially on the everyday familiarity and moving power of television.

And, yet television, indeed the media as a whole, cannot contain every aspect of Diana. Her life was not a script, her death was not staged; and the public response, although choreographed by the media, sometimes exceeded its mediation. The silence of the crowd at Diana's funeral was broken as it applauded her brother's tribute. Were the people watching on the big screens in Hyde Park assuming the role of mourners, fans or protesters? As the applause rolled into the Abbey itself, what kind of spiral was set up between the outdoor screens, the public, the Abbey and television?

The limitations of an exclusively media-based analysis must also be recognized at another level. The myth of Diana now reaches beyond the confines of the media, and its meanings cannot be understood through analysis of media content alone. How did people make sense of and work with Diana's image as a vehicle for their own aspirations, fears and desires? How did her image take on its own momentum in a particular historical and political context? What forms of cultural production took place beyond the screen? How did people's experience of her death intersect with what they saw and heard around them in the streets? While writing this essay in the immediate aftermath of Diana's death, I repeatedly asked people I met to describe their most memorable image from the previous two weeks. I was struck by the extent to which they not only described television images but also their encounters with strangers, the reactions of friends and relatives, their own direct experiences of the rituals of mourning. The 'Diana-phenomenon' was created through the mass media, but has become imprinted on the collective memory. Diana the media-created icon outlives and now overreaches its progenitor.

Bibliography

Appleyard, B. (1997) 'The triumph of magic over message', *Sunday Times,* 7 September: 6.

Brunt, R (1998) 'Icon', *Screen,* 39(1): 68–70.

Cameron, D (1998) 'Not a happy ending: a gilded cage', *Trouble and Strife,* 36: 69–70.

Carlin, J. (1997) 'The site that is bringing home entertainment to millions', *Independent,* 26 September: 7.

Geraghty, C (1998) 'Story', *Screen,* 39(1): 70–3.

Kane, P. (1997) 'The stench of a rat called guilt', *Herald,* 4 September: 17.

Kelly, L (1998) 'Not a happy ending: including others', *Trouble and Strife*, 36: 67–8.

Kitzinger, J. (1994) 'Visible and Invisible Women in AIDS Discourse', in L. Doyal and T. Wilton (eds), *AIDS: Setting a Feminist Agenda*, London: Taylor and Francis.

Kitzinger, J. (1998) 'The Gender Politics of News Production' in C. Carter, G. Branson and A. Stuart (eds), *Gender, News and Power*, London: Routledge.

Kuhn, A (1998) 'Flowers and Tears: The Death of Diana, Princess of Wales', *Screen*, 39 (1): 67–8.

Lamb, C. (1997) 'Yes, I was a cynic until I met her', *Sunday Times*, 7 September: 7.

McCollum, H (1998) 'Not a happy ending: surviving in public', *Trouble and Strife*, 36: 65–7.

Miller, D., Kitzinger, J., Williams, K. and Beharrell, P. (1998) *The Circuit of Mass Communication: Media Strategies, Representation and Audience Reception in the AIDS Crisis*, London: Sage.

Scanlon, J (1998) 'Not a happy ending: the horrors of heterosexuality', *Trouble and Strife*, 36: 70–2

Snow, J. (1997) 'A death like no other', *Guardian*, 8 September: 7.

Troon, A. (1997) 'Caught in lens of the people', *Scotsman*, 8 September: 20.

5

The Children's Princess

Jenny Hockey and Allison James

In 1981 a nineteen-year-old children's nanny moved out of social obscurity to take up a centre stage position within national narratives which were to unfold into the next millennium. By the time she met her accidental death in a Paris car crash in 1997, Diana, Princess of Wales, had become a focus of attention throughout the world. In the public events which followed, described universally in the press as an 'outpouring of grief', children had a prominent presence and were made a particular focus in newspaper reporting. Thousands of child mourners lined the path of the funeral procession; their teddies, their bunches of flowers and their poems were picked out for special mention; their accounts of her life, character and charm were widely reported. For example:

> Dear Diana, said one, your house is in heaven. Love Laura aged 6. (*Guardian*, 2 September 1997)
> Kate (12) Amy (10) . . . yesterday was Kate's birthday and she had chosen to spend it in London, at Kensington Palace and camped out at Westminster Abbey. (*Guardian*, 6 September 1997)

This chapter asks what was accomplished through the prominence of children during this period of national mourning when, for many twentieth-century children, death has become masked or hidden and their participation in mourning is often downplayed (Young and Papadatou 1997).

The extent of children's involvement in mourning Diana has been remarked by many and it took place in a variety of different ways. In classrooms, supermarkets and at royal and religious sites throughout the UK, children became visible, either in person, in writing or via their toys, paintings and drawings (Figures 1.1, 9.8). The *Mail on Sunday*, among many newspapers, commented that 'the young outnumbered the old'. The aerial photographs of Buckingham Palace and Kensington Palace showed these buildings as never before – wreathed in 15,000 tons of tributes, among which children's cuddly toys and messages were prominent. On the funeral route away from London, children's presence was also felt: crowds gathered around a brightly adorned traffic bollard on top of which sat flowers, a white teddy bear and a compilation tape of pop music bearing a message written in a child's hand: 'William – music gets me through my hard times. I hope this helps you get through yours' (*Mail on Sunday*, 7 September 1997). Another message from a nine-year-old girl read: 'You were a nice lady. I am sad that you died. You did lots of things for people and the world' (*Express on Sunday*, 7 September 1997). In this way, ordinary children became extraordinary through taking on the role of public mourners; the words of young children, which in more ordinary times are often discounted, were taken as somehow signalling the essential truth about Diana's life.

However, another aspect of the funeral which received even more media exposure also had children as its focus – but its representation was very different. Here death rendered the extraordinary childhoods of Prince William and Prince Harry somehow more ordinary and mundane. Highly visible in the wreath on Diana's coffin was a simple card bearing the handwritten child's message 'Mummy'. Behind her cortège walked two boys, her sons following their mother's body on the final stage of its journey into Westminster Abbey. The impact of their mother's death upon these particular children stirred great public emotion. The edition of the *Sunday Post* (7 September 1998) signalled this through a series of headlines:

Wreath from Diana's sorrowful sons simply said 'Mummy'

Courage of Diana's boys – but song brought sobs

There were gasps and cries of 'Oh the poor boys'

It was the look on the faces of the boys which broke my heart yesterday

We will protect your beloved boys

In the public imagination, the elite positions of 'Princess' and 'Princes' were replaced by the close and loving familial bonds which unite more ordinary mothers with their sons (Figure 2.1).

Through an account of both the life of Diana and press reports of her funeral this chapter explores this constant and diverse imaging of 'the child' in the mourning of Diana. As we shall see, it was an imaging which included both real and metaphoric children. What we argue is that this was a process of re-presentation which allowed some resolution of the contradictions and ambiguities which Diana had through her life come to embody: through the evocation of 'the child' and images of childhood, her death – premature, surrounded in controversy and occurring at a high point in a life often beset with sorrow – was rendered, conceptually, a good rather than a bad death (Kellehear 1990; Bradbury 1996).

Managing Death: Infantilization and the Role of Children

Billig argues that to attend to ordinary accounts of the extraordinary lives (and, by implication, deaths) of royalty is 'to investigate the tones and patterns of contemporary consciousness' (1992: viii). Thus, when we examine the prevalence of the images and voices of children within the accounts through which the life and the death of Diana has been described, and later constructed, we find out more about the ambiguous 'tones and patterns' of contemporary childhood. We discover, in effect, the facets of 'the child' which make it a resonant figure within the popular imagination – and so enable it to take on such a powerful metaphoric role. The discourses through which 'the child' and 'childhood' are contemporarily understood are both diverse and contradictory, spanning the range from the evil to the innocent child (James, Jenks and Prout 1998). However, the image which contemporarily commands the most powerful ideological role is that which centres on children's passivity, vulnerability and dependence. And as argued elsewhere (Hockey and James 1993), it is through the positively perceived image of the child as passive, vulnerable and dependent, an image which underpins the process of infantilization, that some of the more problematic aspects of social life and human frailty can be metaphorically reconfigured.

For example, in a culture such as Britain where youthfulness commands respect (Featherstone 1991), deep old age is often negatively perceived as a time of personal dependency. This disrupts the cultural emphasis placed on the importance of independence in adult life, an independence achieved through the acquisition of the status and personhood of 'adult' which is then threatened or lost by the encroachment of age upon the body and the mind. Infantilizing practices, whereby elderly people are treated as if they are children, have been documented as a characteristic of those who care for them but, although experienced as deeply humiliating by those who are their focus, these practices are nonetheless explicable: invoking images of 'the child' is one way in which, culturally, the contradiction of dependent adulthood is conceptually reconciled, softened and transformed. In effect, the loss of the independence which characterizes adult life is made more manageable for those who care through recourse to the positive images of dependency and of a hopeful future which the child invokes (Hockey and James 1993; Jenks 1996).

But infantilization has a wider remit than masking the finality of the ageing process. Ideas of the 'child' and of 'childhood' are also invoked to disguise those other aspects of social life which are equally perceived as dangerous, problematic or ambiguous. In the Valentine messages sent between lovers, for example, potent and passionate sexuality is rendered safe through 'child-ish' naming practices. Sick people may similarly have their disease and temporary dependency eased and rendered less threatening through the gift of a cuddly toy from one adult to another or the encoding of teddy bears, kittens and puppy dogs on get well greetings cards. Given these wider infant-ilizing practices which work to ease that which is difficult or problematic in cultural life, it is perhaps unsurprising, therefore, that we also discover children and metaphors of childhood playing a key role in the mediation of the death of Diana. As a royal Princess, she refused to conform to the public expectations traditionally associated with that role. In her life she was someone who transgressed and flouted the boundaries between royalty and commoner, a dangerous practice which both threatened to 'strip away the mystery from royalty', but paradoxically also led to the 'demand that that mystery continues' (Billig 1992: vii). She was, as Gerrad notes, someone who 'broke taboos' (*Observer*, 7 September 1997), a marginal and an outsider and yet someone who could always command powerful attention and respect (Turner 1974). This status and role ambiguity was mirrored in accounts of her character and personality: 'She was always the lost girl. She was the victim, passive and abused. She was the strong woman fighting back' (Gerrad, *Observer*, 7 September 1997). Images of 'the child' have the power to infant-ilize and thereby render safe disturbing ambiguities (Hockey and James 1993). This, we suggest, is a key explanation for the prominent representation of children in the anomalous death of a royal Princess in a mundane car crash.

Children and Diana

A first point of departure for exploring the ways in which the idea of 'the child' and children themselves have helped to shape and make manageable the death of Diana is to examine the literal figuring of children in both her life and her death. It is, for example, quite clear that in her life, Diana had a great deal to do with children. Described as the 'Princess who captured all the children's hearts' (*Mirror*, 7 September 1997), she was frequently photo-graphed and imaged in the company of children and she made children's charities a focus for her work. Indeed children became a central icon for her life and work and, thus, in death acquired an even greater resonance. One reason for this may be that perhaps, more than any other social category, children signalled Diana's ability to move across the immense divides which go to make up British social hierarchies. Long before Tony Blair coined the phrase, photographs which showed her kneeling at the feet of a child in a crowd or in informal poses on the beds of sick children, revealed a people's and a children's princess. 'Children hung on her skirts, they loved her because they knew instinctively that she loved them.' (*Mail on Sunday*, 7 September 1997) Always strikingly well turned out, in these images Diana bridged the gaps of class and wealth which separate royal palaces and state vehicles from high streets and NHS hospital wards. At the core of such occasions was the royal touch – the arm round a child's shoulders, an elite hand clasping a dying hand. Photographed in 1997 at an orthopaedic workshop in Luanda, she holds the crutch of thirteen-year-old Sandra Thijika, badly injured by a landmine, whilst stroking the girl's cheek with her other hand. To all these mundane settings Diana brought, quite literally, a touch of class:

> In one of the final images of the Princess, which she herself favoured, she is clasping a blind and dying child to her breast and gazing downwards at his scarred head with her soft unshuttered eyes; she has become a beautiful pieta, the chaste and dolorous mother, our new Mary burdened by the sorrows of the world. It is a picture that dazzlingly mixed selflessness and self-regard. (*Observer*, 7 September 1998)

And contained within this maternal image was the other aspect of children's engagement with Diana. Not only was she a princess; she was also a mother and her loving and caring relationship with her sons was made much of in the mourning. The *Mail on Sunday*, for example, described her as 'a singular mother' and as '. . . a complex symbol of modern parenthood in all its fraught and troubled devotion'. Self-proclaimed as the Queen of Hearts, Diana's nurturing of her sons was seen as distinctive in its ordinariness. In contrast to the childhoods of other royals, 'her boys' were encouraged to have a 'normal' childhood and her mothering was regarded as both natural and instinctive. Echoed across the full range of news reports, her role as a mother was unquestioned: 'She had sons which was after all her raison d'etre, and took pleasure in bringing them up to the best of her abilities' (*Mail on Sunday*, 7 September 1997). 'Their mother, sometimes accused of being superficial, had a real depth of feeling towards her children, and expressed it instinctively. Children crave emotion, and she was, after all, an emotional being' (*Mail on Sunday*, 7 September 1997). In his funeral oration her brother, Earl Spencer, located these maternal instincts way back in her own childhood when he described her recent holiday with him in South Africa: 'It was as if we had been transported back to our childhood when we spent such an enormous time together ... fundamentally she had not changed at all from the big sister who mothered me as a baby, fought with me at school.' And it was this capacity for mothering which seemed to strike a chord with ordinary people, as one woman described: 'I looked at my children and realised I was there to help them through their sadness but now Diana's boys have no mother to do that for them' (*Mail on Sunday*, 7 September 1997).

But yet, in this compassion for children Diana was herself rendered childlike. Through an emphasis on her natural and instinctive capacity to care, she was metaphorically aligned with children who, similarly, are regarded as driven largely by instinctual feelings and natural desires (Gittins 1998: 22–43). As noted in the *Express on Sunday*: 'Diana, in a way that no one in modern times has ever done, touched the child in each and every one of us' (7 September 1997). Thus it was that through her capacity to care for and about children during her life that in death she became in part infantilized through the representation of her Self as being like a child. It is this which the next sections explore.

Metaphors and Marginality

A first point to note is that in the conduct of her own life parallels can be drawn between the position which Diana was seen to occupy and that of 'the child'. Like children, she was positioned, and indeed at times often chose to position herself, temporarily on the margins of society. Made to stand apart, whether as members of particular categories or as individuals, such marginals may be outsiders, members of elites or indeed liminal beings who can move betwixt and between the stable points of a society's classificatory system (Turner 1974). In the case of Diana, it was the latter kind of marginality which was most often remarked and which positioned Diana in a status position parallel to that of children.

Described as a commoner, this marginality, for example, enabled Diana to epitomize the possibility of personal transformation, a transformation which in many ways mirrors the child growing into adulthood. From the moment that she emerged like a butterfly from her wedding car in a Cinderella bridal gown to the final high-life weeks in love with a foreign playboy in Mediterranean yachts and exclusive Parisian hotels, we can chart her personal growth and development. In this sense Diana also achieved that longed for personal transformation that characterizes the lives of many more ordinary women. Depicted, for example, through the 'before' and 'after' images and accounts of dieting, divorce and death of a spouse, such stories commonly found in women's magazines offer inspiration to others.

Jenks notes that the child is familiar to us, but strange, inhabiting our adult world and yet not really belonging to it (1982: 9–10). Just so, Diana. It was in her ability to embody and conjoin such opposites that the powerful appeal of her marginality was realized. She moved, for example, incessantly between outsiderhood and an elite royal centre. And it was through such movement that she was able to fulfil the public's twin desires of royalty: 'mystery' and its stripping away (Billig 1992: vii). In her commoner role she slipped out of royal palaces to appear at the bedsides of the terminally ill and knelt down to hug children wherever she went. But, when she inhabited her elite persona, no member of UK royalty more closely approximated to the vision of a glittering and stunningly beautiful princess. Diana was both like, and not like us. Photographed at fitness studios, fairgrounds and confessional interviews, Diana the commoner revealed the fascinating ordinariness of the Royal Family. Adultery, divorce, bulimia and low self-esteem were points of contact for women and men throughout the country. And yet glimpsed dancing at gala occasions in glamorous designer clothes, Diana also restored to the monarchy a mystique and a glamour which made it an immensely sought-after and lucrative topic for the world's media.

Her positioning as someone who in her life was able to successfully mediate very different worlds, as someone occupying society's margins, was reaffirmed and restated in the highly selective media accounts of who attended her funeral and in the accounts volunteered by mourners :

Wide boys, punks, lads, young and old. Some stoop with age and hold on to sticks. Businessmen are here, the homeless. Ghanaians, Scots, Colombians, Americans. Two Hasidic Jews lean over the railings, their hands clasped in prayer . . . here are the AIDS victims, the Falklands, the Gulf War veterans, the homeless, the divorced, the mentally ill, the unemployed, those who have also mourned the loss of loved ones.

Almost to a person they say that Diana spoke to them personally and gave them hope when they were at the bottom. Ex-prisoners, single mothers, the deaf, the lame, the crippled, lie down together. She cared, they say. Others who should have known better did not. (*Guardian*, 6 September 1997)

I met the princess at Oxford where she opened some sports facilities for disabled people. She was just like us. (*Disability Now*, October 1997)

People loved her because she was just like they were. She was just one of us. (*Mail on Sunday*, 7 September 1998).

But she was also, of course, importantly not one of us. Like children are to adults, her fascination and her power derives from this necessary difference and distance. And in this Diana was literally made childlike.

Thus, not only are there parallels to be drawn between the way Diana was positioned, like a child poised for transition on society's margins; more fundamentally, in her marginality she was also, at times, actually transformed into a metaphoric child. The next section suggests how through a process of infantilization, Diana was literally rendered childlike, dependent and vulnerably innocent.

Infantilization of a Princess

Although in her life Diana moved from childhood to adulthood and from society's margins to its royal centre, this movement was never unidirectional. During the intervening seventeen years, from her marriage to her death, Diana constantly re-enacted the possibility of personal and social transformation. And in this there was ever a movement back towards 'the child'. In the ways in which she publicly positioned herself – or was positioned by others – was exploited the power residing within the image of 'the child' and the power to be found in transgressive movement itself. In this it is the themes of childish innocence and vulnerability which are the most obvious. These themes were explicitly drawn on by her brother in the funeral oration which movingly highlighted her bulimia and her innocence as important for the vulnerable victim of the world's press which she became and at whose hands she died:

> Diana remained throughout a very insecure person at heart, almost childlike in her desire to do good for others so she could release herself from deep feelings of unworthiness of which her eating disorders were merely a symptom. The world sensed this part of her character and cherished her for her vulnerability while admiring her for her honesty . . . It is a point to remember that of all the ironies about Diana, perhaps this was the greatest – a girl given the name of the ancient goddess of hunting was, in the end, the most hunted person of the modern age.

Described by her brother as 'almost childlike' in her life, it was, however, in her death that this process of infantilization was metaphorically completed. It took hold in a number of different ways: i) in the re-representation of her life story as a princess, ii) in the re-representation of her personhood, and iii) through the highlighting of children as proxy mourners. In combination, these cultural devices ensured that Diana was drawn back into the safety of the child's world, and the potential threat to social values which her 'bad' death posed – a death which was sudden, violent, premature and with no leave-taking (Kellehear 1990) – was avoided. Instead, the powerful image of 'the child' , with its representation of hope and of the future (Jenks 1996), of life rather than death, worked to soften not only the death itself but also to repair and restore to accounts of her life an aura of innocence and compassion which had in recent times been seen to be at risk.

Clearly Diana, Princess of Wales was not a child and yet in the accounts told of her life she was often metaphorically repositioned as one. Beginning with the story of the virginal child bride, one narrative of her life charts a passage from innocence to knowledge, the transition which all children make from childhood to adulthood. The loss of innocence for children begins with the recognition of their sexuality; and for Diana this was made visible early in her marriage in the birth of her sons. Bradford (1996) describes Diana as Charles's 'child bride', citing a letter written by Charles which describes Diana on her honeymoon cruise 'dash(ing) about chatting up all the sailors and the cooks in the galley'. 'He might just as well have been describing a puppy as a wife,' says Bradford (1996: 443). In other representations Diana is pictured as a playmate-mother to her sons, imaged most famously riding the roller coaster with them.

As in life so in death. During the mourning the troubling biographical details of her life – the fairy-tale wedding and marriage to a prince which ended in divorce – was quickly recast as a rather different child's fairy story. This medium lends itself to the task since it is in childhood fairy tales that we first encounter those marginal beings – frog princes – who straddle the diverse realms of the magical, the royal and the animal kingdoms. Diana's story was represented as a rags to riches tale, in which the princess eventually finds her true love, after a time spent alone or cast out in the wilderness. Like other heroines of fairy tales – Snow White who was poisoned and placed in a glass tomb or the Sleeping Beauty who fell into a deep sleep having pricked her finger – Diana was discovered by the man who was to be her true love and with whom, if she had not been killed, she may indeed have lived happily ever after. The *Yorkshire Post on Sunday* drew on this image explicitly, as follows: 'Cinderella found her true Prince but it was too late' (7 September 1997). And in her death she found her resting place in an island grave ringed with trees where she truly became the Lady of the Lake, a persona which is echoed in Graham's post-mortem tribute volume where Diana finally becomes 'the children's princess' (1998: 64).

In this way Diana's life story became retold as a media fairy tale from her child-bride beginnings to her final resting place on 'the island . . . pleasure garden where she played as a girl' (*Observer*, 7 September 1997). And, once dead, her power appeared ineradicably enhanced. Indeed those close to her expressed regret that Diana could not witness the country's adulation, an overwhelming sop to the personal insecurities which she was said to have suffered, a testimony to the goodness of a woman whose saintliness eclipsed her prior associations with sexual liaisons and anti-cellulite fitness regimes. And in this final period of re-representation, children were, as we showed at the outset, everywhere prominent.

Conclusion

The infantilizations which surrounded the death of Diana, Princess of Wales, were not however without their dangers for, in death, she lost the ability to affect shifts or transformations in her own persona, to move between a royal and a child/Other domain. Death made her inexorably Other. Hence the poignancy of images within which she, for the first time, was instead moved by others – the troops bearing her body; a gun-carriage trundling her exposed coffin through the city which she had previously dazzled. By the early summer of 1997 she had become visible everywhere, yet belonged nowhere. She was the property of everyone and no one. Once dead, however, her own, non-royal family reclaimed her – via her lineage through her children and in her brother's funeral denouncement of her Royal Family's parenting style.

And yet other more popular claims on her image continue to be made and in these the iconography of 'the child' and 'childhood' still play their part. Thus, while a six-year-old disabled girl was the welcomed choice of substitute for Diana at a charity event which would have been her first formal engagement after the summer break, other child-substitutes for Diana have proved to be distinctly more contentious (*Guardian*, 5 September 1997). For example, in Pennsylvania in the Unites States the Franklin Mint company have produced a series of Diana dolls for children, the latest of which models the outfit she wore during her campaign against landmines in Angola. This Cindy-style doll, destined for the toy market, is in stark contrast to the porcelain Diana replica dolls produced for the adult collector market. The trustees of Diana's memorial fund have decided to pursue the Franklin Mint through court for producing this toy. 'How can you do this?' they said. 'Diana is not a plaything, a toy'. Yet, as Ros Coward points out, 'the manipulable Diana doll offers the possibility of adapting it to memories and associations, which the stiff distance of an "heirloom doll" cannot express' (*Guardian*, 21 May 1998). And this is precisely the point. In the ambiguous heirloom doll, the toy which is no toy at all, we have an entirely appropriate icon for a commoner princess who moved incessantly between Western high life and the world's troubled poor, sick and endangered. In the Diana toy doll we risk the dangerous but inevitable outcome of a process of infantilization, the final democratization of a royal princess, ironically, at the hands of small children.

A similar set of tensions and concerns surround the plans for a memorial garden in the grounds of Diana's former home, Kensington Palace, as described by Helen Carter in the *Guardian* (10 July 1998). The proposals are for one part of the garden to have 'a children's theme'. This would be a 'secret garden' with an emphasis on 'an exciting and imaginative play area'. It would be a garden for children. However, dismissing this idea as a 'Disneyworld for Diana', its opponents reject such a reclaiming of the People's Princess through a process of infantilization and insist, instead, that the garden should remain as an adult space for quiet contemplation as it was when she was alive. And finally, the makers of a children's cartoon, which depicts Diana's life, has come under fire from Church leaders who claim that 'cartoons are by their nature tacky' and thus not a suitable medium for depicting her story (*Guardian,* 27 July 1998). And in response it is to the importance of children for Diana that the film makers turn to justify their right to make the film: 'It's not tacky, it's a delightful look at her life. Diana played a very important part in children's lives – they grieve as much as adults' (*Guardian,* 27 July 1998). Animation, like infantilization, makes that which is dangerous or ambiguous more manageable.

In the post-mortem struggle to re-animate Diana, Princess of Wales, we find the twin aspects of her life as commoner and royalty continuing to be played out through images of childhood. Those who marshal her life time associations with children in support of the sale of toys, films and adventure playgrounds stand accused of trivializing, and thereby degrading and rendering ordinary her memory in death. But in their defence the marketeers call on the innocence and purity of children, claiming child's play as an appropriate site within which to sanctify and preserve her identity as a saintly royal princess.

Bibliography

Billig, M. (1992) *Talking of the Royal Family*, London: Routledge.

Bradbury, M. (1996) 'Representations of 'Good' and 'Bad' Death among Death-workers and the Bereaved', in G. Howarth and P. Jupp (eds) *Contemporary Issues in the Sociology of Death, Dying and Disposal*, Basingstoke: Macmillan.

Bradford, S. (1996) *Elizabeth. A Biography of her Majesty the Queen*, London: QPD/ Heinemann.

Featherstone, M. (1991) 'The Body in Consumer Culture' in M. Featherstone et al (eds), *The Body. Social Process and Cultural Theory*, London: Sage.

Gittins, D. (1998) *The Child in Question*, Basingstoke: Macmillan.

Graham, T. (1998) *Diana, Princess of Wales: a tribute*, London: Weidenfeld and Nicholson.

Hockey, J. and James, A. (1993) *Growing Up and Growing Old*, London: Sage.

James, A., Jenks, C. and Prout, A. (1998) *Theorising Childhood*, Cambridge: Polity Press.

Jenks, C. (ed.) (1982) *The Sociology of Childhood: essential readings*, London: Batsford.

Jenks, C. (1996) 'The Postmodern Child' in J. Brannen and M. O'Brien (eds), *Children and Families*, London: Falmer Press.

Kellehear, A. (1990) *Dying of Cancer: the final year of life*, Chur: Harwood Academic Press.

Turner, V. (1974) *Dramas, Fields and Metaphors: Symbolic Action in Human Society*, Ithaca: Cornell University Press.

Young, B. and Papadatou, D. (1997) 'Childhood Death and Bereavement', in C.M. Parkes, P. Laungani and B. Young (eds), *Death and Bereavement across Cultures*, London: Routledge.

Acknowledgement

Our thanks to Jo Heslop, University of Hull, for giving us access to her newspaper archive of Diana's death.

6

A Nation Under Stress: The Psychological Impact of Diana's Death

Mark Shevlin, Mark Davies, Stephanie Walker and Tina Ramkalawan

Wilson (1994) described the historical development of the concept of traumatic stress, in particular the concept of post-traumatic stress disorder (PTSD), from Freud to the criteria specified in the revised third and fourth editions of the Diagnostic and Statistical Manual (DSM III-R, IV) of the American Psychological Association (APA 1987, 1994). The psychological literature has considered traumatic stress responses to a number of stressors aligned with the DSM III-R/IV criteria for PTSD such as threats to life (Cella et al. 1990), threats to psychological well-being (Amick-McMullen et al. 1989), threats to physical/psychological well-being of others (Fullerton & Ursano 1997), witnessing traumatic events (Herlofsen 1994), and involvement in a human or natural disaster (McFarlane 1989; Hodgkinson & Stewart 1991; Curle & Williams 1996). However, more recently it has been argued that people may experience severe psychological distress in response to events in which they are not participants or situations that pose no physical threat. Examples of such events include a spouse's affair (Helzer et al. 1987) or the result of football matches (Masterton & Mander 1990; Steels 1994). From a lay perspective the impression of severe psychological distress among many individuals was witnessed during the public mourning following the death and funeral of Diana, Princess of Wales. Although the media covered the psychological reaction to the death of the Princess in detail, little actual quantification of the degree of psychological distress was made. One such preliminary piece of research was undertaken by Shevlin et al. (1997) who attempted to objectively measure the degree of psychological distress felt by individuals by the application of the well established Impact of Events Scale

(Horowitz et al. 1979). In this chapter this early work has been extended to explore possible age and gender relationships.

The Impact of Events Scale (IES) was designed to assess the impact of any specific traumatic event. The scale is comprised of two sub-scales measuring intrusion and avoidance which are dimensions included in the DSM IV criteria for post traumatic stress syndrome (American Psychological Association, 1994). With the IES, respondents are required to rate the frequency of intrusive thinking and avoidance tendencies during the previous seven days in relation to a specific event. Scores for the avoidance and intrusion sub-scales can be summed for a total score. The IES has been shown to have sound psychometric properties. Satisfactory estimates of test-retest reliability and internal consistency have been reported (Horowitz et al. 1979; Zilberg et al. 1982). In addition, evidence for a clear factor structure (Robbins & Hunt 1996), convergent validity (Neal et al. 1994) and discriminant validity (Zilberg et al. 1982) has been reported for the IES. Researchers who have previously used the IES suggest that total scores of 0–8 may be interpreted as sub-clinical, 9–25 as mild, 26–43 as moderate, and over 43 as severe, and that a score of 26 or over may be regarded as a 'clinically significant reaction' (Shapiro 1996).

Shevlin et al. (1997) administered the IES to a random sample of 205 respondents three weeks after the death of Princess Diana. This opportunity sample was drawn from a city in the East Midlands, and of those indicating their age (47 per cent), the mean was 40.97 years (SD=17.45, range 17–82). Either the *death* or the *funeral* of Princess Diana was used as the specific traumatic event for 102 and 103 respondents respectively. The IES was found to be internally consistent, with a Cronbach's alpha of 0.854 for the full scale. Slightly lower, but acceptable, estimates were found for the intrusion (α=0.792) and avoidance (α=0.765) sub-scales. A correlation of 0.61 (p<0.05) was found between the scores of the two sub-scales, consistent with the findings of Robbins and Hunt (1996), which indicated that the scale was measuring two related but relatively distinct dimensions.

The mean total IES scores for the death of Princess Diana was 16.94 (SD=12.75) and 19.17 (SD=13.32) for the funeral. Descriptive statistics for the avoidance and intrusion sub-scales and the total scale score for the total sample are presented in Table 6.1.

The mean total IES and sub-scale scores reported in Table 1 show that for this sample the responses are similar to those reported for events involving physical threats and natural disasters. McFarlane (1992) reported similar mean IES (17.4), intrusion (11.5) and avoidance (6.1) scores for fire fighters. Johnsen et al. (1997) reported mean IES (19.7), intrusion (9.1) and avoidance (10.6) scores for victims four months after an avalanche, and mean IES (19.0),

Table 6.1. Descriptive statistics for IES scores.

IES Dimension	N	Mean	Minimum	Maximum	Standard Deviation
Intrusion	205	9.141	0.00	33.000	7.459
Avoidance	205	8.917	0.00	32.000	7.442
Total	205	18.05	0.00	57.000	12.968

intrusion (8.7) and avoidance (10.0) scores for rescuers four months after an avalanche. Higher mean scores have been reported for the South African police exposed to violence during the preceding year (Total=24.4, intrusion= 8.7, avoidance=15.7; Kopel & Friedman 1997) and Vietnam War combat veterans (Total=40.7, intrusion=20.4, avoidance=20.3; Wilson et al. 1985). Therefore the mean scores in this study suggest that the psychological consequences of the death and funeral of Princess Diana were significant. The mean scores on the sub-scales and total scale score are consistent with those studies that examined the impact of traditional traumatic stressors such as threats to personal well-being and natural disasters.

The percentages of total IES scores within each category of severity proposed by Shapiro (1996) are presented in Table 6.2.

Table 6.2. Percentages of IES scores by severity categories.

Category description	Death of Diana		Funeral of Diana	
	IES score	Percentage	IES score	Percentage
Subclinical	0 – 8	33	0 – 8	26
Mild	9 – 25	36	9 – 25	39
Moderate	26 – 43	30	26 – 43	29
Severe	43 – 75	1	43 – 75	6

The categorized percentages presented in Table 2 and the range of scores presented in Table 1 indicate that there was variability in the psychological response to the death and funeral of Princess Diana. The IES scores ranged from 0 to 44 (Mean total=16.9, Intrusion=9.0, Avoidance=7.9) for the death of Princess Diana and from 0 to 57 (Mean total=19.2, Intrusion=9.2,

Avoidance=10.0) for the funeral. Diana's funeral elicited a higher total score and total mean score than her death. This may be due to the fact that individuals had had time to reflect on the events between the death and the funeral. It is also feasible that the media may have influenced the manner in which people addressed the events portrayed.

For the death and funeral, 33 per cent and 26 per cent of the sample respectively indicated a relatively low level of psychological distress. Such data should not be interpreted as evidence that these individuals experienced no distress. Any scores above zero signify that the events are of psychological importance, but their response was not indicative of post-traumatic stress symptomatology. Alternatively, a small percentage of people experienced severe psychological distress at the death (1 per cent) and funeral (6 per cent) of Princess Diana. The symptomatology associated with such extreme scores is consistent with post-traumatic stress syndrome as defined in operational terms of avoidance and intrusion. Evidently, individuals reacted at both extremes of the IES continuum, but the most interesting finding is that a significant percentage of those surveyed responded to a 'clinically significant' degree. In relation to the death of Diana 31 per cent of respondents scored above the diagnostic cut-off score of 25, while 35 per cent of respondents asked to focus on the funeral had scores greater than 25 (Shapiro 1996).

Gender Effects

To investigate any gender differences in the response to the death and funeral of Princess Diana a series of t-tests were carried out on the total IES scores and the intrusion and avoidance sub-scales between men and women. The results show that women had a significantly higher mean intrusion score (t=-3.66, df=203, p<.05) and a significantly higher mean total IES score (t=-3.06, df=203, p<.05). No significant mean differences were found for avoidance scores (t=-1.68, df=203, p>.05). Although the total female IES score is significantly higher than the male score, this is probably due to differences on the intrusion dimension. This higher incidence of intrusive thoughts may represent a real difference in the manner by which men and women dealt with the events. However, the commonly held position that men deal with difficult issues through denial and women prefer to talk through and embrace the issues is not fully supported by the data, as there was no significant difference between the avoidance sub-scale scores. An alternative explanation may lie with the difference between the genders in expressing their psychological experiences. A related example of this is given with respect to pain perception. Through carefully controlled experimental investigation it has been demonstrated that the pain threshold between two cultural groups (Nepalese porters and Western mountain climbers) does not differ, but the criterion for reporting pain does (Clark & Clark 1980). Perhaps a similar situation occurred with respect to reporting a psychological response to Diana's death in relation to intrusive (painful) thoughts. In other words, it is possible there is no difference in the degree of intrusive thoughts between the two groups but rather they have different criteria for when to decide to report such intrusive thoughts.

Age Effects

The relationship between IES scores and age was examined using Pearson product moment correlations as a positive linear relationship was predicted. Moderate and statistically significant correlations were found between age and Intrusion scores ($r=0.265$, $p<0.05$) and age and total IES scores ($r=0.235$, $p<0.05$). The correlation between age and avoidance scores was not statistically significant ($r=0.158$, $p>.05$). The correlations suggest that the level of distress experienced was related to age; increasing age being associated with increased levels of distress.

Conclusion

Overall, the results show a high level of psychological distress as measured by the IES. This suggests that for individuals the psychological response to the death and funeral of Princess Diana was not trivial and is consistent with the findings of Masterton & Mander (1990) and Steels (1994) in that non-traditional psychological stressors can produce significant levels of psychological disturbance. Moreover, the analysis indicated that IES scores were higher for females and increased with age.

The fact that the sample was essentially opportunistic in nature should not negate the substantive finding that the majority of the respondents were suffering significant psychological distress. The IES has been demonstrated to have sound psychometric properties and is used extensively in the trauma literature (Weiss & Marmar 1997). On the anniversary of the death of the Princess, the media chose to change their focus from one supporting public mourning to a position challenging the genuine nature of the 'rightness' of the public grief on the scale witnessed. The work reported here lies outside this debate. Whether the people who felt moved by the tragic events in the autumn of 1997 were genuinely moved to mourn for the Princess, irrespective of media coverage, or whether there was some form of grief-fest orchestrated by the media is irrelevant to the topic at hand. From the work by Shevlin et al (1997) and the additional material reported here, it is clear that the people involved were psychologically affected. The crucial issue that strikes the authors about the events in 1997 (and the anniversary) is the willingness of commentators and pundits to blindly make judgements and protestations about people's behaviour without data to support their personal opinions. Deaths of high-profile popular figures, like Diana, have occurred in the past (e.g. Rudolf Valentino, Elvis, Eva Peron, River Phoenix) and they will of course occur in the future. In terms of future work in the field, we would encourage social scientists to begin to explore the response of people affected by such events through objective data collection so that the psychological phenomena can be better analysed and understood. Work on the psychological impact of the death of public figures may also benefit from the consideration of the impact of the 'death' of virtual characters (soap opera characters, animated characters, cyberpets) on the psychological well-being of their fans.

Bibliography

American Psychological Association (1987) *Diagnostic and Statistical Manual of Mental Disorders*, 3rd edition, Washington DC: APA.

American Psychological Association (1994) *Diagnostic and Statistical Manual of Mental Disorders*, 4th edition, Washington DC: APA.

Amick-McMullen, A., Kilpatrick, D.G., Veronen, L.J. & Smith, S. (1989) 'Family Survivors of Homicide Victims: Theoretical Perspectives and an Exploratory Study', *Journal of Traumatic Stress*, 2: 21–35.

Clark, W.C. & Clark, S.B. (1980) 'Pain Responses in Nepalese Porters', *Science*, 209: 538–9.

Cella, D.F., Mahon, S.M., Donovan, M.I. (1990) 'Cancer Recurrence as a Traumatic Event', *Behavioral Medicine*, 16: 15–22.

Curle, C.E. & Williams, C. (1996) 'Post-traumatic Stress Reactions in Children: Gender Differences in the Incidence of Trauma Reactions at Two Years and Examination of Factors Influencing Adjustment', *British Journal of Clinical Psychology*, 35: 29–309.

Fullerton, C.S., Ursano, R.J. (1997) 'Post-traumatic Responses in Spouse/Significant Others of Disaster Workers' in C.S. Fullerton, R.J. Ursano, (eds), *Post-traumatic Stress Disorder: Acute and Long-Term Responses to Trauma and Disaster*, pp. 59–75, Washington: American Psychiatric Press.

Helzer, J.E., Robins, L.N., & McEvoy, L. (1987) 'Post-traumatic Stress Disorder in the General Population: Findings of the Epidemiologic Catchment Area Survey', *New England Journal of Medicine*, 26: 1630–4.

Herlofsen, P. (1994) 'Group Reactions to Trauma: An Avalanche Accident' in R.J. Ursano, B.G. McCaughy, & C.S. Fullerton (eds), *Individual and Community Responses to Trauma and Disaster: The Structure of Human Chaos*, pp. 248–66. Cambridge: Cambridge University Press.

Hodgkinson, P.E. & Stewart, M. (1991) *Coping with Catastrophe: A Handbook of Disaster Management*, London: Routledge.

Horowitz, M.J., Wilner, N. & Alvarez, W. (1979) 'Impact of Events Scale: A Measure of Subjective Stress', *Psychosomatic Medicine*, 41: 209–18.

Johnsen, B.H., Eid, J., Løvstad, T. & Michelsen, L.T. (1997) 'Post-traumatic Stress Symptoms in Non-exposed Victims and Spontaneous Rescuers after an Avalanche', *Journal of Traumatic Stress*, 10: 133–40.

Kopel, H. & Friedman, M. (1997) 'Post-traumatic Symptoms in South African Police Exposed to Violence', *Journal of Traumatic Stress*, 10: 307–17.

Masterton, G. & Mander, A.J. (1990) 'Psychiatric Emergencies, Scotland and the World Cup Finals', *British Journal of Psychiatry*, 156: 475–78.

McFarlane, A.C. (1989) 'The Aetiology of Post-traumatic Morbidity: Predisposing, Precipitating and Perpetuating Factors', *British Journal of Psychiatry*, 154: 221–8.

McFarlane, A.C. (1992) 'Avoidance and Intrusion in Post-traumatic Stress Disorder', *The Journal of Nervous and Mental Disease*, 180: 439–445.

Neal, L.A., Busuttil, W., Rollins, J., Herepath, R., Strike, P., & Turnball, G. (1994) 'Convergent Validity of Measures of Post-traumatic Stress Disorder in a Mixed Military and Civilian Population', *Journal of Traumatic Stress*, 7: 447–55.

Robbins, I. & Hunt, N. (1996) 'Validation of the IES as a Measure of the Long-term Impact of War Trauma', *British Journal of Health Psychology*, 1: 87–9.

Shapiro, F. (1996) *EMDR: Level 1 training manual*, Pacific Grove: CA.

Shevlin, M., Brunsden, V., Walker, S., Davies, M. & Ramkalawan, T. (1997) 'Her Death and Funeral Rate as Traumatic Stressors', *British Medical Journal*, 315: 1467–8.

Steels, M. D. (1994) 'Deliberate Self Poisoning – Nottingham Forest Football Club and F.A. Cup defeat', *Irish Journal of Psychological Medicine*. 11: 76–8.

Weiss, D.S., & Marmar, C.R. (1997) 'The Impact of Event Scale – Revised' in J.P. Wilson & T.M. Keane (eds), *Assessing Psychological Trauma and PTSD*, pp. 399–411, New York, NY, USA: Guilford Press.

Wilson, J.P. (1994) 'The historical evolution of PTSD Diagnostic Criteria: from Freud to DSM-IV', *Journal of Traumatic Stress*, 7, 681–98.

Wilson, J.P., Ken Smith, W. & Johnson, S.K. (1985) 'A Comparative Analysis of PTSD Among Various Survivor Groups' in C.R. Figley (ed.), *Trauma and its Wake: Vol. 1. The Study and Treatment of Posttraumatic Stress Disorder*, pp. 142–72, New York: Brunner/Mazel.

Zilberg, N.J., Weiss, D.S. & Horowitz, M.J. (1982) 'Impact of Event Scale: A Cross Validation Study and Some Empirical Evidence Supporting a Conceptual Model of Stress Response Syndromes', *Journal of Consulting and Clinical Psychology*, 50: 407–14.

7

Secular Religion and the Public Response to Diana's Death

Chris Harris

The public response to the death of Princess Diana is evidence that Britain is still a very spiritual country. (The Archbishop of Canterbury)

Can sociology assist in the task of evaluating the Archbishop's remark? Any such attempt obviously depends on the exact meaning of the term 'spiritual', which is surely an issue that belongs more properly to the theologian than to the sociologist. This paper will substitute 'religious' for the term 'spiritual'. Clearly the Archbishop as the head of a religious institution can scarcely object to the rephrasing and, faced as the Church of England is with declining membership, attendances and revenues (Church of England, Central Board of Finance 1997) he needs to believe that the answer to the rephrased question is 'yes'.

Answering the question then requires a specification of the meaning of the term 'religion' in sociological discourse. Unfortunately sociologists have as much difficulty in producing such a definition as would be encountered by a theologian asked to define 'spiritual' (see the discussion in Hamilton 1995: 11–18). Has sociology nothing to say therefore? On the contrary, this paper will argue, first, that the categories developed by the classical sociologists for the analysis of religious phenomena can usefully be employed in analysing the response to the death of Diana and, secondly, that the utility of such religious categories does not, in itself, qualify it as being a religious response. The applicability of the categories of the sociology of religion does not warrant the conclusion that the phenomena to which they are applied are *ipso facto* 'religious'. In so doing the paper seeks to make a modest contribution to the issue of the sociological definition of religion.

The social disciplines have responded to the modernistic world view by accepting that the history of modern European thought is, to adopt the title of Edwin Chadwick's book, the history of *The Secularization of the European*

Mind (1975). This is the chief strand in what sociologists of religion have come to call the 'secularization thesis'. However, though the classical sociologists contributed some elements of that 'thesis', there is a tension in their work between the historical meta-narrative of a decline in *religiosity* and a belief in the universality of *religion*, either as a societal or as an anthropological universal. Durkheim and Weber, for example, seem to hold both to a meta-narrative of religious decline and to a belief that religion is a functional prerequisite either of society (Durkheim) or of the individual (Weber). On the other hand Marx, while holding that religion is functional for the maintenance of capitalism, expected religion and all ideology to wither away when its material basis was destroyed by the arrival of a future communist society.

Lesser students of religion have tended, rather more consistently, either to argue in favour of the decline in religious belief and practice over time (see for example Wallis and Bruce, in Bruce 1992) or to argue that religion is of universal importance (for example, Parsons 1951). The latter may however be accused of succeeding in maintaining religion's importance only by adopting implicitly a substantive, sociological definition of religion which is so wide that it empties it of all the qualities that make it a definition of religion in those substantive senses which the term conveys in common language use (see for example Yinger 1970). The most celebrated form of this extension is to be found in the notion of 'civil religion' put forward by Bellah (1967, 1975; Bellah and Hammond 1980; for discussion of civil religion in the British context, see Thompson 1988 and 1992). If you are a universalist you will see religion everywhere: not only in civic rituals but in musical cults and in public outpourings of grief such as that following the Hillsborough football disaster, and in the response to the death of Diana.

To the passenger in the Clapham omnibus the inclusion of these obviously non-religious phenomena within the category 'religious' seems absurd, since they are obviously 'secular'. The term 'secular religion' appears patently self-contradictory. The key question is: can phenomena which are *prima facie* candidates for the title 'secular religion' be regarded as still 'religious' in spite of their secular nature, or are they merely examples of social phenomena which, while not distinctively religious in the substantive sense, none the less possess characteristics which have been the particular focus of attention for sociologists of religion?

In discussing what light the response to Diana's death can throw on these issues, I shall approach the response to her death somewhat indirectly. I wish first to consider metropolitanism, something not at all discussed in any of the reactions to the response to Diana's death that I have seen. London, especially in the imperial age, was a centre of power and influence, a power and influence symbolically and ritually displayed. It was a stage on which drama and tragedy were played out and provided the lower orders within its ambit not merely with a spectacle but also with a sense of participation in great events. London was, in the dramatic sense, *exciting,* and key to this was the crowds, a sense of participation in something self-transcendent, of participation in something bigger than oneself.

Of course, it can be argued that the ability of broadcasting to transmit the public life of the capital into our homes renders actual participation redundant. On the contrary, I would suggest that the images of the crowds swirling around at the 'mighty heart' of things portrayed by the television, while it provides access to the spectacle, only emphasizes provincial exclusion. 'I saw it on the tele' is no substitute for 'I was there'. A chorister from St David's Cathedral, interviewed on television, listed the royal events of the 1980s and 1990s which she has 'missed', adding: 'I am travelling up overnight for the funeral because I am determined not to miss this one.' The reviewer of Martin Amis's latest novel in the *London Review of Books* remarks on 'a curious paradox of contemporary life: the more we are told by . . . TV that there is more out there than ever before, the more we feel trapped in our own lives. The more there is the more we feel excluded from.'

Now the experience of transcendence in large gatherings whose members congregate together in numinous places is characteristic of the members of religious groups across cultures and throughout the ages. To make his stand against the authorities of his day, Jesus had to go to Jerusalem, the central place of a people defined by the worship of their God. But Jerusalem was as much a symbol of Judah's nationhood and the seat of secular power. Jesus would have gone there even if the Jews had had no central place of religious worship. To produce phenomena of the kind which are associated with religion, the numinousness of the central place does not have to derive from the other world – its special character does not need to arise from its association with spiritual forces. Its locus as a centre of secular power will do just as well to stimulate the crowds, the pilgrimages, the transcendence.

Much has been written about the role of the broadcasting media in shaping the response to Diana's death. This role was central for two reasons. The first is fortuitous – the timing. She died after the Sunday papers had gone to press thus privileging broadcasting over the press. The second reason broadcasting was important was what it decided to do, particularly what the BBC decided to do. Traditionally the BBC has been a national institution dedicated to public service, a role which it took very seriously. While much has changed within the BBC in the last thirty years, its outer surface is still recognizably the descendant of the BBC of the war years. It is still a national institution and its news coverage is still regarded as authoritative. This perception provides a context which gives meaning to what it does.

Now the news service is of course no longer staffed by public servants but by journalists and I define journalists as a profession whose chief orienting concept is that of the 'story'. The head of news at the BBC justified (on 'Feedback') his decision to run a continuous 'Today'-type news magazine programme non-stop for the whole of Sunday on all channels in terms of its 'news-value'; Diana's death was 'the most important *story* the BBC has ever reported'. My point is that because the BBC is the BBC and not the *Sun*, *Times* or other organ of the Murdoch press, this decision was 'read' by the audience as signalling the national significance of Diana's death. But there was a problem. There was simply not enough information to warrant the coverage. So they covered the reaction to the coverage; but not overtly: the reaction to the saturation coverage was reported as the reaction to Diana's death. The BBC's saturation coverage was 'read' as indicating that Diana's death was an event of supreme national importance, and the reaction to the coverage was read as a national reaction to her death, the reporting of which amplified the very reaction which it reported.

The coverage defined the story as a 'human interest' story. Since they could not interview the chief actors in the drama, human interest had to be provided by interviewing the public. This involved interviewers going on about how sad it all is until the interviewee started to blub and the camera zoomed in on the tears. If this didn't work, they went on about how sad everybody else was, at which point the interviewee usually obliged. Such manipulation by interviewers of their subjects then provided a warrant for a *new* news item about the depth of the grief of ordinary people for someone they had never met. After three days of this anyone not already near to tears felt there was something wrong with them. In the case of the funeral, the media told the nation that the nation was upping sticks and going to London, thus making everyone feel that they ought to be coming too or that they might be missing something if they didn't. It was no surprise therefore that one interviewee, self-described as a college lecturer, was unable to explain why he and his whole family were getting up at three in the morning to attend the funeral: 'I don't know why we are going really. I just felt we had to.'

All this is very familiar to a student of religion. In evangelical Christianity people leap from their seats and declare themselves for Jesus after an hour of emotional blackmail which tells them that they are morally worthless if they don't and when everyone else in the arena seems to be doing so. What is distinctive about the Diana event is that the engendering of this response is *mediated*: instead of being engendered by membership of a crowd, it is experienced individually via the media but in a way that is signed as collective. This deprives the experience of the cathartic effect that crowd participation creates, while at the same time creating a need for that catharsis. Hence the trip to London or some other public place where the individual response could be given an expression both public and collective. But why was Diana's death experienced as a national loss? Empirically because of her long domination of the popular media, but symbolically because she was royal – HRH or no HRH – and royalty, like the capital, are national symbols.

Thus far the account given is consistent with the claim that event and response were unique, but only in the sense that they constituted a unique conjunction of elements and processes already existing and operative in contemporary Britain and, as Wollfe's chapter demonstrates, have historical precedents. Beneath this account however runs a Durkheimian theme. At one point I felt the scenes relayed by the television depicted an 'effervescent assembly' which Durkheim, in the *Elementary Forms of the Religious Life* (1915), claims functions both as a reaffirmation of existing religious beliefs and the site of the emergence of new beliefs and practices. It can certainly be claimed that the ambivalent attitude of the crowds reflected exactly this dual function: there was a simultaneous acceptance of the monarchy as a national symbol and a rejection of its traditional (i.e. early twentieth century) forms. But the crowds of condolence signers, flower layers and funeral mourners were not effervescent assemblies, though their members were certainly in the grip of what Durkheim would have called a *courant sociale*. Evangelical meetings are frequently effervescent assemblies and the techniques of manipulation employed in such assemblies had certainly been operating on the mourning crowds. But the manipulation was employed by the media reaching out to isolated individuals and not dependent upon changes in consciousness which individuals undergo through crowd membership. The assemblies were the *result* of media-amplified emotion, not its site and origin. In any case, though the concept of the effervescent assembly is used by Durkheim in his discussion of religion, there is nothing specifically religious about this phenomenon; moreover it could be argued that such phenomena are primarily psychological rather than social in character. However what makes such assemblies social phenomena for Durkheim is that their participants constitute a totality: the assembly is the coming together of otherwise separated subgroups so that the experience it engenders is that of being made 'whole'. But whereas for Durkheim the assembly engenders the effervescence, in the Diana case the media-generated effervescence created the assembly. In order for this to happen the media had not only to amplify an emotional response but also to create the impression that such responses are nationwide thus creating the need to express the emotion through some sort of congregation.

It is through the category of totality that we begin to approach religion in the Durkheimian sense. In the *Elementary Forms* Durkheim defined 'religion' as a set of beliefs and practices related to sacred things, that is things set apart and forbidden which unite their members in a moral community or 'church'. A central argument in the *Elementary Forms* is that the superposited, extrinsic quality of sacredness is the result of the fact that sacred things symbolize a totality whose reality transcends that of the individuals which compose it. Sacred signifiers are sacred because the signified is just such a reality, namely, 'Society'. The difficulty of this definition arises from the fact that, as long as people live in groups and express their dependence on and respect for the group through ritual practices, then they are practising religion, however secular their conception of external reality. Hence the veneration extended to, for example, any symbol of nationality – whether a national team, a national flag, a national institution, a nationalized industry or a national person – is, on this definition, religious. But what sort of religion would this be? Why, 'secular religion' of course, since the content of the *conscience collective* of a modern society (i.e. one with an organic structure) is necessarily diffuse, general and rational.

How were the media able to do this? Because they had made Diana? If we answer 'yes' to this question another arises: why did the media make Diana? Because she was the consort of the heir apparent and, as a mother of his children was a future queen mum – a mother of our national future. Royalty are sacred – set apart and forbidden – because they symbolize the totality of which we are part. But they are not gods, a crucial feature of Weber's definition of religion as opposed to magic.

This, of course, is not to ignore the importance of Diana's personality in creating her fame/notoriety. But it is to point out that it is not the person themselves but the *relation* between the person and their office that is crucial. In the case of the Queen there is rarely a glimpse of the person behind the mask, let alone any discrepancy between the institution and the person. Occasional breakings of the formal mask associated with the sacred social position, the momentary lifting of a curtain, generate a susurration of excitement. It is as if the sacred Host winked, or the Royal Standard stubbornly refused to be unrolled to drape a royal coffin. The fascination of royalty is that these sacred symbols are, contrary to all appearances, actually human – just like you and me. But the key phrase is 'contrary to all appearances'. The fascination with the humanity of royalty derives from its being customarily concealed and it is this concealment that results in the frisson created by the rare and occasional revelation.

Diana in contrast went full frontal and forced Charles to go full-frontal in self-defence. This posed a problem for the paparazzi. Their stock in trade is getting behind the curtain, levering off the royal persona (mask) to reveal the person beneath. When royalty cast aside the mask, the media become frantic in their search for something else to reveal. Diana personified the end of monarchy, the end of the sacred, of things set apart and forbidden. Her fascination depended crucially, however, on her being *royal,* on the contradiction between her formal status and the interpretation of her role, a contradiction which depended on the existence of a traditional Royal Family of which she was, so signally, through the revelation of her vulnerable humanity, not a part.

Now the tension between the extra-ordinary qualities of a person and the office which they occupy is one of the main themes of Weber's sociology of religion (Weber 1965; 1968: Chs 3, 6, 14, 16) and is encapsulated in his distinction between prophets and priests, between the charismatic domination of the prophet – 'ye have heard it said of old time, but *I* say unto you' – and the legal rational domination of the priesthood in which the person is subordinate to the office. The essential problem of religious groups is their need to interpret an eternal message in the light of changing historical circumstances. The source of social change for Weber lies in extra-ordinary individuals. The existence of prophets is functional for the maintenance of religious organizations since prophets are the source of those adaptations which faiths must make to changed cultural and social circumstances. Yet radical ideas won't catch on unless they have legitimation: Jesus spoke 'with authority, not as the scribes'. The personal authority of the prophet is necessary to secure the acceptance of the adaptation he proposes, but at the same time this authority undermines the traditional authority of the priest and thus endangers the very structure of the church whose continued existence is necessary to preserve the faith which the prophet seeks to adapt. Prophets are dangerous. A church cannot survive with them or without them. As for a church, so with the monarchy. Charles, concerned to reform the monarchy, lacks the charisma which would give his adaptations authority. He is not therefore a prophet but an eccentric. Diana had the charisma but instead of using it to transform the institution, by her privileging of the person over the office she tended to destroy it. The Weberian distinction between priest and prophet, between continuity and adaptive change, between office and incumbent are made with reference to the sphere of religion, but apply equally to all social institutions in conditions of rapid social and cultural change; they apply not only to the Church of England but also to the political parties. For example it could be argued that, William Hague, the present leader of the Tory party, lacks both the prophetic vision needed to legitimate the required reforms and the charismatic authority to carry them through.

Conceptual distinctions made in the sociology of religion are therefore highly applicable not only to sacred institutions but to social life in general. However, unless you are a Durkheimian, this does not imply that there is no sociological distinction between the substantive religious sphere and the secular, a distinction which Weber never defines but took for granted in a somewhat conventional way. Religion for Weber is concerned with the worship of a God or gods, and what makes gods divine is not their being signifiers of society but the worship of their followers. The response to Diana's death is not, therefore, for Weber, a religious phenomenon as such, but one to which the categories devised for the analysis of such phenomena none the less apply.

There is however one sense in which it could be argued that it *is* a religious phenomenon and this is the Marxian sense. For Marx, religion was the sigh of the oppressed, who sought refuge from the intolerable present in the hope of a better life hereafter (Marx and Engels 1955). It is the primary manifestation of alienated self-consciousness, the archetypical 'ideology'. Diana is seen as an icon of the oppressed who through courage and suffering broke the suffocating bonds that confined her and in a bound was free. She holds out therefore the hope of personal salvation – but from what? From the oppressive, stuffy old Royal Family which in turn symbolizes the restraints of tradition and convention. She was truly 'modern' in that sense of the term found in the rhetoric used by the then newly elected British Prime Minister, Tony Blair, to describe the difference between his 'new' Labour party and its predecessor. What we have is a myth concerning a suffering heroine who demonstrates the possibility of a triumph over the forces of darkness and through whom we can vicariously live out that triumph. The desire for real liberation is satisfied by a surrogate liberation, the real oppression in society is displaced by an imagined oppression of custom and tradition which can be more easily overthrown. Liberation will be achieved by modernization: new Labour, new Britain, post-Diana. In this sense the triumph of new 'Labour' and the response to the death of Diana are cognate phenomena and both are equally ideological and therefore for Marx 'religious' since they involve the displacement of real onto imagined problems. As one commentator acutely remarked, the ambivalently royalist crowds mourning Diana mistake the problem; it is not the stuffy old Royal Family but advanced capitalism that is doing their heads in.

This paper has argued, first that the categories employed by the classical sociologists of religion are applicable to the event; and secondly, that the fact that they are so applicable does not, *in itself*, imply that the phenomenon to which they are applied is religious.

As to whether, from the point of view of the classical sociologists, the response to Diana's death is a religious phenomenon, the answer depends on which sociologist you choose. I have argued that from a Durkheimian point of view the answer is 'yes'; from a Marxian point of view the answer is 'yes';

from a Weberian point of view the answer is 'no'.

I then glossed these conclusions as follows: Durkheim's definition of religion is so wide as to make trivial the conclusion that the phenomenon is religious, since for Durkheim all group rituals are religious. There's nothing much in this conclusion to encourage the Archbishop.

Nor is the Archbishop likely to be encouraged by the Marxian conclusion which is premised on a thoroughgoing ontological materialism which insists that, even at the phenomenal level, what appear as 'spiritual' concerns are in reality 'mystified' social/material concerns. This theoretical standpoint is similar to Durkheim's inasmuch as all forms of 'displacement' are religious/ideological so that there can be no non-religious ideal/mythical constructs or motivations and the claim that the phenomena are religious is therefore also trivial. No comfort for the Archbishop here because Marx's claim is based on the assumption that the British people *cannot* be authentically 'spiritual'. Only from a Weberian standpoint can we arrive at judgement which is non-trivial, i.e. empirically significant in the sense that from that standpoint two different states of affairs are equally possible. Unfortunately, from that standpoint, the content of the judgement must be that the phenomena could have been, but in fact were not, religious.

My quarrel with Marx and Durkheim does not of course involve a rejection of all that they have to say about religion; it is restricted to the utility of their *definition* of religion. My objection is that their esoteric academic definitions depart too far from the exoteric, everyday, meaning of the word. Religion for Durkheim is in the last analysis about group reverence, but though our commonsensical notion of religion does indeed include the notion of group reverence, we do not call every instance of group reverence religious. Equally what have been termed religious phenomena certainly include examples of displacement, and there is a lot of displacement about, but that does not justify calling all displacement religion. It will not do to say that when I use the word religion I mean something else than is commonly meant by it *if* my usage then includes whole ranges of phenomena not generally termed religious and/or excludes other whole ranges which generally are so termed. Weber doesn't get into these difficulties, since he doesn't define religion in general at all except to distinguish it from magic.

My definition would be as follows. A set of beliefs and practices only intelligible to the observer on the assumption that those who participate in them believe in the existence of a non-empirical reality which lies behind or beyond our phenomenal experience may be sociologically termed 'spiritual' beliefs and practices. Those beliefs and practices which are primarily concerned with the manipulation of the reality for the benefit of practitioners may be termed 'magical'. Beliefs and practices which are primarily concerned with the establishment of a right relationship with that reality may be termed 'religious'.

The proper word to use to refer to Diana in discussing the response to her death is 'myth'. She became a mythical figure which people found useful to help them think about their own lives and personal situations. 'Myths are good to think with' (Lévi-Strauss 1966). Many but not all religions express their beliefs in mythical forms. This is unsurprising. Religious beliefs necessarily refer to non-empirical entities. As a result they cannot be thought in concrete terms and are therefore not easily accessible to those who live in the *practico-concrète* except through the device of myth. But this applies to any *abstract* belief whether or not it is concerned with non-empirical 'spiritual' reality. Myths are not distinctively religious, though are commonly so.

A whole range of phenomena associated with religion and therefore nominated 'religious' have this character. We have learnt to see them as religious because historically the religious sphere is where they have predominated. We need to see these phenomena hitherto defined as religious as characteristic of all human groups, not just religious ones. If we make them central to our definition of religion then, given their wide distribution, everything becomes religious. If the term religion is to mean anything it must have a restricted denotation such as that which is achieved by the definition suggested above.

Bibliography

Bellah, R.N. (1967) 'Civil Religion in America', *Daedalus*, vol. 96, no. 1: 1–21.

Bellah, R.N. (1975) *The Broken Covenant. American Civil Religion in Time of Trial,* New York: Seabury Press.

Bellah, R.N. and Hammond, P.E. (eds) (1980) *Varieties of Civil Religion*, San Fransisco: Harper and Row.

Bruce, S. (1992) *Religion and Modernization*, Oxford: The Clarendon Press.

Chadwick, E. (1975) *The Secularization of the European Mind*, Cambridge: Cambridge University Press.

Church Of England Central Board of Finance (1997) *Church Statistics 1995,* London: Central Board of Finance.

Durkheim, E. (1915) *The Elementary Forms of the Religious Life,* London: Allen and Unwin.

Hamilton, M. (1995) *The Sociology of Religion,* London: Routledge.

Lévi-Strauss, C. (1966) *The Savage Mind*, London: Weidenfeld and Nicholson.

Marx, K. and Engels, F. (1955) *On Religion*, Scholars Press: Atlanta, Ga.

Thompson, K. (1988) 'How Religious are the British', in T. Thomas (ed.), *The British: Their Religious Beliefs and Practices,* London: Routledge.

Thompson, K. (1992) 'Religion, Values, and Ideology', in R. Bocock and K. Thompson (eds), *Social and Cultural Forms of Modernity*, Oxford: Polity Press/ The Open University.

Wallis, R. and Bruce, S (1992) 'Secularization: the Orthodox Model' in Bruce (1992).

Weber, M. (1965) *The Sociology of Religion*, ed. T. Parsons, London: Methuen.

Weber, M. (1998) *Economy and Society*, New York: Bedminster Press.

Yinger, J.M. (1970) *The Scientific Study of Religion*, London: Routledge.

Part 3

London

Between a death and the funeral, the body is often the focus for paying respect. Viewing the body is less common in the UK than it was, but it is a key part of mourning ritual in Ireland, the USA and some other countries. At the funeral itself, the last sight of the coffin as it is lowered into the ground or is removed from sight at the crematorium is the emotional crux of the ritual – the body is a sign of the person, and its last exit dramatizes the death of the person.

When somebody famous dies, the body may take on special significance. Many may never have seen the celebrity in the flesh, but in death they may be able to view the body or visit the grave, which thus becomes a place of pilgrimage – as with the graves of John F. Kennedy at Arlington Cemetery and of Elvis Presley at Graceland, not to mention many of the classic places of Catholic pilgrimage over the centuries. Sometimes the place of death, rather than the place of burial, becomes the shrine. This often occurs at the site of murders, road and rail disasters, floods and other natural disasters where the bodies have been removed to a number of diverse locations. Occasionally, another location becomes the prime place of pilgrimage, as in April 1989 when it was the fans' home ground (Anfield) more than the stadium where the disaster occurred (Hillsborough) to which hundreds of thousands flocked with flowers, scarves and other tributes.

Diana's body, so visible in life, was in death hidden. Resting at St James's Palace, it was not accessible to the public. She was then buried on an island at Althorp, out of bounds to the public, in part because the Spencers did not want her grave to attract thousands of pilgrims. A few made the pilgrimage to the Paris underpass where she died, but it was primarily the royal palaces of London, and especially her home, Kensington Palace to which the pilgrims came. It is, after all, to the deceased's home that people go after the funeral, and that Jewish people go to visit during Shiva. Nearby Harrods, the Fayed emporium, also drew very substantial numbers. It was in London that her home was, in London that her body lay, and in London that the funeral took place. For a week, the eyes of the world were on this city, its mourners and its increasingly 'sacred' geography.

Chapters 8, 9 and 10 each look at the behaviour of visitors to Kensington Gardens, but place them within different contexts. Chapter 8, written by an anthropologist with expert knowledge of both garden history and cemetery behaviour, places the behaviour of visitors there within two contexts: the history of the gardens, and the behaviour of ordinary visitors to cemeteries in contemporary London. We find that much of the behaviour that commentators found odd, such as mourners addressing condolence cards to the dead, is in fact to be found everyday in cemeteries around the capital – not to mention at other sites such as the Vietnam Veterans Memorial in Washington DC. Chapter 10 places the same behaviour in Kensington Gardens within the context of those fans who regularly follow members of the Royal Family to their public engagements, the author accompanying two such fans to Kensington. Chapter 9, by a folklorist, looks at the folk religious veneration of the pilgrims to Kensington in the context of centuries of English folklore.

The sense of the crowd is present in each of these three chapters. Using similar ethnographic methods, this time by an insider, Chapter 11 documents how the crowd was policed on the day of the funeral. Royal ceremonials are among the trickier public order operations for the police, since errors are highly visible and there are powerful interests to be offended. Police typically respond by seeking to establish control over the whole event. Establishing control over Diana's funeral would not be easy – given the possibility of the unexpected, a crowd that in the previous six days had been adept at spontaneous creativity, and a short planning period. As it turned out, the crowd controlled itself, most notably at those points of the journey north to Althorp where the police presence was minimal or even absent. One may compare this to Elizabeth's coronation, where police anticipation of pick-pockets and other petty crime proved unfounded.

The funeral itself demanded the creation of a ritual order, also in a very short space of time. Though British funerals have been criticized for being bland and impersonal, when a death affects large numbers of people the communitas generated can enable remarkable rituals to be put together from scratch in a very short period of time. Despite the families involved not having the best of relations with each other (usually a reliable predictor of a fraught funeral), a remarkable funeral was in fact devised and professionally executed, its liturgy and music being the foci of analysis in Chapter 12. Whatever else came out of the week of mourning, the idea that 'the Brits know how to do ceremonial' was affirmed. In death Diana was as effective an ambassador for cool Britannia as she had been in life.

8

Kensington Gardens: From Royal Park to Temporary Cemetery

Doris Francis, Georgina Neophytou and Leonie Kellaher

Following the sudden death of Diana, Princess of Wales, her home at Kensington Palace became the spontaneous focus for public assemblage. However, it was Kensington Gardens, which provided the stage for the ensuing commemorative drama. The crowd's conduct in appropriating and organizing the space on the south lawn and surrounding the Palace evoked and also updated the historical and cultural/religious association between home, death and the garden, between cemeteries and gardens.

It was during the early eighteenth century that the landscape of Kensington Gardens assumed the shape it substantially retained at the time of the death of Princess Diana (Jacques 1998). In the 1700s, such gardens with their groves of trees and secluded wooded walks were seen to offer a palliative for melancholy and a congenial environment for meditative retirement and contemplation (Coffin 1994). In Christian teaching, the garden is a long accepted place for spiritual reflection, a reminder both of the Garden of Eden and of Christ's agony at Gethsemane. The green of nature provided stimuli for formulating and shaping meditation, introspection and imagination (Hunt 1976).

Gardens were not only a suitable location, but also a subject for meditation and spiritual reflection. The seasonal cycle of nature confronts men and women with their own changes and mortality, with the transience of existence and with precarious happiness suddenly subdued by death. Kent's hermitage in Kensington Gardens resonates with allusions to solitary meditation on the brevity of life and the swift passage of time. The eighteenth-century garden also sought to recreate the pastoral arcadia described by Ovid and Virgil, depicted in the paintings of Claude and Poussin and experienced in the Roman *Campagna* on the Grand Tour. Temples, urns, sepulchral inscriptions and columns, dedicated to the memory of specific individuals, were used in these gardens to recreate a pastoral ambience, evoking themes such as *Et In Arcadia Ego* and the Elysian Fields (Panofsky 1951). Such commemorative features could increase melancholic pleasure by associating death and the garden, and by introducing allusions to the classical tradition of burial in the natural landscape (Hunt & Schuyler 1984). It might be argued that the grave of Diana, on a wooded island at Althorp, echoes Rousseau's elegiac burial within an island grove of poplar trees, thereby updating the 18th-century tradition of the 'cult of the tomb' (Ariès l981).

The linkage of death and the garden was continued in the nineteenth century with the promenades of visitors in the newly designed extra-mural cemeteries and with the opening to citizens of the royal parks with their memorial statues (Lasdun 1992). Interestingly, the design of the influential Kensal Green Cemetery was based on Regents Park (Brooks et al. 1989), while the layout of the prominent municipal City of London Cemetery resembles Loudon's plans for Derby Arboretum, the first purposely designed public park in England (Elliott 1991). These similar open landscapes offered the restorative properties of a green retreat to combat the dense, sunless, industrial metropolis.

In the twentieth century, this continuing dialogue between 'man' and nature on the themes of transience and commemoration is located in both cemetery and Kensington Gardens. These bounded spaces are alike in offering a quiet retreat from the hurly-burly of the high street, while long avenues of trees and grassy lawns similarly offer the spiritual resource and refreshment of perfected nature (Jenkins 1992). At Kensington Gardens, the Albert Memorial commemorates the tradition of memorialization in a garden setting. Indeed, Foucault (l982) places gardens and cemeteries in the same category of 'heterotopic space', allowing disparate uses and alternative visions of society (Greenhalgh & Worpole 1995).

This chapter suggests how the public displays of mourning following the death of Princess Diana might be viewed within the context of mourning behaviour in contemporary cemeteries. It offers an interpretation of how the eighteenth-century Kensington Garden landscape was so readily translated into a 'landscape of mourning', which both gave to and also gained from the significance of this historic landscape (Harrison 1992).

This reading of the events at Kensington Gardens (briefly detailed below and obtained from field observations over the period of 'Diana Week') is informed by the authors' recent study of the behaviour of people in six culturally and religiously diverse London cemeteries (Francis et al. 1997).

Our research argues that with the increased medicalization and professionalization of death, there has been a parallel increase in the secularization of religious beliefs relating to death and the afterlife, and a decline of prescribed rites of mourning. Our thesis proposes the continuing cultural elaboration of the cemetery as the site of more idiosyncratic, collective and eclectic expressions of grief, which are infused with secular and spiritual meanings, activities and symbols. In this chapter, we refer to our interviews and observations at Muslim, Greek Orthodox, Roman Catholic, Orthodox Jewish and Christian churched and unchurched groups to understand the commemorative rituals which emerged in September 1997 for Diana. Here we contextualize and explain the make-up of the 'Diana rituals' in terms of the deployment of the same repertoire of flowers, cards and actions which are used in London cemeteries today. It is argued that while extraordinary in terms of scale and intensity, these public memorializations are a part of, and contribute to, an evolving range of bereavement practices, particularly cemetery mourning rituals.

Field Notes

The following quotations, abstracted from personal notes written following Princess Diana's death, are included to provide a first-hand view of events. In collecting this material, the first author utilized a combination of anthropological methodologies of informal interviews, quantitative surveys and participant observation to research mourning behaviour and bereavement rituals which appeared similar to those observed recently during two years of cross-cultural field research in six London cemetery sites. During 'Diana Week' and after, the first author also interviewed cemetery study participants to assess the impact of the Princess's death on their bereavement activities, and sought their interpretations of her findings and analyses about behaviour at Kensington Palace. Thus, research at Kensington Gardens was informed by previous study in London cemeteries, and observations made in Kensington Gardens were cross-checked, discussed and analysed with the help and insights of cemetery visitors.

Sunday, 31 August. Princess Diana Is Dead. My friend called at 6.30 a.m. from the US to tell us Diana was killed in a car crash, having been hounded by the Paris paparazzi. Later Tony Blair on TV, shaken, remarks: 'By how many faces we knew her'; truly the 'princess of the people'. News media show a range of young people leaving flowers at Kensington Palace.

I walk to Kensington Palace to see the flowers brought in tribute. The MacDonald's on Kensington High Street has the TV on, and people are watching Princess Di programmes; they are sold out of ice-cream cones. Many people are on the street carrying bouquets and flowers; it is more crowded than usual at 5.00 p.m. When I near the Palace, I see the many bunches of flowers piled up along the west boundary entrance. The police direct us down to the further entrance at Victoria Gate, where we then turn back into the Gardens and to the west boundary wall where there is a raft of flowers and candles. Each bouquet has a card or sheet with a message – these are not concealed in envelopes, but are open and meant to be read. Indeed, people are filing along, looking at the flowers and reading the tributes. (I have observed similar activities when funeral flowers are displayed on the lawn, or with bouquets placed in the cremation area of the municipal cemetery at Christmas time.) The messages say that they will 'never forget Diana'; that she 'is in heaven'; that they 'identify with her pain, but now her suffering is over'. The tributes are from people of many different racial and ethnic groups, and mention all she did to help others. Many bunches of flowers with handwritten notes are tied to the perimeter railings along Kensington High Street, and people stop to read them. The bells in the nearby church sound. There are single roses strewn on the lawn.

People are orderly, quiet, restrained and wanting to be with others in public and to seek some comfort from seeing others acting in a similar way. As people read the notes and watch others, they are both expressing and learning mourning behaviour, demonstrated in an open, public way.

Monday and Tuesday, 1 and 2 September. Diana's body lies in state in the Chapel Royal at St James's Palace. But behind the gates, the Palace is empty and silent, like a tomb. The Al Fayed funeral is held at the London Central Mosque, Regents Park. The coffin faces Mecca, the Imam stands near the deceased, forgives the departed, asks rest for his soul and blesses all Muslims. Dodi is buried within twenty-four hours, as is the Muslim custom, in Brookwood Cemetery, Surrey, near Woking.

I walk to Kensington Palace, where an all-night candlelight vigil took place; Kensington Gardens remained open past its usual dusk closing. In the morning, there are remains of burned candles, some still burning, with wax and flowers like a shrine (Figure 8.1). There are only a few people in the morning; but by noon, many more are arriving. My radio reports over a hundred people a minute; and, indeed, from my vantage point on the broad-walk embankment, the crowds seem to be streaming in. Among these, there are many men, some in suits, coming during their lunch hour, walking purposefully and carrying flowers with cards: 'I love you', 'I'll never forget you', 'Dodi and Diana together forever' (Figure 8.2). Many people of colour are leaving flowers. There are also many parents with young children, who are encouraged to bring and place flowers and write notes; also babies in

Figure 8.1 Tree shrine, Kensington Gardens, Sunday, 7 September. *Doris Francis*

Figure 8.2 Placing flowers on the gates of Kensington Palace, Monday, 1 September. *Doris Francis*

pushchairs. Many photographs are taken of the flowers on the iron pillars and gates in front of the house.

People have chosen to make Diana's residence into a shrine, a monument/ memorial in place of a tombstone or an opportunity to view her coffin, which is kept only for the private family to view. People say that it is comforting to be at Diana's home, to read the words of others and to be with other people, rather than to grieve alone at home. It is also the tourist season and many people have themselves photographed in front of the Palace, or take pictures of their children and grandchildren to document their presence at this extra-ordinary event. They comment that there will never be such an outpouring, even for the Queen or the Queen Mum. People come and stay longer than on ordinary days. I speak with visitors from Kent, who bring flowers to both Kensington and Buckingham Palaces, and who will also sign the Book of Remembrance at St James's Palace. The usual people are also in the park at lunchtime – roller skates, dogs, lunch, ice cream – the normal park atmos-phere. Here the imagery of the house/shrine/memorial/garden of rest/park are all mixed.

In the evening after work, the crowd again increases. It is quiet, sombre; few talk. People just walk around, file past and read the flowers posted along the railings. Through these flowers, they express their personal feelings and also bear witness to others' private/public expressions. It is both public and private in complex ways. Some try to differentiate their flowers from those of the mass: they tie them to places on the railings where they stand out, or to branches of the trees along the Dial Walk. Here nature, death and mourning are reunited as autumn approaches. I speak with the Notting Hill Gate florist, who tells me that there is no particular colour or type of flower that people are choosing, but perhaps roses, he adds. When I ask, people tell me that they choose the flowers they like, particularly the colour.

Thursday, 4 September: Buckingham Palace. Everyone at Green Park is carrying flowers; the tube station posts directions to Buckingham and St James's Palaces. There are long queues at Buckingham Palace; it takes a minimum of an hour and twenty minutes just to place flowers and to get close enough to read others' cards and notes. Today the Palace looks like a shrine: notes are positioned, placed and framed. There are toy animals, home-made flags, signs, pictures, rows and rows of flowers, many very expensive, placed all along the fence. It feels a more orderly, more directed and more formal setting – surrounded by concrete and asphalt – than the park-like atmosphere of Kensington Gardens. I stand in the queue in front of two women, who came today from Surrey. They will also walk to Kensington Palace and Harrods, where the whole front of the store is piled high with flowers and cards to Di and Dodi. They have bought flowers in the colours they like: autumnal shades and red roses. The women recall coming to London for Diana's wedding and sleeping all night on the street to have a good vantage point to view the procession. The royal landscape of London is now the landscape of Diana. These women will also come to the funeral, and like many, will remember her life through urban landmarks. Here weddings and funerals are linked. They are also coupled in news items as people to be married this weekend, or to be guests at weddings, decide how to include reflections and memorials for Diana.

Thursday Evening. Go at 6.30 p.m. to St James's Palace. Met a woman this morning who has been there three times: 'You can see the Chapel where she's resting, the light; it's the place closest to where she is.' There are huge crowds at Green Park; the platforms for the funeral procession are mostly in place. As I arrive at the Palace, the mullioned window of the Chapel where Diana's body is resting, is illuminated. It appears to give off a kind of spiritual glow. Many, many people are standing, leaning on the barricades just looking and watching the window, as if something were going to happen. There are flowers and candles everywhere. I walk through heavy crowds to the queue where people wait to sign the Books of Remembrance. The line extends all the way down the Mall, and then backs-and-forths on itself five times. There are two stalls selling food, and the Women's Royal Voluntary Service and Salvation Army canteens give out tea and chocolate bars. The average wait to sign is seven hours, although there are now forty-two books.

Walking back, there are many flowers and candles on a black statue of a Madonna/mother figure. Again around the Royal Chapel with its light and hushed atmosphere, there is a kind of apotheosis, a definite site of pilgrimage, with the body somehow not yet dead, not yet buried and put away. Notes from school groups and individuals, all addressed to Diana, saying they 'miss her', 'thanking her for the meaningful life she led', 'wishing her peace'. People all read these and bring candles and flowers.

Friday afternoon, 5 September. At St James's, the Queen is in the Chapel and then walks among the crowd, picking up their bouquets and notes, and thereby validating everyone's tokens of remembrance and affection (it is too crowded for me to see). I then return to Kensington Palace and see that enormous cornucopia; that huge carpet/sea of flowers with their pungent smell now covers the entire lawn in front of her home gates and around to the Orangerie (Figure 8.3). An extraordinary sight of tribute, flowers from at least a million people. When the body is brought back from St James's Chapel Royal to her home, small shrines with candles, which will burn throughout the night of candlelight vigils, are already prepared. I hurry home to watch the Queen's Speech, but clearly not everyone does. Many hundreds of people pass me still going to the Palace with flowers, or dressed in dark

Figure 8.3 Flowers in front of Kensington Palace, Thursday, 11 September. *Tony Walter*

suits to view Diana's body being brought in a hearse to the Palace.

Saturday, September 6. This morning we rise about 6.00 with a feeling almost of excitement. We join other people also walking quickly on the street. We turn in at the Park, and find places near the Albert Memorial directly along the route. At about 8.50, everyone stands up; many people are wearing black ribbons. Absolute quiet and silence reign as people stand waiting for the procession, which leaves Kensington Palace just after 9.00. From where we stand, it is not possible to hear the muffled bell toll. There is total silence; stillness with a sense of anticipation; still and quiet. Part of the wedding route is now the funeral route. First, the dark horses and dark riders come into view – silence; then the guards in black uniforms with gold; and then the coffin on the gun-mount draped in the yellow, black and red cloth – an image that stays (Figure 8.4).

Then, when it has passed, we join the huge number of people who go to Hyde Park to watch the funeral on the giant TV screens. At the end of the funeral, people walk, stopping along the Serpentine for a funeral repast, to picnic, smoke and chat to friends. Many, many people return to Kensington Palace to view the flowers and read the cards (in the same way that mourners view the flowers after an ordinary funeral). They go back to Kensington Palace, back to the home of the deceased (again, in the same way that

Figure 8.4 Diana's funeral cortège, Saturday, 6 September 1997. *Ross Lambert*

mourners often return to the family home for the funeral tea). Back home, the TV shows the flowers strewn on the hearse as it drives north to her country family home. It carries 'her home, to the cedars, villages and green fields of England'. Here the line separating the public from the private, the public and the private funeral, is redrawn when the iron gates of the Spencer family home separate the public funeral from the private family burial. The funeral and cortège ended, the TV begins to normalize life with the regularly-scheduled programmes. The shops reopen.

Interpretation

Having completed the field account of the events observed, what follows is an interpretation of the various elements, both religious and secular, which were appropriated as part of the improvised commemorative rituals during the week before the funeral:

Flowers

Flowers have always been the traditional gift of mourning, remembrance and love. One connection of flowers and gardens with death may lie in the fact that plants die. A garden unremittingly reveals the actuality of death, yet provides consolation that the skilful gardener can keep plants alive. A well-tended garden is a 'symbolic bulwark' against disorder and the randomness that death introduces. Gardens and flowers are also emblematic of the human life course and suggest ideal relations between individuals, the community and the divine order, as in the Garden of Eden. The descriptive terms applied to a plant's progress are often used to parallel human development: to put down roots, to blossom, to flower, to come to fruition, to unfold (Miller 1993). A second interpretation of the symbolism of flowers lies in the biological and cultural similarities between humans and plants. Both grow, mature, age and die, flourish or wither in the particular environment for which each is dependent for sustenance and support. Furthermore, flowers, in particular, are connected with reproduction, generation and continued development (Goody 1993). Their evocative fragrance has come to signify sanctification: the sweet smell of heaven, the graves, relics and tombs of the saints.

The emblematic association of Diana with the rose (Figure 8.5) draws upon traditional connections with England's royal history and the War of the Roses; with the Virgin Mary and the *hortus conclusus*; with the image of the English

Figure 8.5 *Goodbye England's Rose*, Kensington Gardens, Thursday, 11 September. *Tony Walter*

countryside and country home, as well as with rose me.
parks and cemeteries and with roses planted on graves
regeneration. Less well acknowledged is the latent symbol,
with sexuality, romantic love, affluence, generosity and the 'fa

Beautiful flowers taken to Kensington Palace, like those
cemeteries (Figure 8.6), are physical acts of caring which expre   motion.
As in the cemetery, people observe and learn from each other, adopting a
current practice to their own needs and preference. At Kensington Gardens,

Figure 8.6 Attendant arranging funeral flowers on a family grave, City of London
Cemetery, 1997. *Doris Francis*

the fashion was to bring cut flowers in cellophane/paper wrappers, similar
to the sheathes displayed at the cemetery following the funeral, thereby
bounding the space as similarly 'special'. There did not appear to be the
customary funerary displays ordered in advance from a florist, such as those
spelling out the letters of Diana's name in flowers, or floral arrangements on
a heart-shaped styrofoam base. Each group/family member often brought
his/her own floral tribute, purposely selected for the aesthetic appeal of their
colour or form to the giver. These sprays were often not unwrapped, but left
in their sleeves as if to protect their temporal delicacy from the elements.

Rather than seeing these cut flowers wilt and die, their freshness and vitality were continually renewed as mourners denied the symbolism of death by adding fresh new bouquets to the ever-growing field of flowers. Their vitality, thereby, denying the fragility and corruption of the dead body. As in the cemetery, the floral tributes were laid out for display: their number, size and expense exhibiting the standing of the deceased, and their totality manifesting shared caring and grief. Three weeks after the funeral, these flowers were recycled and the compost used to replenish the soil and to promote new growth, thereby renewing the cycles of life, regeneration and rebirth and providing the 'soothing influences of nature' to the bereaved.

Cards

In addition, many people wrote notes and cards, which they attached to their flowers. As if the transient, perishable flowers alone were not adequate to the task, these more permanent notes articulated their individual feelings about Diana, and verbally expressed what her life had 'meant' to them personally. As with flowers for a funeral or those brought to the cremation area at Christmas, such accompanying notes may not be enclosed in an envelope, but are left open allowing others to read them and thereby to affirm, normalize and validate their contents. Both the communal placing of flowers in a central area, and the open writing and public reading of cards helped to construct a shared image of Diana and to develop a sense of community among the bereaved. Many people were comforted knowing they were not alone in feeling grief, and were supported by reading other people's cards. Public statements of private feelings in the bounded grounds of Kensington Palace momentarily turned the park landscape into a 'garden of remembrance', a sacred space, 'of time-out-of-time', similar to a cemetery.

Our research supports an evolving acknowledgement of death as a part of life, in which public/private expressions of grief in the cemetery are accepted as appropriate and helpful to healing. As part of this new openness, gifts of toy animals may be placed at the tombstone of a young person to provide comfort and support, and other mementoes are left on the grave of adults as tributes and reminders that they are not forgotten. Similarly, such tokens were left outside Kensington Palace. In Kensington Gardens, as in the cemetery, it was often believed that the deceased is aware of the purposeful activities of people and could somehow receive love and comfort from their flowers, gifts, cards, words and actions. The hanging of cards on trees (Figure 8.7) is also something people do in cemeteries, using nature to display their emotional tributes and evoking historic arboreal symbolism linked with community, continuity and divinity (Thomas 1983).

Figure 8.7 Tree shrine, Kensington Gardens, Thursday, 11 September. *Tony Walter*

Candlelight Vigils

Candles are used in Orthodox and Catholic wakes and funerals. The tapers placed around the body form a boundary, which both guards the spirit of the deceased and protects the attendant mourners. A lit candle (Figure 8.8) calls the spirit of the deceased down from the 'space of time', and provides a focus for the person: its warmth, liveliness and comfort contrasting to the cold stone of the grave. Candles lit in memoriam chart the ascension of prayers for the deceased to Heaven. At Easter in the Greek Orthodox Church, for example, Christ's resurrection is both physically and symbolically represented and announced by the priests entering a darkened church to bring forth the light. The holding of a lighted taper evokes the mysteries of medieval death pageantry, and forms a sacred community among the assembled mourners in the quiet of the night. In the home, candles and fresh flowers are often placed next to a photograph of the deceased.

Crowds

At memorial services and cemetery funerals, it is not uncommon to have large gatherings of many hundreds of people when a young person dies. In Western society, death in the prime of life, alone and in tragic circumstances is considered a 'bad death'. Many people attend such funerals when someone

Figure 8.8 Lighting candles at a tree shrine, Kensington Gardens, Sunday 7 September. *Doris Francis*

their own age or younger dies tragically. At major religious holidays, and Mother's and Father's Day, thousands of people congregate at the cemetery. Many visitors come a long distance and may go to more than one site, making a type of pilgrimage by visiting a number of cemeteries at these significant times (Francis et al. 1997). Similarly, large numbers of people chose to visit and leave flowers at the various locations associated with Diana.

Through observation of the crowds who assembled at Kensington Palace following the death of Diana, and through surveys of mourners at cemeteries on Mother's Day (as well as through counts of those who regularly used Kensington Gardens – Jenkins 1992), we were struck by the similarity of visitors in terms of age and gender. Here it is important to emphasize the large representation of men, for it is commonly assumed that most males do not openly express their feelings and are, therefore, unlikely to use public spaces for mourning. However, our research reveals a relatively high proportion of men, particularly older men, who tend graves regularly. Thus the more public emotions of men, supposedly engendered by the open grief for Princess Diana, is a phenomenon we have previously observed in cemeteries. In addition, our research also reveals that children are brought to cemeteries, where they are taught about their deceased kin and about the rituals which help preserve their memory. Kensington Gardens, with its statue of Peter Pan and children's play areas, has always been a more domestic space than Hyde Park, and family groups visit together. Likewise, children were brought to the Gardens by their parents following the death of Princess Diana and were similarly taught and encouraged to place their memorial flowers and notes in an appropriate way (Figure 8.8).

In the bounded space of shared mourning that Kensington Gardens became in early September 1997, as in the enclosed landscape of the cemetery, all were equal in the face of death, the great leveller. Individuals from different social classes and ethnic/religious groups, who did not know each other and who might normally never speak, joined together in improvising commemorative rituals, which drew on their different cultural and folk traditions. People spoke with us about the impermanence of relationships and the fragility of bonds with loved ones. Our research further reveals that the events surrounding Princess Diana's death affected the behaviour of some people visiting cemeteries that week. Mourners watched the behaviour of others on TV and gained both courage and reassurance. One of our study participants, for example, took stock of the fleeting character of life and the unexpected nature of death and decided to fulfil her duties to kin, including visiting the cemetery. She explained why she had decided to come to the cemetery alone for the first time and to spend as much time as she needed despite usually becoming depressed by the visit: 'When you loose someone, it's so sad. Diana's death made me sad and made me think of my own lost ones who passed away. She brings things home more. It brings things home to you.'

Kensington Gardens past and future

The Palace is presently remembered as Princess Diana's London home, where hundreds of thousands of people were drawn following her death. The surrounding Gardens were the setting for a display of memorialization of extraordinary proportion, often assumed to signal a transformed society. Once again, competing political agendas vie for this space. The New Labour government and Kensington residents are in contention over 'ownership' of the Gardens. This contest is expressed in the language of garden design and what the landscape will record and commemorate about the meaning of the events of September 1997. Will the historic Gardens remain intact, as many residents and garden historians (Sewell 1998, Strong 1998) insist they should? Or will there be a new 'enhanced' design commemorating Diana and her diverse community of mourners, whose membership cuts across class, age, gender and ethnic lines (and whom the government wishes to count among its constituency) to affirm the legitimate place of emotions in public life? The case is made by conservationists that to overlay or destroy archaeological evidence by reconstructing the landscape would be to eliminate an important strand of garden and social history. And yet, there is a strong counter-argument which says that a new and special commemorative landscape is warranted to mark the unique person who has died; that things are no longer as they were.

Interestingly, the landscape surrounding Kensington Palace is underlain by a series of contrasting historic gardens, where nature had been used before in various ideological and emotional ways. An examination of the design history of this landscape during the last three centuries affords a better understanding of how the events following Diana's death resonate with the multi-layered meanings embedded within Kensington Gardens.

The land comprising Kensington Gardens was developed from part of the original sixteenth- and seventeenth-century Hyde Park, used by Henry VIII as a royal hunting ground (Weinreb and Hibbert 1983). In 1689, William III purchased Nottingham House, later Kensington Palace, for £14,000. The villa was chosen as a private rural retreat where the King could relax from the pressures of Whitehall power. With the assistance of Daniel Marot and George London, William and Mary developed the twelve-acre Slope Garden stretching away from the south front of Kensington Palace in the Franco-Dutch style (Jacques & van der Horst 1988). A gravel central-axis walk

Figure 8.9 Kensington Palace and Gardens, 1715. *Royal Borough of Kensington & Chelsea Libraries & Arts Service*

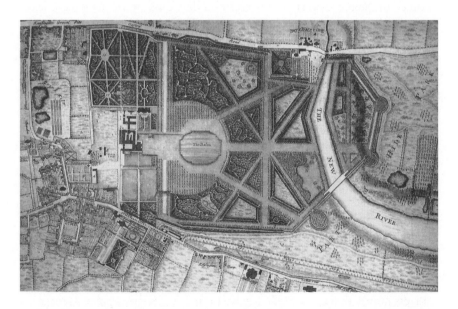

Figure 8.10 Bridgeman's plan for redesigning Kensington Gardens. *Royal Borough of Kensington & Chelsea Libraries & Arts Service*

focused attention on the main facade of the royal residence, while on either side there were geometric parterres defined by low box hedging with formally planted copses beyond (Figure 8.9). This compartmentalized 'artificial environment', with bushes clipped into immaculate topiary pyramids and globes, symbolized the power of the monarchs over all their domains, which thrived under royal order and husbandry, as well as the sumptuary wealth to collect and display rare, exotic plants from distant lands.

Under Queen Anne, Kensington Gardens was expanded, while the southern Slope Garden was altered by the removal of 'Dutch William's' box hedging, reasserting a more 'English' style. With the help of Henry Wise, the Royal Gardener, Anne created a thirty-acre formal wilderness (an ornamental woodland of geometric shady walks bordered by tall, clipped hedges) north of the palace, which also included mock mounts of evergreens, and a sunken terrace garden. It was in Kensington Gardens that Queen Anne sought solace and diversion when her only surviving son died aged twelve. With the subsequent changes in garden design later in the century to more meditative and expressive landscapes, the appearance of Kensington Gardens was radically altered. Today, only the central path leading to the Palace (Dial Walk), Vanbrugh and Hawksmoor's Orangery and Wren's Garden Alcove remain as markers of these earlier garden styles.

During the early eighteenth century, the landscape of Kensington Gardens assumed the shape it substantially retains today. This landscape is significant in the evolution of the revolutionary new English style of gardening and illustrates the history of garden developments of the period 1726 to 1735 (Strong 1992). The present layout reflects the transition from the formal Franco-Dutch geometric layout of order to an ever more irregular, asymmetrical, 'natural' form of gardening and design of the later part of the eighteenth century (Landuse Consultants 1982).

It was under the direction of Queen Caroline, wife of George II, and George Bridgeman, the Royal Gardener, that this new lawn and forest garden was laid out in the area of the open deer park to the east of the Palace (Figure 8.10). The Queen directed that George I's enclosed hunting park be replaced by a garden to walk and meander through with avenues, vistas and curving walks among groves and woods. The resulting ground plan of the forest and lawn garden consisted of a circular lawn, radiating tree-lined avenues and serpentine walks, with the Round Pond as the focal point of the scheme (Landuse Consultants 1982). The Gardens were open to the aristocracy on Saturdays; full dress was *de rigeur*, and dogs and servants were banned.

Bridgeman's designs included a bastioned ha-ha to replace George I's enclosing wall. This ha-ha was important for the development of the new style of garden by allowing the landscape beyond to form part of the garden experience (Strong 1992). The bastions and Kent's revolving summer house further provided views over the new gardens and Hyde Park. At this time, too, the Long Water was extended and the irregularly shaped Serpentine Lake, a radical contrast to the more formal Round Pond, was created. In 1728, the southern Slope Garden was converted to a fashionable 'plain parterre' (unembellished lawn), and a new mount in the south-east corner was planted with evergreens, forest trees and shrubs. In adopting and supporting this revolutionary new English landscape style with its complex political iconography, the German-born Caroline expressed her identity as Queen of Great Britain (Strong 1992).

It was the combination of formal and informal elements that helped make Kensington Gardens a meditative and expressive landscape in the eighteenth century. Bridgeman's ornamental woodland/forest with its variety of trees, complicated network of wandering paths and frequent clearings with intimate recessed seating provided a congenial context for retirement and meditation. Here the empirical exploration of nature was linked with contemplation and psychological self-exploration (Hunt 1976). The movement between closed forest and open lawn further stimulated thought and varied moods. It initiated the reading of expressive ideas into the landscape and provoked reflections beyond the immediate setting.

With the death of Queen Caroline in 1737, the impetus to continue improving the Gardens faded. Since that time, the density of the eighteenth-century planting has deteriorated, although in the past ten years, there has been replanting of the main walks. In the early nineteenth century, the Gardens were opened daily to the 'respectable public' and attracted the local community. In the last forty years, public access has been taken for granted. In the 1980s, with the encouragement of Prince Charles, the south side of the Palace was separated from the Dial Walk by a set of historic gates (these Gates were the focus for many floral tributes). Basically, however, the structure and layout of this landscape garden has remained intact; and the area immediately south of the palace, which became the 'landscape of mourning' for Princess Diana, retains its eighteenth-century design and relationship to the Palace.

Conclusion

Although there will undoubtedly be a memorial to Princess Diana in Kensington Gardens, at the time of writing, it is uncertain as to what form it will take. However, a memorial is already in place as part of the newly-restored Serpentine Gallery, located just at the end of Kensington Gardens, thus giving spatial unity to the 'landscape of mourning' for Princess Diana. Ian Hamilton Finlay's sculpture, dedicated to Princess Diana, former patron of the Serpentine Gallery, reworks the eighteenth-century tradition of the garden in ways which evoke meditation and contemplation (Abrioux 1985). The sculpture is comprised of eight stone benches, a tree-plaque and, at the entrance of the Gallery, a large slate disc set in a field of cobbles, inscribed with the names of trees (in both Botanical Latin and English) found in the classic English landscape of Kensington Gardens. The eight benches, each inscribed with pastoral poetry, are arranged in two arcs on a circular mound with *Calipinia* trees. This site recalls a classical grove for retreat, meditation, study, burial. Across the meadow is a handsome horse-chestnut, with a tree-plaque quoting Virgil's *Ecologues X* in the original Latin on the theme of evening. Hamilton Finlay's linkage of elegiac nature, contemplation, memory, transience (death/evening) and classical references, often in their original Latin, is echoed again, but with contemporary meanings, in the poetic quotation by the philosopher Francis Hutcheson, 1725, which is inscribed in the centre of the entrance circle: 'The beauty of trees, their cool shades and their aptness to conceal from observation, have made groves and woods the usual retreat to those who love solitude, especially to the religious, the pensive, the melancholy, and the amorous.'

In the small book which accompanies the sculpture, Hamilton Finlay (1997) re-asks the question about the dissonance in Arcady between human suffering and superhumanly perfect surroundings. Death in life's prime, landmines, AIDS suffering, the contemporary world in relation to the past, the Garden of Eden and the wilderness – these are all questions which Hamilton Finlay suggests that death and the garden evoke, and also which Kensington Gardens seems to always have been about.

Acknowledgements

The authors wish to acknowledge the Economic and Social Research Council for its support of *Cemetery As Garden*, on which the analysis for this chapter was partially based.

The first author wishes to thank Tim Rock, Brent Elliott, David Jacques and Ann Dill for their helpful conversations, and to acknowledge the generous assistance of Nick Butler, Manager, Kensington Gardens; and Carolyn Starren, Local Studies Librarian, Royal Borough of Kensington & Chelsea Central Library.

Bibliography

Ariès, P. (1981) *The Hour of Our Death*, New York: Alfred Knopf.

Abrioux, Y. (1985) *Ian Hamilton Finlay*, London: Reaktion Books.

Brooks, C., Elliott, B., Litten, J., Robinson, E., Robinson, R. and Temple, P. (1989) *Mortal Remains*, Exeter: Wheaton and The Victorian Society.

Burton, R. (1827) *The Anatomy of Melancholy, Vols I & II* (originally published in 1636), London: Longman, Rees, Orme & Co.

Coffin, D.R. (1994) *The English Garden: Meditation and Memorial*, Princeton: Princeton University Press.

Elliott, B. (1991) 'City of London Cemetery', *Victorian Society Notes*.

Foucault, M. (1984) 'Of Other Spaces', *Diacritics* (Spring): 22–7.

Francis, D., Kellaher, L. & Lee, C. (1997) 'Talking to People in Cemeteries', *Journal of the Institute of Burial and Cremation Administration*, 65(1): 14–25.

Goody, J. (1993) *The Culture of Flowers*, Cambridge: Cambridge University Press.

Greenhalgh, L. & Worpole, K. (1995) *Park Life: Urban Parks and Social Renewal*, London: Comedia & Demos.

Hamilton Finlay, I. & Simig, P.M. (1997) *A Proposal for the Grounds of the Serpentine Gallery*, Wild Hawthorn Press.

Harrison, M. (1992) 'Symbolism, "Ritualism" and the Crowds in early Nineteenth-Century English Towns' in *The Iconography of Landscape*, D. Cosgrove & S. Daniels (eds), Cambridge: Cambridge University Press, pp. 194–213.

Hunt, J.D. (1976) *The Figure in the Landscape: Poetry, Painting, and Gardening during the Eighteenth Century*, London: Johns Hopkins University Press.

Hunt, J.D. & Schuyler, D. (eds) (1984) *Journal of Garden History: Cemetery & Garden*, Vol. 4 (3).

Jacques, D., (1983) *Georgian Gardens: The Reign of Nature*, London: Batsford.

—— (1998) 'Kensington Gardens: The Secret History', *Country Life*, Vol. CXCII (31): 66–7.

Jacques D. & van der Horst, A.J., (1988) *The Gardens of William and Mary*, London: Christopher Helm.

Jenkins, I. (1992) *Review of the Royal Parks: Hyde Park and Kensington Gardens*, London: Department of the Environment.

Keegan, J. (1997) 'England Is a Garden', *Weekend Telegraph*, 8 November.

Lasdun, S. (1991) *The English Park: Royal, Private and Public*, London: Andre Deutsch.

Landuse Consultants (1982) *Royal Parks Historical Survey: Kensington Gardens*, London: Landuse Consultants.

Miller, M. (1993) *The Garden as an Art*, Albany: SUNY Press.

Panofsky, E. (1955) 'Et in Arcadia Ego: Poussin and the Elegiac Tradition', in *Meaning in the Visual Arts*, New York: Doubleday Anchor, pp. 295–320.

Sewell, B. (1998) 'The Cowardly Exercise in Deceit', *Evening Standard*, 9 July, p.15.

Simo, M.L. (1988) *Loudon and the Landscape*, New Haven: Yale University Press.

Strong, R. (1992) *Royal Gardens*, London: BBC Books/Conran Octopus.

The Diana, Princess of Wales Memorial Committee, 1998, *Preliminary Consultation on the Proposals for a Garden to Commemorate Diana, Princess of Wales.*

Thomas, K. (1983) *Man and the Natural World: Changing Attitudes in England 1580–1800*, London: Allen Lane.

Weinreb, B. & Hibbert, C. (eds) (1983) *The London Encyclopaedia*, London: Macmillan.

9

Pilgrims and Shrines

Jennifer Chandler

It happened that I was in London the week following Princess Diana's death. It also happened that I was booked into a hotel at the junction of Queensway and Bayswater Road, opposite Kensington Gardens. Still, my curiosity was not piqued until I saw elaborate flower arrangements in the foyer consisting entirely of white lilies. Now the folklorist in me woke up: in Britain white lilies are still widely regarded as unlucky indoors because of their funeral associations (Vickery 1985: 40–1). The receptionist said they were a gesture of mourning for 'Princess Di' and had I been to the Palace? I crossed the road and followed the thin but steady stream of people heading down the Broad Walk towards Kensington Palace. This was Tuesday, 2 September.

What I saw kept me there until dusk, brought me back next day, and again on Friday with a colleague from the Folklore Society and my camera. What follows is taken from my notes on Tuesday, Wednesday and Friday; and my photographs on Friday. It amplifies and adds to points made earlier in *Folklore* (Monger and Chandler 1998).

We notice what we are interested in and we interpret what we see according to our own frame of reference. From observing pilgrimages, I was pre-conditioned both to notice signs of ritual activity and to 'read' what I saw in terms of pilgrim behaviour. Mine is only one way of reading the evidence.

What did I see?

Who Came

The 'tide of flowers' that gradually flowed through Kensington Gardens was documented by pictures worth a thousand words (see especially *The Times*, 9 September 1997: 5), and the single blooms, bunches, pot plants and funeral wreaths making up this floral sea are described in *Folklore*. The messages attached to those flowers, pinned on a noticeboard near the Palace gates, or hung on the railings, are what I want to look at here: the things that tell us who came and what was on their minds.

Both individuals and groups had their say: the inmates and warders of a prison; 'all the cadets and staff at 1239 sqn Air Training Corps'; the 'Rotary Club of Sarasota'. People wrote in many languages – Chinese, Japanese, French, Turkish, varieties of Arabic, Greek, Welsh, Brazilian Portuguese – or identified themselves as coming from abroad:

> Princess Di
> You are
> D – demure,
> I – informal,
> A – amiable,
> N – never-to-be-forgotten,
> A – angel of goodwill
>
> Love,
> Ramani XX
> SRI LANKA

A bright yellow notice shouted 'Brasil' from the Palace railings. A page from a loose-leaf pad read: 'Dear [ ]iana, I Shock hand w/ you [sic.], when you visited my country KUWAIT. Now that I'm studying in London two blocks away from your palace, I always wished to meet you again . . . !!' The rest was in Arabic. Some people condoled (however unofficially) on behalf of their countries, including Islamic states – Bahrain, Pakistan, United Arab Emirates – and (Figure 9.1) 'the Iraqi Opposition'.

What They Wrote

Messages ran the gamut from conventional regrets to quotations from famous poets – Dante, Virgil, Omar Khayyam (*Evening Standard*, 3 September 1997: 15). Home-made efforts ranged from the simplistic, often voiced through (if not by) children – 'Dear Dodi/Thank you for making Princess Diana happy/ With Love Amelia[?]/ and JG' – to the self-consciously 'poetic'. Some left me in doubt as to whether people were quoting or inventing, like the first of Colin and Jenny Robinson's six stanzas:

> There's passion now,
> But all too late!
> They love her now,
> That used to hate.
> Today we mourn a dead Princess,
> Victim of her own success.

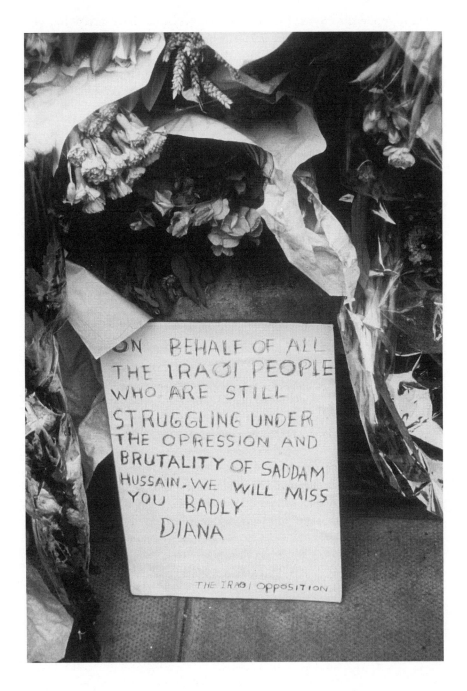

Figure 9.1 Message from the Iraqi Opposition, Kensington Gardens, week 1.
Jennifer Chandler

Many spoke directly to Diana – 'If our love could have saved you you never would have died' (Figure 9.2) – or broke into direct speech at the end of their message: 'Only the envelope that carried "the message" is leaving our Lives. Not its contents . . . You will never die'; or in the poem composed by 'SUE + STEVE D.' on their computer and pinned to the cellophane round their roses:

> A SMILE FOR ALL
> A HEART OF GOLD
> ONE OF THE BEST
> THE WORLD COULDN'T HOLD
> NEVER SELFISH
> ALWAYS KIND
> THESE ARE THE MEMORIES
> SHE LEFT BEHIND
> R.I.P. DIANA
> WITH DODI AT YOUR SIDE

Pop songs were one model, if only indirectly, which people followed:

> Diana,
> Lovely as a summer day
> Distant as the milky way
> Pretty little one that I adore
> You're the only girl my heart beats for
> How I wish that you were still here.

But they had other models, too, the messages in verse constituting a substantial body of folk poetry in the same genre as informal epitaphs on gravemarkers – 'Thoughts of you still bring a tear/ always wishing you were here'[1] – and 'In memoriam' messages in newspapers:

> You were called so suddenly,
> No time to say goodbye.
> You had so much to live for,
> And yet you had to die.[2]

They were especially reminiscent of longer memorial poems, like the elegy nailed to a wayside shrine (see below) in Suffolk which ends:

1. Slab marking interment of ashes of Darin Lee Goate 1965–1987, Loddon, South Norfolk.
2. 'In memoriam' David Jones, 21 October 1994, *Lowestoft Journal*, 16 October 1996: 58.

Figure 9.2 *If our love could have saved you*, Kensington Gardens, week 1. *Jennifer Chandler*

The loss I feel within my heart,
For lost to my embrace
    All of you, but most of all
The smile upon your face.[3]

What They Made

People invested huge amounts of time, thought and effort in the making of hand-made cards, photo montages and hand-drawn likenesses of 'Princess Di'. A parent captioned a child's crude but effortful drawing 'Princess Diana in her Castle, I will miss you/ Love/ Katy (4)'; someone carefully lettered a large, ovoid stone; someone else used computer-graphics for:

PRINCESS DIANA
SHE WAS . . .

[*Rabbit*] SOFT AS A RABBIT   [*Dove*] FREE AS A BIRD
[*Rose*] GENTLE AS A ROSE   [*Lion*] STRONG AS A LION

SHE WAS AND WILL ALWAYS BE LOVED BY THE WORLD
MAY SHE REST IN PEACE

Perhaps the most time-consuming of the tributes I saw was one fixed to the railings along Kensington Road (Figure 9.3). Accompanied by a message in Arabic script, and mounted on a piece of white card was a five-pointed star outlined with small, brightly coloured, three-dimensional stars, modelled from ribbon or paper.

Symbolism and Metaphor

In their flowers, messages and artwork, people drew on symbolism and metaphor. The florist Watkins & Watkins, near St James's and Buckingham Palaces, received orders from mourners in dozens of countries: 'White roses and lilies, the traditional symbols of grief, are especially requested' (*Irish Independent*, Wednesday 3 September 1997: 11). Someone contributed a wreath of artificial red poppies, whether because of the symbolism of the poppies themselves (Funk & Wagnall 1984: 881a; Vickery 1995: 288–9) or from association with Remembrance Sunday.

---

3. Wayside shrine of Kimberley Jary, aged 19, killed on 23 December 1996 at Flixton Holes near Lowestoft, Suffolk.

Figure 9.3 Star tribute, Kensington Gardens, week 1. *Jennifer Chandler*

Many people left a single red rose signifying love, but none had such resonance as the withered rose labelled: 'The last rose cut from our garden in memory of you Diana/Love always/Allison, John and Persephone'. You could all but hear someone singing 'The Last Rose of Summer' – 'Since the lovely are sleeping,/Go sleep thou with them!' (Moore 1863: 49, st. 2). And 'Persephone'! Youth and beauty rapt into the Underworld.

Hand-drawn hearts and Queen of Hearts playing cards were ubiquitous – so ubiquitous that *USA Today* could say it all on the front page on Wednesday 3 September with its main picture: a Queen of Hearts with two pink roses and a guttered-out candle. More original imagery appeared in a careful arrangement of cut-out white letters and shapes applied to a blue ground (Figure 9.4). The design was a circle formed of seven white daisies with golden centres, the name DIANA, and two hands reaching toward each other. The message read: 'Thank you for the kindness of your touch./ Love from Year 3/ Herbert Thompson Junior School/Ely, Cardiff'.

Religious Imagery

Of all the white lilies, how many were customary 'funeral flowers', and how many emblems of Mary? (I spotted no Madonna lilies, L. *candidum*, to give guidance.) And of the roses, how many had secular and how many religious reference? The medieval poet who wrote 'Of a rose is all my song' was neither the first nor the last to use the language of love in praise of the *Rosa sine spina* (Speirs 1958: 70–1, 67).

It was the same with the verbal imagery of light and stars: 'The light you created shone happiness and joy . . .' ; 'Oh, Diana, where have you gone/ You gave us light'; 'Your star will always shine bright'; 'A STAR you were one that will twinkle forever'. These are comparisons anyone might fall back on, including public figures for once at a loss for words and pilloried in *Private Eye* (5 September 1997: 6) for babbling of candles, light, stars and even comets. But though love objects have been compared to light from the Middle Ages to 'You are my Sunshine', this is also the language of the cult of the Virgin, *splendor et lux orientalis*, identified with the 'Woman clothed with the sun' and to this day lauded as *Stella Maris* (Davies 1963: 375, 377–8).

Some evidence was equivocal. The cult of Mary *seemed* to have informed someone's choice in the creation of a small shrine consisting of a small plastic effigy of her, crowned, robed in white and holding a rosary, at her feet two votive lights and a basket of flowers in her special colours: white roses, blue statice, white gypsophila (Figure 9.5). But was this a deliberate grouping?

Figure 9.4 Hands tribute, Kensington Gardens, week 1. *Jennifer Chandler*

Figure 9.5 Marian ground shrine, Kensington Gardens, week 1. *Jennifer Chandler*

When Diana was saluted as 'full of grace' was it an echo of the *Ave Maria*? Are we well beyond 'film star' in this message from Zagreb, Croatia: 'DIANA REGINA IMPERATUM/E NOSTRE STELA./OF THE WORLD./WE WILL LOVE YOU/IN INFINITY . . .' (*Daily Mail*, 2 September 1997: 2)? I am uncertain. But it is tolerably clear from the number of holy pictures of her that Mary had a presence here, and it will not do to underestimate people's range of reference – think of that Dante.

Angel, Saint and Goddess

Cross-fertilization between the language of religion and that of popular song has early precedent and we should not refine on it too much if sometimes we seem back with the troubadours' deification of the beloved within the framework of Courtly Love. But, at the least, it was interesting how readily people fell back on the heavenly hierarchy.

Of many comparisons of Diana with an angel, there was one firmly terrestrial one: a tree decked with a bunch of white lilies bore the message 'I will never forget you, Earth Angel', a reference to the song of that name by Curtis Williams, Jesse Belvin and Gaynel Hodge (1954), perhaps specifically to the first two lines of stanza 2: Earth Angel, Earth Angel, the one I adore/ Love you forever and ever more'. Most people, however, plumped for the comforting nursery myth that we get to be angels when we die: 'DIANA/ GOD HAS CHOSEN/YOU FOR AN ANGEL/REST IN PEACE' ; 'Diana, God's Sweetest Angel' (see the chapter by Bethan Jones in this volume).

Canonization was perhaps inevitable:

> THE SAINT
> THE KINDNESS
> THE BEAUTY
> THE WORLD'S
> REAL PRENCES IS
> GONE

and (Figure 9.6):

> Saint DIANA
> THE IRREPLACABLE
> PATRON SAINT OF LOVE
> In Our Hearts Forever.

Signs of outright deification (I am speaking of imagery still) are more tantalizing. Is there really a reversal of roles in:

> Dear Jesus take this message
> To Diana up above,
> Tell her how we miss her,
> And give her all our love,

which, as far as *words* go, casts God the Son as intercessor? It may be Hollywood talking in 'Diana/ A Goddess of Good'; but that 'Oh . . . where have you gone/You gave us light' (above) echoes like a lament for the nightly setting of some solar deity and 'BEV LACLAUGHLIN – LONDON' had me wondering with this evocation of some vast cosmic being:

> 1961—DIANA—1997
> THOUGH EARTH AND MAN WERE GONE
> AND SUNS AND UNIVERSES CEASED TO BE
> AND THOU WERE LEFT ALONE
> EVERY EXISTENCE WOULD EXIST IN THEE
> THERE IS NOT ROOM FOR DEATH
> NOR ATOM THAT HIS MIGHT COULD RENDER VOID

Figure 9.6 *Saint Diana*, Kensington Gardens, week 1. *Tony Walter*

THOU – THOU ART BEING AND BREATH
AND WHAT THOU ART...
... CAN NEVER BE DESTROYED.
DIANA, PRINCESS OF WALES
MAY YOU REST IN ETERNAL PEACE

Shrines

If the messages were ambiguous, the scene at Kensington Palace Gates was dramatic witness to a mass impulse to establish shrines, in the sense of collocations of objects designed both to memorialize the holy dead and provide a locus for venerating deity.

Someone remarked of the scene that 'we seemed to be in the Mediterranean'. We might as easily substitute Mexico. The components of Mexican table- and shelf-top domestic shrines – flowers, photographs of the departed, holy pictures, candles – were replicated here with some fidelity (Salvo 1997, especially pls 8, 24, 25). So were Mexican shrines focussed on trees (cf. Coleman and Elsner 1995: 127, pl. 46). There were elements, too, of the personalized decoration of grave-sites in parts of the USA (Long 1998; Posey 1998; Heege 1998), and indeed Britain. However, the reference was probably to the kind of permanent roadside shrine (*proskynitari*) erected in Greece at the site of a fatality (Monger 1997: 113).

Wayside Shrines Observation of what happens abroad and the analogy of sending flowers to funerals have probably both contributed to the 'wayside shrine' phenomenon – the deposition of flowers by family members and the general public at the scenes of disasters, road fatalities and other violent deaths. This has been monitored in Britain over the past twenty years (Walter 1996; Monger 1997). Sometimes these temporary tributes lead to permanent memorials (Chandler, forthcoming).

The practice of erecting highly visible memorials to accident victims on or near the spot where they died goes back to at least the eighteenth century (e.g. Westwood 1989: 14, 21). Then there are on-the-spot memorials to wartime casualties and other 'in the course of duty' deaths. These are sometimes maintained as cenotaphs, usually by the deposition of flowers whether regularly, or only periodically, say on the anniversary of death, at Christmas and Easter, or on Remembrance Sunday.

A well-known example of such a memorial is the upright stone in St James's Square, London, erected on the spot where WPC Yvonne Fletcher was shot. It is inscribed: 'HERE FELL WPC YVONNE FLETCHER 17th April

1984'. Underneath is carved the badge of the Metropolitan Police. It is kept decorated, by family, friends and others; in May 1998, a formal 'table arrangement' of fresh flowers, carried the message: 'With deepest sympathy from the Directors and Staff of No. 5'. Less frequented is a wartime cenotaph which stands off a bridleway on Somerleyton Estate, Suffolk. It consists of a small, upright sandstone marker carved with a wreath surrounding a cross.

The inscription reads:
NEAR THIS PLACE
LT J. BLACK.U.S. N.A.T.[F]PILOT
AND
LT T. AIKEN.U.S. N.A.F.[?] NAV-
GAVE THEIR LIVES IN DEFENCE
OF THIS COUNTRY
RETURNING FROM OPERATIONAL
DUTIES ON NOV-14-1944.

GREATER LOVE HATH NO MAN THAN THIS
THAT A MAN LAY DOWN HIS LIFE FOR HIS FRIENDS

In front of the memorial, a wooden rail demarcates a squarish 'grave' planted with daffodils and tulips. In March 1998, it was still decorated with red poppies from Remembrance Sunday the previous November.

The practice of establishing wayside shrines also has something in common with the preservation of the site, memorialization in local tradition and (more rarely) regular decoration with flowers of wayside graves, whether those of gipsies (Monger 1997: 113), or of suicides or executed felons buried at crossroads pre-1823 (Westwood 1985: 129–30; Halliday 1994). One such wayside grave that is regularly maintained is Jay's Grave on Dartmoor, reputedly that of Mary Jay who committed suicide when she was about sixteen. The grave has been marked with stones since 1860, and is always decorated, a custom probably started by the Dartmoor writer Beatrice Chase, who died in 1955. It is unknown who has decorated it since her death, but on 29 September 1998, beside several small pots of flowers, there lay a tied posy, evidently fresh that day.

Given this historical background, the 'true' wayside shrine for Diana was on the spot – or close to it – where she died in Paris, where one indeed developed at the Pont de L'Alma underpass. However, at the time of Diana's death, a number of precedents existed in Britain for symbolic as opposed to on-the-spot sites also becoming the focus of mass floral deposition, for example at Anfield (Walter 1991: 609–10).

Although the wayside shrine phenomenon provides a context for what happened at Kensington, and the whole scene could be viewed as a hugely magnified wayside shrine (Figure 9.7), there was also a proliferation of individual shrines within that setting which spoke rather of a merging of Orthodox and Catholic custom with New Age eclecticism.

Figure 9.7 Kensington Gardens, week 1 – like a wayside shrine. *Jennifer Chandler*

Ground Shrines and Tree Shrines   These individual shrines were of two sorts: 'ground shrines' (i.e. groups of objects evidently placed in association with one another, but not in relation to any fixed element of their surroundings), and 'tree shrines' (i.e. groups of objects placed round the trunks of, fixed to the bark of or hung in the branches of trees). Among the components of both were photographs of the deceased, Diana and Dodi, such as are displayed at the scene of fatal accidents in the Middle East.[4] The ground shrines in particular also displayed holy pictures, not all Christian (see Monger and Chandler 1998: 104).

Lights were much in evidence, including Habitat and Shaker tin lanterns, garden flares, citronella-scented wax in flowerpots, designed for repelling mosquitoes at barbecues, single 'household' candles, coloured and decorative

---

4. Cf. the Muslim shrine to Diana and Dodi in the window of the Di Castro Travel Agency (a Fayed Brothers company), Alexandria (Hamilton 1998: 16).

candles, white church candles and tapers, and votive lights in holders. Though the lighting of candles (Figures 8.1, 8.8) was one of the things that struck commentators as 'foreign', the practice was lent moral support by candlelit vigils for Diana in several cathedrals, reported in papers with photographs and captions such as 'Her candle will never burn out' (*Norwich Evening News*, 6 September 1997: 12–13). It was not unique to British mourning (see *Evening Standard*, 5 September 1997: photo on 7). Nor perhaps was it unique to mourning for Diana (Chandler forthcoming).

With the ground shrines, lapped as they were by flowers, it was hard to decide which objects were intended components of the group and whether it represented a single deposition or was built up incrementally. Easier to 'read' were the tree shrines, scarcely begun on the Tuesday, but by the Friday proliferating, existing shrines having been added to and new ones started. A sheaf of white lilies leant against the bole of a tree attracted a single sunflower, which attracted votive candles, which attracted sprays of flowers and so on (Figures 8.7, 8.8). A pair of worn ballet shoes hanging from a branch early in the week perhaps inspired the lading of other branches with 'offerings' by the funeral. As well as the lanterns, candles, flowers, photographs and toys shared with the ground shrines, such offerings included tie-dyed silk scarves fluttering from boughs (see below).

A tree shrine near Kensington Road developed thematically. On Tuesday it had one tribute but by Friday had become virtually an altar consecrated to love. The key message began:

DIANA X DODI
Together in this Life
Together in the Next
RIP

Pilgrims

There is an obvious parallel between the journey to Kensington Palace Gates and the purposive journey to some sacred place which is the core of most pilgrimage. Like early Christians visiting the shrines of the martyrs in the cemeteries outside Rome, the Kensington pilgrims abandoned their daily routine to embark on a journey to a green and pleasant space, where in comparative tranquillity they reverenced the holy dead – one whom many perceived as a martyr. Given broad similarity, is there resemblance in detail?

Few of those who came to Kensington openly declared their religious baggage, unlike the creator of a folded card with a message (inside right) beginning: 'NAM MYO HO RENGE KYO' and the salutation (inside left):

'Thank you Diana with all my life A Buddhist view'. Nor was there much overt religious activity, although a number of people on Tuesday (harder to spot later as the crowds grew) appeared to be praying or meditating on the grassy bank to the right of and overlooking the Palace Gates, and I saw a woman in *hejab* sit for more than an hour alone on the grass near the apron of flowers at roughly the time of sunset prayer in what looked like a vigil.

But although the evidence is unclear, there *did* seem to be some points of comparison:

Hardship   In 'The Shrine' (dir. Richard Alwyn), shown on BBC 2 on Tuesday 30 December, one of the interviewees herself remarked, apparently un-prompted: 'We're like pilgrims.' She had come to London before the funeral and slept out in the park, enduring the privation popularly regarded as a fundamental concomitant of pilgrimage – she mentioned lack of sleep, lack of food, backache and headaches.

Offerings   There were depositions implying some degree of sacrifice – several pot plants were mature, apparently not bought for the occasion but someone's favourite. They seem of a piece in intention with some if not all of the many toys: a 'family' group of four teddies of different sizes and styles, perhaps belonging to different children in the same family (Figure 9.8); a bear and a rabbit posed together; a fake fur hedgehog; a woolly knitted hedgehog; a badger; a brown teddy with on its chest a message from its child owner. (How many of these were willingly given up, and how many testify to parental pressure? Parental *suggestion*, at least, perhaps lurked behind the offering of two teddy bears grouped with a copy of the young child's book by Sam McBratney, 'Guess how much I love you').

Here, too, seem to belong personal items – a pair of biker's boots against railings, the ballet shoes mentioned above. Though the scarves also mentioned looked like a touch of India, given the revival of interest in holy wells they may be conscious echoes of the traditional offerings at 'cloutie' (rag) wells in the British Isles, sometimes in the course of customary folk 'pilgrimages' (e.g. Buchan 1994: 265–6).

There is a broader aspect, too. Official spokesmen (and others) were haunted by the spectre of 'waste', fretting over the salvaging of flowers for 'hospitals and old folk's homes' (*The Times*, 9 September 1997: 5). The third leader of the *Daily Telegraph*, however, put its finger on essentials:

All these offerings . . . will soon fade and die . . . That is part of their value to those seeking to express their inner feelings. They represent . . . a small sacrifice, an act of love . . . (*Daily Telegraph*, 5 September 1997: 23).

Figure 9.8 Family of teddy bears, Kensington Gardens, week 1. *Jennifer Chandler*

Function not Form It vexed journalists that the wrappings were left on flowers on 'that astonishing Cellophane meadow' (*Evening Standard*, 3 September 1997: 13). 'This lovely parade of flowers . . . would have looked even lovelier without their cellophane wrappings . . .' (*Daily Telegraph*, 5 September 1997: 23). '[W]hy . . . do we leave them wrapped in cellophane, not properly open?' (*Independent*, 3 September 1997: 15) The broadcaster Libby Purves had an answer: 'Cellophane and ribbons mean "look, I didn't nick these from the park, I paid good money for them, to prove I care"' (*The Times*, 9 September 1997: 18). This is one (somewhat élitist) reading, but misses the point that what was 'proper' in the context seemed to almost *everyone*, regardless of economic status, in both England and France (see *International Herald Tribune*, 2 September 1997: front page), to leave the flowers wrapped. Wrapped is how bunches of flowers (as opposed to florists' arrangements) are often laid on new graves: and wrapped is how pilgrims fix them to ropes for hauling saints' reliquaries (Monger and Chandler 1998: 108, n.4). In both cases, the act is more important than the effect.

Ex-votos There is a parallel, too – in result if not motivation – between the outpouring of artwork at Kensington and that of folk-art in the form of ex-votos at Catholic pilgrimage sites. Ex-votos generally speaking are material objects, including framed written testimonies and pictures, left by pilgrims at shrines as thank-offerings. The pictures – for example, of shipwrecks and other disasters miraculously escaped – share with the Kensington artwork a desire to communicate with both the object of devotion and other pilgrims through a visual image. It was the pictures that made Kensington *look* so much like a pilgrim shrine.

Healing   In the context of Kensington, read 'catharsis'. Although journalists spoke of 'synthetic grief', the messages suggested genuine mourning, including the resolution of incomplete personal grieving: 'My immediate junior sister died last year and what I feel now is identical to what I felt last year . . .'; 'I also lost my mother when I was fifteen. She went to a dance and came back dead' (this last written impromptu, on a scrap of tissue paper).

'Fringe' Beliefs   Pilgrimages worldwide often accommodate beliefs and practices belonging to folk religion rather than sanctioned by theology. At Kensington, we were perhaps given a glimpse of popular eschatology: though the Victorian notion of soul-sleep – 'Sleep well and rest in perfect peace' – was frequent as in any cemetery, here and there were hopes (who knows how serious?) for the vigorous enjoyment of a conscious afterlife: 'Dearest Diana and Dodi/Have fun in heaven/Lots of love/Mark'; and:

> DIANA AND DODI
> R.I.P.
> GOD BLESS YOU BOTH
> THE WORLD WILL NEVER FORGET YOU
> MAY YOU HAVE AS MUCH
> FUN IN HEAVEN AS YOU DID IN ST TROPEZ
> WITH LOVE
> REBECCA
> XXXX

Pilgrim-tourists   If any one label has to be given to all those who came to Kensington Palace, 'pilgrim-tourist' best fits, relating them to that growing category of people who can be observed at major pilgrimage sites filtering past or through saints' shrines (reliquaries or buildings), agog to see what is to be seen but also to receive any blessings on offer. As far as Kensington is concerned, it covers that complex motivation which combined genuine mourning with a sense of seizing the historical moment.[5] As a young mother

---

5. Not to mention the age-old element of one-upmanship, cf. Hill (1993).

with two fairly bewildered toddlers said to me: 'They don't understand what's happening but I'll be able to tell them they were there.'

Conclusion

What I saw at Kensington was a mass visitation by people from different national, social and religious backgrounds, often entailing effort and forward planning, and engaging the deepest human sympathies. Its focus was a site associated with the 'holy dead'. It seems to me that this was a pilgrimage – one cobbled out of odds and ends by people many of whom were outsiders to a tradition which in Britain received its official quietus at the Reformation. Like pilgrims, these people assumed privileged status – in their case the freedom to annexe 'public' space. Like pilgrims, they enjoyed an expressiveness probably not permitted them in synagogue, mosque or church. Like pilgrims, they were unaware or unafraid of exposing themselves to censure (which they got) on the grounds of being sentimental, tasteless, subliterate, wasteful. Whether or not they *also* wanted to give the Queen a piece of their mind, express solidarity with an underdog, or protest the transitoriness of life in the person of one who died too young, what they did at Kensington with flowers, pictures, lights and their own bodies was to make a secular space sacred. This is how pilgrimages are made. Perhaps this is one reason why, although (barring a few exotic threads) it was woven from homespun, so many commentators perceived the event as 'un-English'.

Bibliography

Buchan, D. (ed.) (1994) *Folk Tradition and Folk Medicine in Scotland: The Writings of David Rorie*, Edinburgh: Canongate Academic.

Chandler, J. (forthcoming) 'A Suffolk Wayside Shrine'.

Coleman, S. and Elsner, J. (1995) *Pilgrimage Past and Present*, London: British Museum Press.

Davies, R.T. (ed.) (1963) *Medieval English Lyrics*, London: Faber and Faber.

Funk & Wagnall (1984) *Funk & Wagnall Standard Dictionary of Folklore, Mythology and Legend*, (ed.), Maria Leach *et al*, San Francisco: Harper & Row.

Halliday, R. (1994) 'Wayside Graves and Crossroad Burials', *Norfolk Archeology* 42: 1, 80–3.

Hamilton, I. 'Taste, Tact and Racism', *London Review of Books* 20: 2 (22 January 1998), 16–21.

Heege, K.V. (1998) '"They're Pretty, But They're Work": Shell-Decorated Graves as Community Art', *Folklore Forum* 29: 1, 65–98.

Hill, J. (1993) 'Pilgrimage and Prestige in the Icelandic Sagas', *Saga-Book* 23: 6, 433–53.

Long, C.M. (1998) 'Folk Gravesites in New Orleans: Arthur Smith Honors the Ancestors', *Folklore Forum* 29: 1, 23–49.

Monger, G. (1997) 'Modern Wayside Shrines', *Folklore* 108, 113–14.

—— and Chandler, J. (1998) 'Pilgrimage to Kensington Palace', *Folklore* 109, 104–8.

Moore, T. *Moore's Irish Melodies* (1863) London: Henry Lea. Originally published as *A Selection of Irish Melodies*, 10 parts, 1808–34.

Posey, S.M. (1998) 'Grave and Image: Holiday Grave Decorations in a Southern California Memorial Park', *Folklore Forum* 29: 1, 51–63.

Salvo, D. (1997) *Home Altars of Mexico*, London: Thames and Hudson.

Speirs, J. (1958) *Medieval English Poetry The Non-Chaucerian Tradition*, 2nd imp., London: Faber & Faber.

Vickery, R. (1985) *Unlucky Plants: A Folklore Survey*, London: Folklore Society.

—— (1995) *A Dictionary of Plant Lore*, Oxford: Oxford University Press.

Walter, T. (1996) 'Funeral Flowers: A Response to Drury', *Folklore* 107, 106–7.

Westwood, J. (1985) *Albion: A Guide to Legendary Britain*, London: Granada.

—— (1989) *Gothick Norfolk*, Princes Risborough: Shire.

10

A Bridge of Flowers

Anne Rowbottom

> ... flowers are also part of culture ... they are used throughout social life ...
> but above all in establishing, maintaining and even ending relationships, with
> the dead as with the living, with divinities as well as humans (Goody 1993: 2).

The day before the funeral of the Princess of Wales, I stood at the edge of
the vast expanse of flowers that had been laid outside the gates of Kensington
Palace. In describing the scale of these tributes many newspaper reports called
upon the metaphor of 'a sea', an image which also sprang to my mind, but
with a somewhat different connotation. Surveying the scene, I had a strong
image of the flowers flowing from my feet, deepening in number until, many
yards away, they moved up onto the gates of the Palace, to break like waves
against the bulwark of a sea wall (Figure 10. 1). In practice, of course, they
began at the gates and moved outwards, but the metaphor of an advancing
sea held back by walls and gates reveals the often transparent relationship
between spatial organization and social meaning. Proximity carries cultural
connotations about the strength or weakness of social relationships (Hall
1966), as is evident in the placing of the flowers of the most intimate kin of
the divorced Princess (i.e. her two sons and her brother) upon her coffin
and, therefore, in closest proximity to her body. Conversely, the public flowers
placed outside the walls and gates of Kensington Palace, Buckingham Palace
and St James's Palace are, literally and figuratively, distanced from the
Princess. My concern in this chapter is with the use of flowers in the negotiation of this spatial and social distance.

An Overview of the Flowers

From the announcement of her death in the early hours of Sunday 31 August,
to her burial the following Saturday, flowers formed a central motif in the
public mourning for Diana, Princess of Wales. The first press reports show

Figure 10.1 'Like waves breaking against a sea wall'. Kensington Gardens, week 1. *Anne Rowbottom*

that as early as the dawn of the day she died flowers were being fastened to the gates, inserted between the railings, and laid on the paths and pavements outside Kensington Palace and Buckingham Palace. When her body was taken to rest in the Chapel Royal at St James's Palace this became a third major focus of public grief in central London. By midweek an estimated £30 million worth of bunches and bouquets had been laid at a multitude of sites throughout Britain, with orchids from Thailand, carnations from Kenya and sunflowers from Israel being flown in to meet the continuous demand (*Sun*, 4 September 1997: 7). By the end of the week 50 million blooms, weighing some 10,000 tons were said to have been laid outside Buckingham Palace and Kensington Palace (Jack, 1997: 15). On the day of the funeral thousands more flowers were strewn on the cortege, not only on its procession through London, but throughout the 76-mile journey to Althorp, the family estate where the private burial took place. At times so great a number of blooms rested on the hearse that the driver had to stop and remove them from the windscreen in order to be able to see the road ahead. So many flowers had been laid at the gates of Althorp that, when Earl Spencer had them unwrapped and ferried to the island where his sister was buried, they covered the ground in a carpet of colourful blossoms.

The form and especially the scale of the public response has aroused much academic interest, with continuity and change in mourning practices providing an immediate and highly relevant context. However, to frame the public response solely in this context is to isolate it from the broader pattern of public participation in events centering on the Royal Family. Research interest in this particular social phenomenon has been sadly lacking over the years, a situation complained of by Shils & Young (1953) at the beginning of the present reign that still persists four decades later (Billig 1992). As a result there is no substantial body of data against which the public mourning can be compared and it is, therefore, easy to assume that what took place represented a totally unique moment in British cultural life. One consequence of this assumption is that it is unlikely to sustain much more than a short-lived flurry of interest, and so the wider implications of the relationship between popular royalism and the production and reproduction of the institution of constitutional monarchy will remain unexamined. Consideration of these wider implications is, however, beyond the scope of the present chapter, where my more modest aim is to discuss the flowers and to draw comparisons with their use at other royal events.

Observation and Participation

When the Princess died I was invited to go to London with two ardent royalists. Their intention was to take flowers to Kensington Palace on the Friday morning, then to secure a place on the front row of the funeral route by sleeping out overnight in The Mall, the ceremonial avenue which connects Buckingham Palace with Whitehall. The two royalists, Daniel who lives in the north of England and Patricia who lives in the Midlands, are part of a loose-knit network of men and women from all parts of the United Kingdom whose ages range from teenagers to the retired and whose occupations, although varied, are predominantly those of the lower-middle classes. They are united by their support for the monarchy expressed through their practice of regularly travelling to towns and cities throughout the country to stand for hours, in all weathers, to offer flowers to members of the Royal Family as they make official visits to a wide variety of civic, commercial and charitable organizations.

The Princess had been a particular favourite with many of the royalists, who often likened their interactions with her to meetings with an old friend, as she would laugh and joke with them, in many cases addressing them by their first names. It is through the regularity of such encounters that the royalists stand out from the anonymity of the crowd. Daniel, for example, had seen her on more than one hundred occasions, and given her flowers on sixty-two occasions, and many of the others could claim a similar total. The royalists are not by any means the only members of the public to offer flowers to, or exchange a few words with members of the Royal Family. At the end of a visit it is not unusual for the rear-window shelf and the boot of at least one of the royal cars to be full of flowers. Regularity of attendance may single the royalists out from the crowd, but the form of their activities is neither unique nor extraordinary. What the royalists represent is an especially active expression of widely established practices through which members of the public approach members of the Royal Family.

I first met the royalists during fieldwork for my doctoral thesis and regularly travelled with them during 1989 and 1990 (Rowbottom 1994) and again in 1996 and 1997 (Henley & Rowbottom 1997); in between these periods of intensive fieldwork I have maintained contact with key informants and travelled on a more intermittent basis. The account provided in this chapter is based upon two days' participant observation with Daniel and Patricia during the public mourning, with comparisons drawn from my earlier fieldwork amongst the royalists.

Closeness and Distance

In the announcement of the death of the Princess and in the subsequent media coverage the national audience was positioned as having suffered a loss, as being bereaved. If 'power is visible only through its consequences' (Westergaard and Resler 1976), then the cultural dominance of this discourse is evident in the negative case that those who rejected this positioning experienced difficulty in expressing their views (Jack 1997). In a similar way the discourse on the monarchy positions its audience as loyal subjects and, again, dominance is demonstrated in the negative case that republicanism lacks a strong political voice (Wilson 1989). Difficulties in finding expression are not, however, restricted to the dissidents. Those drawn into an emotional engagement with the death of the Princess were physically and socially distanced from the centre of events as, unlike family and friends, they had no right to view the body, be physically present at the funeral service and the burial, and had no means of offering consolation in person to the bereaved relatives. This contradictory combination of involvement and social distance is not peculiar to the death of the Princess, but is characteristic of the relationship between commoners and royalty as currently constructed. Through the media, mass audiences are brought into an intimate communion with the lives of the Royal Family, but however involved viewers and readers become they remain 'an abstract crowd of invisible and anonymous spectators' (Chaney 1993: 183). For those accepting the position of loyal subject and/or mourner this particular identity remains a virtual, rather than actual one, unless and until it can be confirmed through social interaction with others (Goffman 1968). Offering flowers provides such an opportunity.

The Central Sites

When attending royal visits the royalists are faced with choosing a place to stand. In doing so their guiding principle is that of finding somewhere that will bring them into close proximity with the royal. At the public mourning, where contact could not be achieved physically, it had to be sought at a more symbolic level. (I would suggest that this motivated the throwing of flowers onto the coffin on its journey to Westminster Abbey, and the showering of the hearse during its journey to Althorp.) When faced with the choice of taking their flowers to Kensington Palace, Buckingham Palace or St James's Palace, Daniel and Patricia had no hesitation in choosing Kensington Palace. As Patricia explained:

I want to go to Kensington Palace because that was where she lived, it was her home, and if she had returned from Paris she would be there now. I know lots of people are taking flowers to Buckingham Palace (which must be a comfort to the Royal Family) and I know she is in the chapel at St James's and that lots of people are going there, but tonight [Friday] they will take her to Kensington Palace and that's where the funeral will leave from tomorrow. If we were short of time I would suggest going to St James's, but we are not and as Kensington Palace is where she lived and where I'll feel closest to her, that's where I want to go.

Kensington Palace stands within the royal park of Kensington Gardens to which there is free public access (Chapter 8). The park is separated from the busy traffic thoroughfare of Kensington Road by a type of boundary wall typical of many public parks and private gardens. Consisting of some nine or ten courses of brickwork topped with coping stones and four-feet-high iron railings, it would not normally be a focus of attention, but now it had been transformed (Figure 10.2). Bunches of flowers had been inserted horizontally between the railings creating solid stretches of bright colour, complemented by the paler colours and glistening cellophane of their wrappings. In other places bunches, fastened vertically to the railings, were accompanied by pictures and drawings of the Princess, as well as cards, verses

Figure 10.2 The wall between Kensington Gardens and Kensington Road, week 1. *Anne Rowbottom*

and messages. Where there was room the coping stones served as a shelf for free-standing wreaths and candles. The overall effect was to turn a dull wall into a stunning visual display. As we made our way slowly through the crowds converging on the gates into the park, we regularly stopped to look at the flowers, read the messages and take photographs. Very little was said, except to comment on how overwhelmingly sad it all was. Inside the park more flowers, messages and candles doubled back along the length of the wall but, although plentiful they were not so densely packed as on the street side, presumably because the park offered other options.

Across the grassland, between the boundary wall and the ornamental gates of the palace, mature trees and saplings alike had flowers, cards and pictures fastened to their trunks, hanging from their branches and encircling their roots. Although there were thousands of people moving around, many of whom had brought young children, there were no loud noises, no one was running, or even moving quickly. When tears were shed they were shed as privately as possible, hidden by hands, lowered heads or the shoulders of companions. Although quiet and self-contained, those present demonstrated awareness of and consideration for others by making way for people to pass through the crowds and allowing each other sufficient space and time to look, take photographs, read the messages, or lay flowers. The gravity and decorum, also noted by Monger & Chandler (1998), is the type of behaviour usually considered as appropriate at English funerals (Walter 1997). By acting in this way the people in Kensington Gardens were expressing their identity as the bereaved and, through the reciprocal actions of others, having this identity confirmed.

On reaching the front of the crowd the royalists stood for a while gazing over the sea of flowers towards the palace gates. At the start of the week media reports had shown bunches of flowers, cards and other objects being fastened along the length and height of the fifty-yard-long screen of ornamental railings and gates (Figure 1.1; *Guardian,* 6 September 1997: 7). As this filled up, the tributes had been laid on the ground, and by Friday morning spread for many yards in each direction making the gates inaccessible (Figure 1.2). Many of the trees which had been decorated earlier in the week were now engulfed in this spreading tide, along with lamp posts, park benches and litter bins. It was here, as close as it was now possible to get to the Palace, that the royalists wanted to leave their flowers.

After taking in the whole scene they both in turn bent down to gently lay their flowers amongst the others. Patricia gave a bunch of mixed chrysanthemums and white gypsophila, Daniel pink roses and white freesias, which they left in the wrapping paper. They did this, they said, because it was how they would have given her flowers in life, also it was what everyone else appeared to be doing, and looking around they felt that the wrapped flowers gave a better idea of just how many people had been here. In laying their flowers they rested the heads of their bunch on the stem of the one in front, taking care that their dedication card could be seen, but that it did not obscure that of anyone else. Then after saying a silent prayer, they straightened up to stand in silence wiping away quiet tears. Then, after spending several minutes taking photographs of the whole scene and of the individual tributes lying at our feet, Patricia said quietly 'I think we should go now and let someone else have our places.' At this we made our way back through the crowd to look at as many as possible of the tributes left on and around the trees.

Later in the day we found similar scenes on The Mall. Deep lines of flowers ran along the length of the boundary wall of St James's Palace. A permanent notice fixed to wooden gates inset into this wall warned, 'Access is required at all times for emergency vehicles. Please do not obstruct.' This warning had been completely disregarded. Flowers, drawings and even twelve small teddy bears individually in cellophane were fastened to the gates, while in front of them the lines of flowers continued unbroken. At the end of the wall they continued around the gatehouse of Clarence House, the home of the Queen Mother, to pile up against the railings of the gateway which gives access to the entrance. At the gatehouse the windowsills, doorstep and mail box were used to hold flowers with more tributes fastened to the door and walls. As at Kensington Palace the trees and lamp posts were decorated, and flowers and banners were beginning to appear on the crush barriers erected to control the crowds expected at the following day's funeral. At the top of The Mall, the railings and gates of Buckingham Palace also held flowers, pictures and other tributes, as did the steps, ledges, plinths and statues of the Victoria memorial.

Letting the Flowers Speak

At royal visits it is officialdom that takes over public spaces, suspending normal activities, restricting access to buildings and constraining the public behind crush barriers in streets where they usually have freedom of movement. In this way official control of public spaces is asserted and mundane places are transformed into an arena for the display of royalty. During the mourning there was a reversal of this situation in that it was the public who took over the park, pathways, railings, gates, walls and trees to display their flowers and claim an identity as the bereaved. As in all social dramas (Turner 1982) they sought to negotiate the official boundaries and definitions of the situation (Barth 1969) and to 'dramatize who they and other people are, or who they hope others will take them to be' (Buckley & Kenney 1993: 211). Their claim to a bereaved identity was, however, threatened by the fact that the takeover was partial, rather than complete.

Although the three royal palaces present readily accessible sites, this is so only to the extent that they are situated amongst the hustle of central London. Within this public location all stand in private grounds surrounded by high walls and gates and are further protected by police and guardsmen from unauthorized public access. The gates which were obstructed by flowers at Kensington Palace were ornamental ones, those used for access were kept open, as was the gateway to Clarence House and to St James's. At Buckingham Palace, the home of the Queen and a symbolic centre of national life, not only was one gate kept free from obstruction, but greater control of the crowds was exercised. Here the flowers were not allowed to spread all over the pavement, and crush barriers were erected to create a walkway in front of them. Access to this space was controlled by the police who admitted restricted numbers of people through at any one time, either to lay more flowers, or to look at those already there. In these architectural and organizational arrangements the weakness of the social relationship between the Princess and the people was most clearly dramatized. It is in the negotiation of these official boundaries and definitions that the cultural conventions attached to gifts of flowers provide a rhetorical resource for claiming closer social ties with the Princess.

The use of flowers in the movement from virtual to actual mourner is hardly surprising given that flowers have an established use in British funeral ceremonies, are placed on graves and, in recent years have been laid at the sites of tragic accidents (Monger 1997). When taken as gifts for the dead, flowers 'mark the bearer as a mourner' (Biddle & Walter 1998) by invoking the widely understood convention that flowers express social and emotional ties (Goody 1993). This general meaning is supported by another conventional understanding: the motivation for the act of giving is the expression of sentiments of friendship, love and gratitude (Cheal 1988: 16–19). Therefore, as both item and act invoke claims to social ties, a gift of flowers is a particularly suitable medium for bridging the distance between the self and the other, whether living or dead, royal or commoner.

These conventional understandings can be seen in the meanings that the royalists attach to their flowers. At an operational level they may, as the royalists readily admit, serve to gain admission into the company of the royals for a few moments, but they stress that this is not the sole reason that they take them. Their motivation, in the words of one royalist, is 'to show our respect and affection and to say thank you for all they do'. For Daniel and Patricia, purchased bunches of flowers are sufficient to make this point, while others gave extra emphasis to the conventional meaning by fashioning their flowers into more elaborate forms, such as bouquets, posies and arrangements in small wicker baskets. In taking the time and trouble to make their flowers 'a little bit special' they undertook a labour of love, and they were sure their efforts were recognized and appreciated by the royals. Although bunches of flowers were the most prevalent type of mourning flowers, there were some baskets, posies and bouquets taken to the royal palaces, but whether these were home made or purchased I have no means of knowing. More widely represented exceptions to the bunches of flowers, were the funeral flowers purchased from professional florists which are known as Special Tributes.

Florists' Special Tributes

The most elaborate example of the purchased special tributes that I saw is the one described in the Interflora catalogue as 'The Gates of Heaven' (Figure 10.3). Standing around two feet high and topped by a golden cross, it was made up of white chrysanthemums decorated with red carnations and a corner spray of red roses. These were fashioned into a free-standing arch, under which two golden gates stood slightly ajar. A black and white picture of the smiling Princess, cut from a magazine, had been inserted behind the gates and in front of them burned two small votive candles. Retailing at over £100 this was probably the most expensive of the tributes and the only example I saw was on the boundary wall at Kensington Palace. More plentiful were the special tributes that drew upon the personal name of the Princess, either by taking the shape of the initial letter 'D', or having 'D' or 'Di' picked out within another shape, usually a heart or square cushion. Depending upon the overall size and the type of the flowers used these fell into a price range of around thirty-five to eighty-five pounds. Although costing less than the 'Gates of Heaven' they are still much dearer than the bunches of flowers which, from what was on sale at the time, were likely to have cost between five and twelve pounds. In addition to a higher price, the florists' categorization of these items as 'special tributes' indicates that they are intended to signify close social ties between the donor and the deceased. Therefore, in making this purchase the donor is laying claim to an intimacy, a claim which is more explicitly stated in the socially familiar use of the personal name, whether as an initial or a diminutive. Many donors further strengthened this claim in the wording of cards they attached to their gifts. For example, the card attached to 'The Gates of Heaven' read, 'Diana, Loved you so much, missing you so badly. God Bless' .

Figure 10.3 'Gates of Heaven', purchased floral tribute, Kensington Gardens, week 1. *Anne Rowbottom*

Labours of Love

As already noted, when making their bouquets and baskets of flowers the royalists felt themselves to be adding to the message of respect and affection through the time and trouble they took over their gifts. A similar expression is suggested in the home-made tributes of the mourners. These were not floral arrangements, but combined fresh flowers with pictures and messages onto sheets of paper, or thin card. One example had fifteen purple orchids, grouped in five bunches of three sprays, fastened onto a sheet of A3 size card by a pink ribbon, with multi-looped bows in the top left and bottom right corners. A picture of the Princess, cut from a newspaper or magazine, was stuck in the bottom left-hand corner with a handwritten message on the opposite side in a script and language which I could not understand. Such expensive blooms were not the norm, roses or carnations being a more popular choice. A flower would often be fastened to each corner of a sheet of card, or a small bunch placed in the centre at the top. One drawing of the Princess had red and white carnations draped down from the top to represent a crown.

Although obviously the work of young children, one example is of particular interest for the way it incorporates the main themes characteristic of the adult versions namely, royal status, love and continuity, as well as the motifs of crown, heart and angels. It was made from a sheet of thin card cut into a heart shape and painted pink. Two, by now very wilted, sunflower heads had been glued to the right and left of the centre, below which a smaller heart shape was outlined in (wild) daisies. Within this floral heart there was a felt pen drawing of the head and shoulders of a female figure, signified by large red lips and long hair, wearing a crown. Written above this drawing was the statement 'You are an angel'. The top right- and left-hand sections of the heart shape appeared to be the work of even younger children. On the left side, above a rudimentary outline of a figure, was written 'you are the best princess in the hole (sic) wide world'. In the other corner, below the words 'Eli loves Diana for ever', were three kisses and what appeared to be a crown.

Discussion and Conclusion

A wide range of flowers was used in the bunches, special tributes and labours of love with roses, chrysanthemums, carnations and lilies being very well represented . However, in accordance with English tradition, no flower was of itself particularly marked as a gift suitable for the dead. All or any of the blooms could equally well have been given to the Princess during her lifetime,

Figure 10.4 Many messages incorporated a *Queen of Hearts* playing card, Kensington Gardens, week 2. *Tony Walter*

and in addition there seemed to be a conscious desire amongst many donors to give the Princess in death what was understood to have been pleasing to her in life (cf. Goody 1993: 292). Daniel was particularly explicit about this. He took pink roses to Kensington Palace, 'because they were one of her favourite flowers', and chose a card with a picture of ballet dancers, 'as she loved ballet'. A more general expression of this desire to please can be seen in the way many people addressed their cards and messages to 'Her Royal Highness' or alternatively referred to 'HRH' . This title, accorded only to senior members of the Royal Family, was taken away from the Princess following the divorce – a loss which, according to media reports, distressed the Princess. Drawing upon their knowledge of this situation, these donors enhanced their gifts by returning her lost title. Other references to royal status were made in the drawings, pictures cut from magazines and use of the cutout portrait postcards usually sold to tourists, which pictured her wearing the definitive attribute of a true Princess, a diamond tiara.

Giving what was known to please her was also apparent in the widespread use of the heart motif. During a television interview the Princess said that as she would never be Queen of England, she hoped she could become the Queen of people's hearts. Like flowers the image of the heart conveys love and this motif was widespread, not only in the labours of love, but also in the cards and messages attached to the bunches of flowers. Once again in many of the messages the conventional meaning was explicitly stated. One donor wrote: 'Dearest Diana, You touched the aids patient and the cancer victim. And by touching them, you touched us, everyone.' Others declared a love for her so great that 'our hearts are broken' by her death. In expressions of love, written and visual references to The Queen of Hearts were made (Figure 10.4). Actual playing cards, or colour printed copies were attached to flowers and dedication cards. Enlargements of photocopies were also turned into posters and fastened to tree trunks and railings often accompanied by messages on the theme, 'You will always be the Queen of our hearts'.

The idea of continuity was also strong. Like young Eli many promised, 'We will love you for ever' (Figure 10.5). The donor's flowers might soon fade, but the sentiments of love and affection expressed by their gift would continue for ever. Many gave the Princess immortality, picturing her as an angel, or addressing her as one. Variations on this theme gave her the happiness and true love in heaven that she had not found on earth, as they partnered her with her companion in death, Dodi Al Fayed. In giving her their love they gave her something else, the idealized version of herself that they had rhetorically constructed. Forever young and beautiful, caring and worthy, happy and in love, she would live in their hearts for ever. Through their gifts the donors claimed the intimate social ties acquired through knowledge of the needs and desires of another person. As the messages and special tributes show, spatially the public flowers may have remained outside the palace gates, but rhetorically they allowed the donors to bridge the social distance between themselves and Diana, Princess of Wales.

Bibliography

Barth, F. (1969) 'Introduction' in F. Barth (ed.), *Ethnic Groups and Boundaries: The Social Organisation of Cultural Difference*, London: Allen & Unwin.

Biddle, L. & Walter, T. (1998) 'The Emotional English and their Queen of Hearts', *Folklore* 109: 96–99.

Billig, M. (1992) *Talking of the Royal Family*, London & New York: Routledge.

Buckley, A. & Kenney, M.C. (1995) *Negotiating Identity: Rhetoric, Metaphor and Social Drama in Northern Ireland*, Washington & London: Smithsonian Institute Press.

Chaney, D. (1993) *Fictions of Collective Life*, London & New York: Routledge.

Cheal, D. (1988) *The Gift Economy*, London: Routledge.

Goffman, E. (1968) *Stigma: Notes on the Management of Spoiled Identity*, Harmondsworth: Penguin.

Figure 10.5 Many messages referred to the love of either Diana or her mourners for her, Kensington Gardens, week 2. *Tony Walter*

Goody, J. (1993) *The Culture of Flowers*, Cambridge: Cambridge University Press.

Hall, E.T. (1966) *The Hidden Dimension: Man's use of space in public and private*, London: Bodley Head.

Henley, P. & Rowbottom, A. (1997) *Royal Watchers*, Mosaic Productions for BBC2 Television.

Jack, I. (1997) 'Those Who Felt Differently', *Granta 60*, Winter, 10–34.

Monger, G. (1997) 'Modern Wayside Shrines', *Folklore*, 108: 113–14.

Monger, G. & Chandler, J. (1998) 'Pilgrimage to Kensington Palace', *Folklore*, 109: 104–8.

Rowbottom, A. (1994) *Royal Symbolism and Social Integration*, unpublished PhD thesis: Department of Social Anthropology, University of Manchester.

Shils, E. & Young, M. (1953) 'The Meaning of the Coronation', *Sociological Review (ns)* 1: 63–81.

Turner, V. (1982) *From Ritual to Theatre: The Human Seriousness of Play*, New York: Performing Arts Journal Publications.

Walter, T. (1997) 'Emotional Reserve and the English Way of Grief', in K. Charmaz, G. Howarth and A. Kellehear (eds), *The Unknown Country: Experiences of Death in Australia, Britain and the USA*, Basingstoke: Macmillan.

Westergaard, J. & Resler, H. (1976) *Class in a Capitalist Society*, London: Pelican.

Wilson, E. (1989) *The Myth of British Monarchy*, London: Journeyman.

11

Policing the Funeral

Tom Laidlaw and P.A.J. Waddington

The Metropolitan Police, especially those responsible for the centre of London, are extremely familiar with large gatherings in public places of various kinds. Protest demonstrations occur on average more than three times a week, added to which carnivals, festivals and royal ceremonials are common. The habitual response of the police to such gatherings is to seek to establish extensive control over the entire event (Waddington 1994b). Not only must protest demonstrations be peaceful, they must *minimise* disruption to others (Waddington 1994a, 1996); people gathering to celebrate New Year in Trafalgar Square are protected not only from crime and disorder, but are subject to many restrictions in the name of public safety; royal ceremonials not only are protected from terrorist attack, but also from anything that might detract from the dignity of the occasion. Of course, the achievement of these aspirations is variable. It depends on a variety of factors: first, whether the event is organized or spontaneous. Organisers can be persuaded to accept the police agenda, something that officers are very skilled at doing, but an event like New Year's Eve has no official organiser to impose restrictions and so the police must do so themselves directly. Secondly, those with vested interests can be more or less powerful. Most protest organisers are pretty powerless, whereas commercial companies, foreign embassies, government departments, and, of course, royalty, wield enormous power. Thirdly, police must have sufficient knowledge of what is to take place in order to prepare for it: the more predictable events are, the more comfortable senior officers feel. Fourthly, comfort is engendered when there is time for preparation – for deliberating over the 'what ifs' and making arrangements to 'cover their backs'.

The funeral of Princess Diana lacked most of the elements that give comfort to senior police officers: it was unexpected; suffused with uncertainties and ambiguities; open to public spontanety; involved a complex set of powerful vested interests; and had to be concluded swiftly. Police were denied what they value most – control.

A Royal Funeral?

Royal ceremonials are usually remarkably comfortable occasions for senior officers since they are exquisitely controlled. They are pre-planned with interested parties who share common goals to maintain the security and dignity of the occasion, and police are subject to few restrictions in imposing control over space and members of the public. Roads are closed and searched long before the event takes place and spectators enter territory that the police 'own'. Whilst there is the threat of terrorist action or lone assassin, security measures are extensive.

All of this applies to royal funerals. Long before death is imminent, members of the Royal Family are consulted, through the Lord Chamberlain or Earl Marshal,[1] about their funeral arrangements (Bland 1986). Unexpected deaths can readily be accommodated by any of a set of 'off-the-shelf' 'templates'. Members of the Royal Family normally have personal police protection, so the moment a death is confirmed the plans held by police and other agencies are activated starting a process to produce the required ceremonial. Interested parties, from the major broadcasters to the street sweepers, have details of their roles together with the luxury of some time to prepare and rehearse.

This would have been the case with the funeral of Diana, Princess of Wales, *had she been royal,* however since her divorce from the Prince of Wales her position and standing within royal circles were unclear. Yet, there was a clear royal interest in the funeral. There was no plan or protocol to cover these quite peculiar circumstances. The unexpectedness and circumstances of her death, a lack of awareness as to the whereabouts of her body and the vagueness of her royal position contributed to uncertainty and some confusion in commencing the planning of the police operation.

Police learned of her death, like everyone else, through the news media. Realizing the significance of what had happened, officers responsible for public order operations and their staff assembled hastily to begin preliminary planning. Arrangements needed to be made immediately for the return of the bodies of Diana and Dodi Al Fayed later that Sunday. The airfield at Northolt needed to be secured and provision made for the attendance of the official party. The Special Escort Group (responsible for guarding the Royal Family whilst in transit) were alerted, its inspector returning from holiday, and a motorcycle escort provided. But from the outset there was uncertainty and vacillation. Initially arrangements had been made to convey the body of

1. The Lord Chamberlain arranges the funerals of all members of the Royal Family apart from that of the Monarch, which is the province of the Earl Marshal.

Diana to the royal undertakers in north London but this was altered and the body was escorted to the Royal Coroner's mortuary at Fulham and then conveyed to the Chapel Royal at St James's Palace. Ambiguities of status extended beyond Princess Diana. An extraordinary decision was taken at the highest level in the police hierarchy to provide a motorcycle escort for the body of Dodi from the Battersea Heliport to the Royal Coroner's mortuary, thence to the mosque in Regents Park for a service and on to Surrey for burial before sunset in accordance with Islamic practice.

This ambiguity of status continued to be felt as the week unfolded in the absence of any definite lead from the Lord Chamberlain. Senior officers made initial preparations using as a template a 'standard' royal funeral, but in the knowledge that much still needed to be decided. It was with a mixture of relief and some despair that police heard the announcement on Monday that the funeral was to be held the following Saturday. Planning that would normally take months of negotiation needed to be concluded in days and involve not only the Lord Chamberlain but also the Princess's own family. Inevitably arrangements were agreed, only to be revoked and renegotiated. For instance, the state funeral plan being used as a template had a processional route from St James's Palace to Westminster Abbey. But estimates of the size of the crowd led to concerns that this route would provide insufficient public viewing space, threatening crowd safety and control as spectators pressed to watch the cortège. At Wednesday's tense meeting between senior police officers and the Lord Chamberlain's office, a decision was arrived at to provide additional public viewing by extending the processional route, to start from Kensington Palace, go alongside Hyde Park, past Buckingham Palace to join the original route at St James's Palace from where those mourners walking in the procession would join in. This significant alteration required planners to work through the night, hastily recruiting additional officers and other public services for the operation. By the conclusion of this process the operation directly entailed the deployment of over 4,000 officers, including officers of the City of London Police. Many civilian support staff were also needed to transport and cater for this temporary army.

Police welcomed whatever assistance was offered, not always with satisfactory results. The BBC was in the process of installing two giant screens in Hyde Park for the following week's Proms in the Park concert. They agreed to make the screens ready in time to show a live telecast of the funeral service and procession. A similar screen was also to be erected in Regents Park and together it was hoped that this would inhibit any vast movement of spectators towards the Abbey. The Department of Culture, Media and Sport (DCMS), responsible for the royal parks, hired private stewards to undertake crowd safety and control at these sites. Stewards were also hired to assist at other locations where the DCMS had responsibility. In the tight time-scale the late introduction of stewards and a breakdown in communication between DCMS, police and the stewarding companies resulted in confusion on the Saturday as to roles, jurisdiction and the suitability of high-visibility clothing on this sombre occasion.

A distinguishing feature of royal ceremonials is the need to ensure security. The ultimate disaster for public order policing in the capital is not a riot, but an assassination attempt on members of the Royal Family. The ceasefire in the Irish conflict had been holding for some time and there was no intelligence to indicate a change nor was activity by other terrorist groups thought likely, nevertheless significant precautions were taken. The more likely threat to members of the Royal Family or other VIPs was a lone assassin or attention-seeker such as the man who fired blanks at the Queen during Trooping the Colour in 1982. This funeral procession would see four royal princes, including the line of succession to the throne, walking before the public in the open. Moreover, in anticipation of huge crowds, it had been decided, in a change from traditional methods, to narrow the processional route by placing the crowd control barriers into the carriageway rather than along the kerb edge thus bringing the royal party and public into close proximity. Protection officers feared that the security of their 'principals' was being compromised to assuage the public mood.

The public mood also created a quite unusual source of anxiety regarding the safety of the Prince of Wales. Speculation was rife that controversy surrounding the royal divorce and the response of the Royal Family to Diana's death had engendered public hostility which, it was feared, might be expressed in some extreme fashion. The action of members of the Royal Family, including the Prince of Wales, in walking amongst the crowds at Kensington and St James's Palaces the day before the funeral allayed these fears.

Public Interest and Reaction

The public mood was the driving force behind much of what took place during the week preceding the funeral. The intensity of public interest added to the pressure on planners who were acutely aware that, despite the ambiguity that surrounded arrangements, they could not fail to 'make it all happen' whatever 'it' was. In the absence of a clear lead from the authorities there was apprehension that the initiative would pass to the public and the media. Saturation media coverage and increasing hype was seen as drawing increasing numbers of people into the area. There were also early fears that the media might organize some form of book in which to record condolences in advance of the official one provided by the Lord Chamberlain's Office and so attract even greater numbers before adequate facilities had been arranged. Interim plans to police the increasing numbers in the royal parks were introduced with arrangements to draw police officers from other parts of London if that became necessary at the cost of financial expense and disruption to normal policing activities.

International media interest in the aftermath of Princess Diana's death also had direct implications for the policing operation. They collectively inflicted upon already strained police resources insatiable demands for information and facilities. Intense competition amongst broadcasters (many of them unfamiliar with covering major ceremonial events) for facilities in the restricted space available and the involvement of the Department of Culture, Media and Sport soured normally cordial working relationships and led to some acrimony. Principal UK broadcasters, frustrated at the delays, alleged that police were prevaricating and an exchange took place at the highest level between them and the police.

Police

The police operation was massive not only in size, but also complexity. The Metropolitan Police were assisted by the Royal Parks Police especially at Kensington Palace Gardens. The City of London Police provided manpower, and close liaison was maintained with British Transport Police amid fears of overcrowding in the Underground. Plans for the cortège journey to Althorpe were agreed with Hertfordshire and Northamptonshire Police. Within the Metropolitan Police the two principal branches involved were Royalty Protection and 1 Area Headquarters Ceremonial Office. Such complexity was bound to create conflicts and it did.

One of the first issues was the appointment of a 'Gold' commander to be responsible for the co-ordination of all policing arrangements. The appointee would normally be responsible for strategic decision making within standing policy on all policing arrangements but on this occasion it became apparent from the outset that tensions existed within the organization about who should assume ultimate command, resulting in delay and frustration for their subordinates who were eager to commence preparations. The overweening concerns of the highest echelons continued to be felt through the planning and execution of the police operation. Normally, briefing the media at ceremonial events would be undertaken by the Gold commander familiar with operational details, but the importance of this occasion saw the police press conference, characterized by the general lack of factual information, led by the commissioner flanked by his two assistant commissioners. On the Saturday morning in the hour before the procession was due to leave Kensington Palace, the assistant commissioner responsible for No. 1 Area rode the length of the route, checking and pausing to issue directions where the policing activities did not meet his expectations. Having one officer senior to the Gold commander taking an active interest is not unusual for ceremonial occasions but such was the perceived significance of this occasion that Gold came under scrutiny from both assistant commissioners of the two branches involved and the Metropolitan Police commissioner himself. Fortunately, the operation satisfied this intense scrutiny.

The reaction of subordinates was no less unusual. Normally, operations arranged at such short notice would result in many officers being unable to attend briefings for a variety of reasons, not least apathy, but not on this occasion. Such was the apparent desire to be part of this unique event that the New Scotland Yard briefing room was overwhelmed and relay broadcasts were needed to adjoining rooms. During the early hours of Saturday morning the mammoth tasks of transporting and feeding several thousand police officers began. On any major event involving large numbers of police officers there are invariably some who are late, some who complain about the catering and a number of general grumbles about having leave days cancelled or having to leave their home division for the particular duty. Senior officers were pleasantly surprised to have all personnel on time with none of the usual complaints. Everyone involved was keen to ensure that nothing, as far as police could influence, would mar the dignity of what was clearly to be a unique occasion. These same officers the previous day had been policing in all areas of London dealing with every manner of police activity, but this day was something different. Not only were they immaculately turned out but some, being aware of the emotional state of the crowd, had brought supplies of tissues for use by anyone overcome in their immediate section of crowd.

Policing Grief

The police operation fell into two natural stages: the days following the announcement of Princess Diana's death and the funeral ceremony itself.

Aftermath

The scale of public reaction to Princess Diana's death was such that a police operation of sorts commenced almost immediately as mourners flocked to the royal palaces to leave flowers and other mementos. By Sunday evening considerable crowds were assembling outside Kensington Palace, Buckingham Palace and, when the place of rest of Diana's body became known, St James's Palace. All three locations are within royal parks and the jurisdiction of the Royal Parks Police whose officers undertook the initial policing of the gathering crowds. As the week wore on arrangements had been made to draft in additional Metropolitan Police officers for round the clock policing of the growing crowds outside Kensington Palace and the queues waiting to sign the increased number of books of condolence at St James's Palace.

Royal Parks officers used to policing large crowds at major events in the parks soon became aware of a different atmosphere in this crowd. There was an unusual quietness, people were not sure what to do, some were in shock and many distressed. At Kensington Palace people were arriving with flowers, laying them at the gates and as darkness fell lighted candles became evident. Not only flowers were laid but bottles of wine and champagne, teddy bears, framed pictures and other items. Initially police officers helped in the laying of flowers but soon organized children from the crowd to assist. Hundreds of candles were lit with some setting light to paper-wrapped flowers. They found a difficult task in sensitively controlling these small conflagrations to prevent more serious incidents. The amount of candle wax on officers' boots became an indication of how long they had been on duty. The policing task in the sense of crowd control was not a problem but the sensitivities of every action with such great emotion around proved more testing. Officers quickly realized the importance of accepting letters, cards and gifts and giving assurance that they would be passed to the addressees, mostly the two young princes. The only moments of contention were when police had to move crowd control barriers denoting the public areas. This was done as the area required for flowers grew and more urgently when members of the Royal Family arrived unexpectedly for a walkabout.

Another different aspect to the occasion noted by police officers was the reserved behaviour of the press during the week who, unusually, presented no problems and some of whom were seen to be caught up in the collective emotion.

The Funeral

Police arrangements for the funeral were subject to a severe test on Friday evening when the body of Diana was moved from St James's Palace to Kensington Palace. Initially it had been the police hope that this movement would not be publicized but the ever growing crowds around St James's Palace combined with the intense public and media interest in every facet of the arrangements made this unrealistic. Provision was made for the Special Escort Group to escort the hearse accompanied by a car containing the Prince of Wales, but rather than travelling by the reasonably secure barriered roads forming the processional route, directions were received through the Lord Chamberlain's office to travel on roads outside Hyde Park. Nor was the timing of the movement open to negotiation. The publicity for this movement attracted greater numbers to the area of St James's Palace and especially Kensington Palace. Police resources were severely stretched when the crowd, simply through weight of numbers, threatened to engulf the convoy. Only skilled riding by the motorcycle escorts and deft work by the available police officers saw the hearse and the Prince's car through the throng. It was acknowledged not to have been in the usual neat, orderly and secure style practised on normal occasions and this increased the pressure on the operational senior officers already anxious about the following day's policing.

On the morning of the funeral arriving officers took up their positions, allowing those who had been supervising the gathering crowds overnight to be released from duty. There is a strict routine for such handovers of responsibility to ensure the continuity of security but on this morning the volume of officers seeking to find their respective posts caused some initial confusion. Supervising officers, aware of the gravity of the situation and possible adverse repercussions, quickly resolved any remaining problems on the spot. Some roads forming the processional route had been closed to traffic for several days but now came the task of excluding traffic from the remaining streets so that the crowd barriers could be properly and finally positioned. The build-up of crowd was greater than expected with many having settled into vantage points. The repositioning of barriers following the exclusion of traffic created a number of minor disputes between some members of the crowd and the police officers concerned in the repositioning. Officers who had established empathetic relationships with members of the crowd during the preceding hours were able to resolve these problems by careful explanation and ad hoc negotiation. Thus, whilst difficulties were overcome, it was becoming increasingly evident that the operation was not being implemented like clockwork and control was being ceded to street-level officers.

More comfortingly, across London and northwards towards Northamptonshire the other aspects of the policing operation were falling into place. The security co-ordinator's plan had been implemented, traffic diversions and motorway patrols were operating and the civilian support staff were in position with their communications and closed circuit television equipment. The only significant incident at this time was when a police civilian CCTV operator attempting to improve the camera angle on the gates of Kensington Palace fell off his rooftop perch. Fortunately he was not seriously injured.

Many of the more important mourners were on their way to Westminster Abbey under police motor cycle escort. This arguably was not a police duty but on ceremonial occasions, and especially this one, the police opt for the easier path of facilitating the smooth and dignified running of the event rather than answering subsequent adverse comment. High-level decisions were taken to waive the standing rules governing the entitlement to motorcycle escorts – the late arrival of prominent mourners at the Abbey would not have been in the best interests of police.

Two crowd issues remained a concern. The first was the possibility of the public, overcome in their collective grief, bypassing the barriers and falling in behind the procession. The effect of this would have been twofold. It would have interfered with the official mourners joining in at St James's Palace and then swamped the already crowded area around the Abbey causing friction with those already established as well as obstructing the route of the cortège after the service. Police did not relish the prospect of forcible removal of individually compliant mourners whose collective weight of numbers and emotional state would be a serious disruption to the all-important dignity of the occasion. To deal with this possibility the police used a plan successfully used on previous ceremonial occasions to marshal the crowd behind a moving cordon of officers following at a discrete distance behind the cortège.

The second crowd issue related to safety in the movements of the many thousands of people attracted to the giant screens in Hyde Park. The extended route now presented the opportunity for these people to view the gun carriage procession as it passed along the south side of Hyde Park on its way to the Abbey. They could then watch the live telecast on the screens and after the service move to the east side of the park to view the cortège as it travelled along Park Lane on its way to Althorp. The movement of thousands of people anxious to obtain good vantage points was a real concern for police but the deployment of several hundred stewards together with police officers success-fully reduced this perceived danger.

With the procession under way there was some relief in the police control room that the crowds, vast as they were, did not appear to be as great as the earlier press reports had envisaged. Apart from a few anticipated pinch points there was sufficient public space for safe and relatively comfortable viewing along the processional route. The police officers lining the route mentally adjusted to the calmness and silence so unusual in a crowd of this size. However, they were not prepared for the throwing of flowers as the procession passed. Normally the throwing of any object on a state occasion would be seen as a threat to security demanding swift police intervention. It was quickly realized that such action was inappropriate on this occasion and officers confined themselves to observing sensitivities by attempting to avoid stepping on the thrown flowers, an intention which soon became impossible in places by the coverage of flowers on the ground.

The gun carriage bearing the coffin processed along the barriered and police-lined route. The royal princes and Earl Spencer together with other official mourners joined on foot from St James's Palace. The procession arrived at the Great West Door of Westminster Abbey on time one hour and fifty minutes after leaving Kensington Palace. Although not a police duty the extraneous and critical role of achieving exact timing for the procession was undertaken by a mounted police officer, who without rehearsal, led and judged the pace accurately to provide the dignified arrival at the Abbey. The service was relayed to crowds in the street by loud speakers and telecast to the giant screens in Hyde Park and Regents Park. The crowds were emotional, some distressed but caused no real problem to police. The only aspect which created some uncertainty was not knowing when the minute's silence began.

London away from the ceremonial area was almost deserted and traffic officers worrying about traffic diversions could find little traffic to divert. The police control room using extensive CCTV was monitoring not only the immediate area but also the route the cortège was to take on leaving Westminster Abbey to travel to Althorp. The normal use of police helicopters to transmit pictures to the control room was considered inappropriate in the central area where it was perceived the noise from the machines would have damaged the dignity of the occasion and possibly antagonized the silent mourning crowd. Other aircraft, including media charters were excluded by the application of an overflying ban, ostensibly on the grounds of security.

The cameras covering the post-funeral route through north London towards the M1 revealed almost deserted streets with some pockets of crowding at vantage points along the route. There did not appear to be any problems. Police were deployed to where it was thought crowds might gather but in unprecedented circumstances a best guess was all that was possible. The route was not lined by police but had received wide publicity in the press. By the time the cortège passed, large numbers of people had left their television sets and made their way to seek vantage points. It had been the police intention to allow traffic to run until the last moment when traffic officers would stop it to allow the cortège to continue unhindered at a dignified pace in what police describe as a traffic-free 'bubble'.

It was with surprise and apprehension that the police controllers watched the crowds gather as the live television pictures charted the progress of the cortège on leaving Westminster Abbey. The progression was a return along the processional route already strewn with flowers past the silent crowds. At Wellington Arch (at Hyde Park corner) an escort of police motorcyclists from the Special Escort Group fell in alongside the hearse to secure and control the dignity of the 77-mile journey through north London and Hertfordshire to Northamptonshire and Althorp. A Range Rover communications vehicle in radio contact with the various police forces through which they would pass brought up the rear. Where there were police on the route they were largely overwhelmed but the crowds, although emotional, were calm and compliant. At the parts of the route where there were no police officers the crowd controlled itself, opening to allow passage for the hearse and its motorcycle escort. The police motorcyclists would have preferred a greater width of clear roadway to allay their fear of members of the crowd falling or throwing themselves in front of the cortège. The public knew the exact detail of the route down to which lane would be used and they lined it in such numbers there was no escape. Traffic police finding three straggling buses still on the closed route ahead of the cortège attempted several times to turn them off but rather than upset those mourners who had established their positions they kept the buses going. Instead of arriving at Golders Green passengers were bemused to find themselves many miles further north at Scratchwood Service Area on the M1 but were rewarded with a view of the cortège as it finally passed them. There were few actual incidents of concern to the escort, the most difficult to accustom to was the volume of flowers being thrown, many of which hit the motorcyclists and lodged on their machines. The hearse too suffered from the amount of floral tributes being aimed at it. When the cortège reached the M1 and temporarily away from the crowds but still in sight of television cameras, it stopped while the protection officer travelling in it removed, as carefully as possible, armfuls of flowers obstructing the driver's view, placing them as if by arrangement at the side of the motorway.

Another abnormal feature of this occasion was a ceremonial route that included motorways. Decisions had to be taken at the highest levels to waive the normally strict enforcement of laws designed to ensure road safety in order to allow the expression of public grief. Crowds along the motorway were indeed far greater than anticipated and many drivers, with a disregard for rules and their personal safety, stopped to view the cortège as it passed (Figure 1.4).

Whilst crowds were unexpectedly compliant, the same could not be said entirely for police forces through which the cortège passed. Police officers travelling on operational duty through other police force areas are always aware of the protocol required to avoid inter-force conflict. For this occasion agreement had been reached to allow the Special Escort Group of the Metropolitan Police to escort the cortège all the way to Althorpe with local forces keeping the route clear and providing motorway patrol vehicles at a distance to maintain security and dignity by preventing unauthorized vehicles, including media, approaching too close. However, the Metropolitan Police had no authority to enforce this protocol over other forces. The escort commander travelled in the communications Range Rover at the rear of the cortège to regulate the speed to a dignified pace and also to allow the family mourners, travelling separately, to reach Althorp before the cortège. It was much to his chagrin and that of the New Scotland Yard control room that the cortège, as it passed through other force areas, was surrounded by local police units, headlamps blazing and blue lights flashing. Not only was this considered to be quite unnecessary but was perceived as defiling the dignity so carefully achieved until that time.

Crowds continued to line the route with a large gathering around the gates of Althorp where the police escort peeled off allowing the hearse to enter the Spencer family estate. The police escort motorcyclists, tired and uncomfortable after the long slow ride were trapped within the crowd for some time as local police had been unable to maintain an escape route.

Phew!

From the police perspective this operation had all the hallmarks of disaster in the making: it was unexpected, ambiguous, unprecedented and they needed to compete with powerful vested interests for control. Yet, the whole week was without serious incident. Why? Because mourners controlled themselves. Public order lay in the hands of the public who, despite the unique circumstances, understood what was appropriate and complied with it. Given such compliance, policing was truly 'by consent'.

Methodological Postscript

The data on the policing of the funeral was gathered by Tom Laidlaw, a recently retired Metropolitan Police officer, who held the rank of Commander and had long experience in commanding public order operations. He was employed as a consultant by 'ShowSec International' to co-ordinate the 2,500 stewards hired by the Department of Culture, Media and Sport and to be the liaison point with the Metropolitan Police. Consequently he attended meetings with the police and on the actual day of the funeral spent the entire day in the Special Operations Control at New Scotland Yard. He was also able to exploit his many contacts within the Metropolitan Police who were involved in the policing arrangements, and thus obtain an inside view of the policing operation. A more comprehensive picture was subsequently obtained through a number of interviews after the event with officers of the Metropolitan Police and Royal Parks Police including the Assistant Commissioner in charge of the funeral planning arrangements, the 'Gold' Commander, the Security Co-ordinator, a Royalty Protection Officer, a Diplomatic Protection Officer, the head of the Special Escort Group, the senior Traffic Division officer and the Metropolitan and Royal Parks police planning teams.

Bibliography

Bland, O. (1986) *The Royal Way of Death*, London: Constable.

Waddington, P.A.J. (1994a) 'Coercion and accommodation: policing public order after the Public Order Act', *British Journal of Sociology* 45(3): 367–85.

Waddington, P.A.J. (1994b) *Liberty and Order: Policing Public Order in a Capital City*, London: UCL Press.

Waddington, P.A.J. (1996) 'The other side of the barricades: policing protest' in C. Barker and P. Kennedy (eds), *To Make Another World: Studies in Protest and Collective Action*, Aldershot: Avebury: 219–36.

12

Liturgy and Music

Grace Davie and David Martin

The first week of September was full of formal religious liturgies enacted in the Princess's memory in every city, town and village of the nation. Some of these became gathering points for the population as a whole (they were mostly but not exclusively Christian); others were simple services that would have taken place anyway, but acquired a particular resonance in view of Diana's death. Examples abound: special prayers incorporated into the morning or evening office, a weekday mass said in her memory or a special evensong on the Sunday following the funeral and so on. The three services outlined here have a national rather than local focus and, between them, spanned the week. The first took place in St Paul's Cathedral at 6.30 p.m. on the day that the Princess of Wales died; the second was the Requiem Mass offered in Westminster Cathedral on Friday 5 September; the third was the funeral (technically a memorial service) in Westminster Abbey on the morning of Saturday 6 September. The Abbey service preceded a private burial in the grounds of Althorp Park, the Spencer family home in Northamptonshire. We look first at the liturgical framework of the three public national rites and then at the music employed.[1]

Liturgy

It is clear that some form of formal liturgy was required. Much attention has been given to the improvised and informal gestures of mourning that coloured the week following the Princess's death, whether these be individual (such as the laying of flowers or the lighting of a candle) or collective (the patient queuing to sign a book of condolence, an act that inevitably drew people together). Neither, however heartfelt though they may have been, were

---

1. The liturgical section is by Davie, the musical section by Martin. Both are based on a close observation of the events in question and a careful scrutiny of the very full (print and television) journalistic record.

adequate in themselves to express the feelings of the nation as a whole as they tried to come to terms with the death of an enigmatic, but deeply sympathetic public figure in the prime of her life. Not only enigma but ambiguity pervades the whole affair: Diana was, after all, the *divorced* wife of the heir to the throne and, at the time of death, was keeping company with the son of a prominent Muslim. Why, then, was she was given what was effectively a state funeral in the Church of England? The answer is not self-evident. What is clear, however, that the refusal of the Church to comply with this request would have caused outrage.

The analysis here is offered on the assumption that the churches of this country (including the established Church) still have a significant role to play despite the marked decline in churchgoing in post-war Britain (Davie 1994). It was precisely these institutions that were charged with the task of marking Diana's death on behalf both of her family and the nation. How did they respond? What languages, spoken and sung, were available to express the grief of millions, drawn together not only in person but also, exponentially, through the world's media?

The relationship between the liturgies themselves and their projection on the global media forms a dominant thread throughout. Both are integral to the three occasions that we analyse – producing at certain moments some remarkable (if unforeseen) effects. The St Paul's service on the evening of her death embodied all these features: not only did it become, effectively, the 'Songs of Praise' broadcast for that particular Sunday (watched in the normal way by several million people, this time by several more), it also coincided with the arrival of the plane carrying Diana's body back to Britain at RAF Northolt. The juxtaposition of the singing of Psalm 130 ('Out of the deep have I called unto thee, O Lord') with the landing of the plane produced one of the most remarkable television effects of the whole week. That, probably, was fortuitous and depended for its visual effect on the split-second decision-making of the producer concerned. It is less surprising that the unpreparedness of everyone for an event such as the Princess's death provided the theme for the service as a whole. It was the first moment in which there could be some recollection of what had happened within a Christian context. The structure was simple, combining readings, a short address and a few moments of prayer.

All three were chosen to affirm Christian certainties in face of human vulnerability. They were spoken before a congregation visibly in shock and barely able to comprehend either what had happened or the words that they were hearing. Precisely this, however, gives meaning to the Church's role. At times such as these, the established church does for us what we cannot do ourselves. This is true after any bereavement; in the case of Diana the role was simply magnified to meet the demands of a nation as well as a family. The closing words of the Dean's sermon captured this sentiment:

> These are words that we are scarcely able to hear, to receive, in moments of profound shock, of disbelief, of tragedy. But the words remain and they will speak as the days and the weeks pass because they are tried and tested words that have proved their ability to speak to the darkest moments. But today – now – it is enough to be still, to pray, and to commend into God's hands the one whom we remember and all whom we hold with her before God in love.

It was these words that were followed by Psalm 130 and the arrival of the plane from France.

Five days later, the mood of the nation was rather different. Detailed plans had been made for the funeral in Westminster Abbey and the Royal Family had come to London. On the eve of the funeral, however, a Memorial Requiem Mass took place in (the Catholic) Westminster Cathedral where the principal celebrant (and preacher) was Cardinal Basil Hume, the Archbishop of Westminster. The Mass in itself requires some explanation given that the Princess herself was a baptized and confirmed Anglican and that the Monarch remains Supreme Governor of the Church of England (Maitland 1998). Two factors are significant here. The first concerns the Princess's own family. Frances Shand Kydd, the Princess's mother had become a Catholic and was present with her two daughters, together with more than 3,000 mourners – packed into Westminster Cathedral and overflowing outside. In terms of the religious landscape of modern Britain, however, the Mass represented more than this. The naturalness with which it took its place in the cycle of liturgy that framed the week of mourning reflects the changing role of Catholicism within the nation as a whole. No longer is the Catholic community a beleaguered minority pushed to the margins of British society. It has become part of the mainstream with its leader a highly respected source of religious and moral wisdom (Hornsby-Smith 1988). The role of the Cardinal was, in fact, crucial to the whole week in that his was, effectively, the principal sermon preached in connection with Diana's death. (The funeral itself contained a eulogy in place of a sermon.)

Within the structure of the Mass, the sermon or homily took its normal place in the Liturgy of the Word following the epistle from I Corinthians 15 ('Death is swallowed up in victory') and the Gospel from St Matthew, chapter 5 ('Insofar as you did this to one of the least of these brothers of mine, you did it to me'). With the latter in mind, it is worth recalling that this was the day on which Mother Teresa of Calcutta also died. The homily itself is remarkable in its confident assertion that Diana, assisted by the prayers of those who loved her, was 'on her way to the vision of God, to a happiness this world cannot give, where true peace is to be found'. Diana, frail, imperfect and flawed like the rest of us would be judged mercifully. Recalling the words of the gospel, the Cardinal continued:

> The maimed, the sick, the young, the old, were of much concern to you. You will have discovered that in serving these, you were in fact serving Him, even if you had not realized it at the time. We have the Lord's authority for that . . . '*As often as you did this to the least of these, my brothers and sisters,*' the Lord said, '*you did it unto me.*' (Matthew 25 verse 40)

The second part of the homily concentrated on those left behind: the grieving millions as well as her own family. They (we) were invited to reflect on our own mortality, 'the fragility of all our human joys and sorrows' – with the suggestion that a proper understanding of these things lies within the perspective of the Christian gospel, itself the fount of forgiveness and true charity. These were the lessons to be learnt from Diana's life as well as her death. The homily ends with a prayer that referred to one of the week's major themes – Diana's compassion, born of her all-too-human vulnerability and sorrows:

> Farewell then, Diana.
> The agonies of the hearth and the anguish of the mind
> were often your companions in life.
> They were your teachers too
> for from them you learned understanding, compassion and kindness.
> These are your finest legacy to us.
> Thank you for all the good that you did.
> Thank you for the joy that you gave to many.
> Thank you for being like the rest of us,
> flawed but loveable, and above all loved by God.

The emphasis throughout is on compassion, mercy and a common humanity. There is almost no mention of judgement (apart from the Gospel reading itself) and none of purgatory.

Both the St Paul's service and the Requiem Mass were important markers in the week following Diana's death. But the funeral itself, six days after her death, was clearly the most significant liturgical event of the whole week. Indeed it was the most watched television presentation of all time, with a truly global audience numbered in billions. It contained an unusual combination of elements.

The proceedings started almost two hours before the service itself, as the cortège left Kensington Palace with the coffin, lined with zinc and draped with the Royal Standard, placed (traditionally, but somewhat incongrously for a Princess not noted for her militarism) on a horse-drawn gun carriage, followed by a small number of guardsman. Big and colourful enough to be a manifestly royal cortège, yet small enough to seem dreadfully lonely among the silent, thronged crowds. The route was not self-evident; it had been planned and replanned during the preceding week in order that the anticipated crowds might have adequate sight of the cortège (see Chapter 1). About halfway along its route to the Abbey, just over 500 representatives of the Princess's favourite charities joined the procession, which was headed by Prince Charles, Prince William, Prince Harry, the Duke of Edinburgh and Earl Spencer (Princess Diana's brother). The Queen, having saluted the coffin at the gates of Buckingham Palace, went by car to the Abbey with the Queen Mother.

The liturgy itself was an innovative mixture of Christian invocation, personal tributes (both spoken and musical), and ending conventionally with prayers, the blessing and commendation. It had been billed by the Palace as a unique service for a unique person, lauded by many for catching something of Diana's complex personality, criticized by others (mostly the churchgoing constituency) for being insufficiently Christian. Bearing in mind that the whole thing was constructed in less than a week, it represented an impressive organizational and musical achievement if nothing else.

The beginning and end were uncompromisingly Christian. The service began with the sentences which are read or sung at any Christian funeral, stark in their solemnity: 'I am the resurrection and the life, saith the Lord: he that believeth in me, though he were dead, yet shall he live.' They were followed by the bidding prayer, Diana's favourite hymn and two short readings by the Princess's sisters, interspersed with musical tributes. The well-known words on love from I Corinthians 13 (again unequivocally Christian) were read by the Prime Minister, Tony Blair – some thought brilliantly, others thought rather too theatrically. So far, the liturgy was following an accepted pattern. It was the centrepieces of the service, however, that were not only less obviously Christian, but bound to cause controversy: these were Elton John's singing of 'Candle in the Wind' and the extended tribute by Diana's brother, Earl Spencer.

Elton John was either an inspired choice, humanizing an inevitably solemn occasion and introducing an element of popular culture wholly in tune with the Princess's own tastes, or it was a sell-out, a lapse into the style of 'Desert Island Discs' quite out of place in a state occasion. Whatever the case the song was executed with total professionalism and instantly became a best-seller with the proceeds going to the Princess's Memorial Fund. The eulogy was even more controversial in so far as the Earl used the occasion not only to allude to the difficult relationship between the Princess and the press (Diana 'the ancient goddess of hunting was, in the end, the most hunted person of the modern age'), but also to the tensions that had developed between his sister and the Royal Family. The following became the key, much-quoted passage:

> She would want us today to pledge ourselves to protecting her beloved boys William and Harry from a similar fate [being hunted by the press], and I do this here, Diana, on your behalf. We will not allow them to suffer the anguish that used regularly to drive you to tearful despair. And, beyond that, on behalf of your mother and sisters, I pledge that we, your blood family, will do all we can to continue the imaginative way in which you were steering these two exceptional young men, so that their souls are not simply immersed by duty and tradition but can sing openly, as you planned.
>
> We fully respect the heritage into which they have both been born and will always respect and encourage them in their royal role, but we, like you, recognize the need for them to experience as many different aspects of life as possible to arm them spiritually and emotionally for the years ahead. I know you would have expected nothing less from us.

Such a text could not but be controversial, the more so in that it was followed by spontaneous and heartfelt applause, coming initially from the crowds assembled outside the Abbey but gradually endorsed by those inside. Opinions varied regarding the Earl's address, and probably always will. Was this the moment when the real Diana in all her complexity was revealed, the woman as she should, properly, be remembered? Or was this mischief-making in the extreme, designed to foster family strife rather than 'channels of peace' (the theme of the following hymn), an unforgivable exploitation of a privileged moment, made worse by the presence of the two Princes themselves?

Thereafter the funeral reassumed a more conventional tone. Prayers were offered by the Archbishop of Canterbury for Diana herself, for the two families, for all those who mourn and for the Princess's life and work. The Archbishop concluded by inviting those inside and outside the Abbey, together with the radio and television audiences, to join in the Lord's Prayer. The blessing and the commendation brought the spoken liturgy to a close. One final moment, however, was carefully choreographed. At the west end of the Abbey, the cortège halted for a minute's silence, widely observed by the nation as a whole, before the coffin was placed in the hearse for its journey to Althorp in Northamptonshire, with both the route and the hearse adorned with flowers thrown by the quietly applauding crowds.

The final and probably most poignant liturgy of the week remains, however, entirely private. This was the service that preceded the burial on the island within the grounds of Althorp Park, Princess Diana's family home, an island consecrated for Christian burial just two days before. It was the only part of the day's events conducted strictly according to the funeral rite in the Book of Common Prayer.

Music

When it comes to the music chosen for the three services, the main focus of interest has to be the memorial service in Westminster Abbey because the criteria governing its planning were so clearly distinctive. For the other two services little more was required than the standard resources of the Church, and there was some overlap in the texts of the musical settings, in particular the *Justorum Animae* – 'the souls of the righteous are in the hands of God', as well as a hymn with special royal associations 'The Lord's my shepherd' to the tune 'Crimond'.

Of course, the St Paul's service had its own special character because it was the first televised religious meditation on the day Diana died. But it was not governed by televisual criteria in the way the Abbey service had to be and it did not have to render inclusive and summary account before billions. The television cameras simply looked in on a service improvised with a particular focus, which was the fragility of even the most protected and privileged human life and the sheer banality of malignant circumstance.

Music for such an occasion had to take bewilderment at breakage and fragmentation, and transmute it into stillness and wholeness. That meant a low and steady pulse, almost of incantation, such as was expressed in chanted psalm tone for 'Out of the depths have I cried to thee'. The loud and distracting tensions of the disaster-ridden world had to give way to unemphatic rhythms with extended span, and to sustained melodies capable of carrying burdens forward to interim but restful conclusion. That is precisely what the *Agnus Dei* of the Fauré Requiem achieved – steady luminosity punctuated by anguished discharge. Such music set the pace and tone for spoken words forced out by the necessity of the occasion, as well as giving voice to what cannot be said.

Apart from this mood of questioning meditation set by chant and requiem there was collective hymnody. Responses otherwise dissipated in comment and report were reassembled by totally familiar words and music. By singing Charles Wesley's 'Love divine, all loves excelling' the congregation reanimated a mosaic of quotation and an echo chamber of buried memory. Hopes and recoveries barely believable to the conscious mind, even perhaps among the sacred ministers, are able to surface in such poetry as it touches on the pressure points of love, joy, blessing, glory, wonder and new creation. A hymn is a kind of plangent mass communion in which the mouth commits itself to shared affirmations before the constraining dubieties of individual experience reassert themselves. Like a church it offers a momentary enclave of articulate hope maintained against all the seeming probabilities.

The service at Westminster Cathedral on the Friday following embodied these same musical elements but in the context of a Catholic Requiem Mass. There was no need for those who planned it to take into account anything beyond the inner life of the metropolitan church of a faith community of several millions and the mixture of domestic and public griefs there in the congregation, given that Diana's mother was present as a Catholic convert. The mass was sung throughout to plainsong, with the subdued interventions of European renaissance polyphony in motets composed by Lassus and Lobo. So the musical offering emerged from the more archaic layers of music, less personal and inexpressive, as well as distanced from the English variant on the European tradition. Paradoxically, the other worldly restraint of plainsong, unharmonized and arising out of enhanced speech rhythm, has an extraordinary power to channel as well as to chasten and subdue emotion. Those present testified to an intensely moving occasion.

The memorial service in Westminster Abbey on Saturday was the subject of intense negotiation between all concerned, and its choreography had to be executed with exacting precision. The grim fairy tale of a flawed Princess had to be placed within the foundational narrative of gift, testing, sacrifice and hope told by the Christian community. Such a service had to carry people over the gulf between pantomime and liturgy, between media sentiment (or prurience) and religious scrutiny. Above all, since 'the world' had been invited in, the choices had to be inclusive and comprehensive.

What then was the role of music in so difficult an enterprise? Of course, one element here was the personal preference of those most closely involved, and that meant eclecticism as well as inclusiveness. In that respect the service was no different from most that now occur in the crematoria and burial grounds of Britain. There was a need to mirror the conflicting emotions aroused and resolve them, as well as to give exemplary expression as to how death, especially untimely death, might be handled. Royal occasions are always models for emulation and powerful guides to practice. This service also served to make up what was lacking in thousands of unsatisfactory memorial or funeral services (or both combined in a hurried twenty minutes in the crematorium chapel). Piped music accompanying undischarged griefs over untimely departures was transmuted into true musical splendour to honour the dead, and into full and sufficient absolutions. There are multitudinous emotions lurking in limbo which demand explanations for sheer contingency and which seek scapegoats and/or meaning. Only liturgical drama and musical harmonization can achieve a corporate restoration, which is also by projection available for every man and every woman. That was precisely the task placed on a national church for such a rite, and inclusivity was virtually dictated.

A liturgy for the dead has its entrances and exits, in which the body is processed first from west to east and then from east to west. The corpse is moved while the main body of the participants stand still, and in the rest of the service it lies at rest and the sacred ministers and different participants move round it. These entrances and departures, beginnings and endings, are the defining moments, and on this occasion music and text defined them as Christian. Once that definition was first achieved and finally recovered all kinds of divergent and even discordant messages could be accommodated. Like an egg this liturgy broadened out from its first entrance in and then narrowed once more to its Christian base.

That broadening out under the aegis of text and music was brilliantly backed up by the artwork of the cameras. Initially, the sacred action was framed through Gothic vistas (Figure 4.4) and against symmetrical shapes inlaid in the floor before coming up close to the solitary singer offering his votive song or to Earl Spencer issuing his eulogy and commination.

The congregation assembled to seven minutes of unobtrusive organ music by Harris, sometime organist of St George's Windsor, until the cortège arrived at the west door. Then the eastward procession along the aisle was accompanied by the traditional sentences from the Prayer Book to restrained settings by William Croft and Henry Purcell, both organists of the Abbey. The reverse movement, along the aisle westward and towards closure, was secured by an ancient text from the Orthodox burial service recently set to objective hieratic music by John Tavener. This had been dedicated to Athene, a young woman who herself suffered untimely death, and it offered a stark musical gesture to the word 'Alleluia', repeated with slight variation over a drone. Paradoxically, it is this hieratic music, constrained within strict limits over the most archaic layer of persistent sound, which now in its minimalism has popular appeal as 'ambient music' or even as 'world music'. Tavener's chosen text includes an overlay of the last farewell in Shakespeare's 'Hamlet', 'And flights of angels sing thee to thy rest' leading into 'The rest is silence'. When the sixty seconds of silence in the Abbey (and the nation) were over the cortège moved into the sunlight to the tolling of muffled bells before beginning a final journey through city streets strewn with flowers.

Entrance and exit once secured, choices broadened out in search of inclusiveness, touching on as many bases of multiple meaning as possible. One source of evocation was place, given that Diana was an English Princess of Wales. So the hymn 'Guide me, O thou great Jehovah' to the tune Cwm Rhondda – sung towards the end of the service – evoked the mass non-conformist choirs of Wales and the people of the mining valleys singing at Cardiff Arms Park rugby ground. The other 'standard' hymn, 'The King of love my shepherd is', with its reference to 'death's shady black abode', is the quintessential Victorian hymnody of the Church of England. With words by Baker and tune by Dykes it is English staple, and was presumably preferred over the Scottish metrical version of Psalm 23 used at the two earlier services because the associations with the Queen's wedding were too close.

Another hymn in dedicatory vein, 'Make me a channel of thy peace', is a popular sacred song: soft-focus sentiment to a modest rhythmic beat such as characterized progressive school assemblies in the 1960s and 1970s ('Youth Praise') and innumerable 'Family Services'.

The hymn providing the keynote was 'I vow to thee my country'. The Princess chose it at her wedding to express her sense of dedication. The words are by Edward Spring Rice, British ambassador to Washington in the First World War, and express a sorrow at mass carnage which has remained central to the national experience even up to the present day. The tune was adapted from 'Jupiter' in Holst's 'The Planets' and is one of those expansive melodies in nobilmente mode – Elgar, Parry, Walton – which evoke English history, identity and the countryside.

The theme of dedication was renewed in the short hymn for solo choristers 'I would be true' to what is known in England as the Londonderry Air but in deference to republican sentiment described in the programme as the Derry Air. This Irish folk melody clearly served to recollect the conflict then still continuing in Ulster. Even more potently, the boys' faces and voices, in their imputed innocence and real immaturity, called to mind the bereavement of the two young Princes.

Apart from Earl Spencer's speech with its approaching rain of applause from without to within, the two elements most distant from hieratic constraint were 'Candle in the Wind' sung by Elton John and the *Libera me* of the Verdi Requiem. The song by Elton John stirred a nest of association, beginning with its initial composition for Marilyn Monroe, another broken icon, and including Diana comforting Elton John at Versace's funeral in Milan Cathedral. Now those roles were reversed and the cameras came close up for the climax of intimacy. This was recognized by the huge crowds watching in Hyde Park, who immediately stood as a mark of respect. So an item of popular culture represented the most inclusive reaching out. The world had been installed in sacred space to give whatever it could offer.

There were overlapping 'worldly' as well as personal associations in the

Libera me of the Verdi Requiem. The Requiem was the passionate expression of a virtual agnostic in a tradition of southern and extrovert theatricality, and on this occasion it chimed well with the eclectic Catholicism surfacing in the popular gestures of the previous week. However remote from the musical constraint of entrance and exit it was a necessary discharge of energy as well as providing a potent reference back to the music of the universal church as the solo line sinks down to the invariant reciting note of '*Libera me, Domine, de morte aeterna*'. That this priestly incantation was sung by the fully sexualised female voice of Lynne Dawson literally 'impersonated' Diana and offered a counterpoint to the triumphant baroque of Handel's 'Let the bright seraphim' sung at her wedding.

Once dangerous ambivalent and chaotic emotions had been discharged order might be re-established and closure begin. The enactment of release and absolution goes beyond issues of conscious belief and discloses needs which transcend mere counselling, though thousands besieged churches for just that. By its inclusiveness the Abbey liturgy allowed people to take leave of their own griefs as they took leave of Diana.

Sacred choreography, so carefully planned as to be invisible and seem inevitable, unites personal and universal, private and civic. As an enactment of civil religion it channelled the indeterminancy of turbulent and intimate emotions and focussed multiple and even contradictory meanings. Not only was it 'civic' but musically it was strikingly civilian, perhaps because Diana was a woman and one who had only recently campaigned against landmines. Mysteriously, through psychic transaction and the subterranean linkages of myths, it brought together ancient tales of infidelity, malign fatality, ferrying to the enchanted isles of the dead, and *liebestod*, and placed them within the Christian narrative. Moreover, the Church by the careful and subdued modesty of its prayers distanced itself from false sanctification and the self-amplifying spiral of media sentiment. The aim, triumphantly achieved, was an efficacious rite.

There were, of course, many millions of emotional absentees on that day briefly not counted as part of 'the nation'. To them it was at best a charade, at worst the bedevilment of sacred space. But they preferred not to make their absence public as they quietly tested out who among their friends felt likewise.

Bibliography

Davie, G. (1994) *Religion in Britain Since 1945: Believing without Belonging*, Oxford: Blackwell.

Hornsby-Smith, M. (1988) 'Into the Mainstream: Recent Transformation in British Catholicism', pp. 218–31 in T. Gannon (ed.), *World Catholicism in Transition*, London & New York: Macmillan.

Maitland, S. (1998) 'The Secular Saint', pp. 63–74 in M. Merck (ed.), *After Diana: irreverent elegies*, London & New York: Verso.

Part 4

The Global and the Provincial

This section documents the geography of respect, and in Chapter 17, of disrespect.

Chapter 13, by a sociologist otherwise engaged in an interview study of popular afterlife beliefs, analyses the contents of books of condolence, finding differences between the paper books in a provincial town and the (largely American) messages posted on the Internet. In Chapter 14, Marion Bowman – a folklorist – examines how the smaller shops in her local town memorialized Diana. Chapter 15 expands the gaze to the USA, describing the spontaneous memorials that sprang up, while Chapter 16 theorizes American women's fascination for Princess Diana. Finally, Chapter 17 examines disrespect in the form of the jokes that sprang up immediately Diana died.

Respect and disrespect may be found in academia as well as elsewhere. Whereas most contributors to this book have kept their own feelings about Diana well hidden, Wendy Griffin is clear about her feminist approval for Diana, while Christie Davies' sympathy with the irreverent jokers is equally manifest. This is reflected in Davies's argument that many people identified with Diana the oppressed victim, while Griffin by contrast respects Diana because she moved through victimhood to become a heroic survivor.

The final three chapters all refer to awareness of mortality in a world defined largely by television. Chapter 15 begins by asserting that Americans sense such a mastery over nature that premature death comes as a shock, but Chapter 16 points to the everyday presence of premature death in the news media. Chapter 17 argues that the incongruity of tragic death sandwiched between commercial ads or soap operas gives rise to the jokes that, in the age of television, inevitably follow disaster; jokes are also a form of resistance to media-imposed mourning. The jokers' disrespect is thus the unintended consequence of the media's respect.

13

Books of Condolence

Bethan Jones

Following the death of Diana, Princess of Wales, there was a proliferation of books of condolence in which individuals could express their sympathy and often shock at her loss. These books were in fact so popular in Britain that they were available in many disparate locations, local civic offices and supermarkets, but also hospitals, libraries, universities and churches. The process of writing messages of condolence suggests a reversion to a more traditional form of mourning that was prevalent during Victorian society where bereavement was strictly governed by socially defined rules (Whaley 1981). The death of Diana may be compared with Royal deaths during the Victorian era where the British public were expected to enter a period of general mourning in order to show their respect (Taylor 1983; Wolffe in this volume). While the British tend not to abide by such traditions and rules in today's society, one might see publicly written messages of condolence as a modern interpretation of a more communal form of general public mourning. Marris (1974) argues that loss typically results in a reversion to the familiar through the desire to assimilate new reality into pre-existing conservative structures of meaning.

This chapter is concerned with the comparative analysis of a random sample of messages taken from books of condolence kept at the civic offices located in the central shopping and office area of Reading, a medium-sized town in the south of England, with a similar random sample of messages taken from books of condolence that were available on the world wide web. In both cases the random nature of the sample was achieved by using alternate books, and both samples contained messages written both before and after the funeral – 1,808 messages were taken from the civic office books and 1,017 from the Internet; messages were then coded and divided into categories. This chapter details the different genres of messages in the two types of books and possible explanations for the marked differences in the forms of condolence expressed. The messages in civic office and Internet books did however share common features by virtue of the fact that they were overwhelmingly addressed to Diana personally. Hence they have more in common with messages accompanying funeral flowers, memorial columns in local newspapers and those available on the Internet than with letters of condolence and cards sent to the next of kin. (Figure 13.1)

Figure 13.1 Signing the book of condolence in a provincial town hall. *Bath Evening Chronicle*

Gender

Gender was an important feature of both samples. Among the civic office messages 72 per cent were clearly written by women compared with 16 per cent by men. While the differences in gender were not as large for Internet messages, 44 per cent clearly by women compared to 24 per cent by men, there was still a noticeable disparity. The remainder were written jointly by both sexes or their gender is unclear. Messages from the English civic office books were often written by women on behalf of their children, many of the English female authors referring to Diana enjoying some form of life after death. This ties in with previous observations that women tend to be more religious than men, and therefore are more likely to utilise traditional ways of dealing with stressful situations (Miller and Hoffman 1995). Women may also have greater experience of different forms of spirituality (Bennett 1987), and they typically express grief more than do men (Stroebe 1998).

General Messages of Sympathy

The first group of condolence messages was typical of the types of general consolatory sentiments contained in sympathy cards and letters of bereavement; for example 'please accept our condolences' or 'you may be out of sight but you will never be out of heart and mind'. 33 per cent of English messages took this non-specific format, compared with only 12 per cent of Internet messages. Messages in the paper books often ran in thematic blocks, with authors clearly reading the preceding message before composing their own. The British media frequently ran stories about the popularity of these books after the death of Diana which may have led people to feel it was their duty to convey their sympathy. Given both an emotional reserve and a lack of socially prescribed mourning rituals in contemporary society (Elias 1985; Walter 1997), writers may have reverted back to traditional and well-worn sentiments and phrases.

The procedure of posting a message to one of the books on the Internet was radically different from the paper books which could explain the marked differences in popularity of this type of message. With the Internet, messages are composed in Pine format and then posted to the appropriate site. It is not known if the authors of these messages would spend time reading the electronic book prior to sending their own message, but they did not seem to reveal a pattern similar to those in the civic office. This could however be a result of the sheer volume of mail posted to such sites, hence they would not appear in strict chronological order. As local telephone calls are free in the USA it was possible for individuals to spend time composing their ideas, compared with the English system where people tended to visit the paper books in their lunch hour and may have felt rushed because of their awareness of the queue forming behind them.

References were made to Diana as the people's princess and 'queen of hearts'; for example, 'Diana, you wanted to be known as the queen of our hearts, you never made it to be queen but you are certainly the princess of my heart'. Authors would mention the infamous Panorama TV documentary, her need to be loved by the nation and the fact that she would never be queen. Such ideas were more common among the English condolence books than the ones posted on the net. Internet messages were primarily American in origin, and while their authors may have watched the TV documentary their messages were longer and more focused. Diana would be greatly 'missed' because she was so well loved and respected. Messages emphasized that although Diana was dead she would 'never be forgotten' and would continue to live on in the hearts and minds of 'the people' who loved her. Other messages focused on the 'tragic' circumstances that surrounded the death.

Premature death is especially difficult to deal with in modern society where death typically occurs in old age (Mellor 1993).

Eternal Things

Forty-six per cent of the Civic Office book messages referred to an afterlife, whether it was anthropocentric or theological in content. For example, 'Diana and Dodi I hope that you have now found true happiness and peace, the world is a darker place without you rest in peace'. It has been argued that the continued popularity of religious beliefs may originate from their ability to explain death through the comforting illusion of paradise (Freud 1928), and this may be especially true for Christianity whose theological system rests predominantly upon a belief in the post-mortem resurrection of Christ (Bowker 1991). These messages of condolence enabled the author to make sense of the tragedy: it might be easier to deal with by believing that Diana and Dodi are now reunited in paradise. Such spiritual schemes provide meaning for the bereaved and aid the process of assimilation; they are an important part of early grief and facilitate the creation of positive meaning (Richards and Folkman 1997). Belief in the romantic reunion of loved ones in heaven became increasingly popular during the Victorian period due to the Evangelical idealization of the family unit and the influence of romanticism. This period also saw a declining belief in the literal doctrine of hell that led to increased anticipation of future bliss in heaven; reunion was no longer conditional (Jalland 1996).

The English condolence books contained more references to God than did the Internet messages, although it is important to note that the English messages tended to refer to God in a very general way. This is surprising because Britain is arguably more secularized than America, surveys pointing to the dramatic decline in church attendance during the twentieth century (Brierley 1989, Bruce 1995, 1996). Formal religion declines along with religious images, thinking and behaviour. However, following Davie (1990, 1994) we could argue that these messages reveal a traditional British form of religion, where individuals are happy to believe in God without attending church or analyzing in-depth precisely what their beliefs entail. It may be the case that faith does not develop evenly but in response to crisis (Fowler 1981), in which case traumatic circumstances may elicit otherwise dormant religious beliefs.

The surprising popularity of afterlife beliefs among the English condolence messages may also reflect the fact that in today's society people are unsure how to deal with death and bereavement (Gorer 1965). Untimely and unexpected death could precipitate reversion to more traditional ways of coping like religion, where individuals draw upon the enduring character of the traditional languages of mourning (Winter 1995). But, because we no longer live in a society where such issues are part of the mainstream, the meaning of such sentiments is unclear. Hence people can use phrases like 'God bless' and 'rest in peace' without the researcher knowing specifically what these ideas mean to them.

Messages whose meaning was most unclear were those that wished Diana peace, and were common among the English paper books: 'Diana rest in peace, the press can't get you now', or 'be at peace now'. These might refer to a conscious afterlife, or could simply express hope that the media will now leave Diana alone thereby granting her peace. Similarly images of Diana as a star are unclear as to the sort of post-mortem existence she will enjoy, 'Diana, the world has lost a beautiful person but the skies have gained a beautiful star'. There is nothing in many of these messages to indicate that Diana will have any form of conscious existence; yet they nevertheless refer to things which are eternal, maybe implying that Diana too will be eternal in some way. While people may have vague ideas about what they believe and would like to happen after death they are not detailed because we tend not to think about such issues in everyday life (Houlbrooke 1989).

The majority of messages in this group were nominal in theological content which could explain why they are more common among the English messages than among those posted on the Internet. America is often viewed as being an exception to the secularization thesis, with the continued salience of religion in America reflecting the greater religious choice available there. Pluralism is better suited to meet the universal human need for religion through increased competition (Finke 1997, Stark and Iannaccone 1994). Such studies suggest that declining European church attendance is not due to a lack of popularity for religion but to the failure of existing churches to meet the needs of its would-be congregations. It could be argued that while Americans are more aware of their religion due to high levels of church attendance they are not necessarily more religious. The English are therefore as likely as Americans to write about God and an afterlife but, being less socialized into the language of the churches, are less likely to write in specifically Christian terms.

Other messages in this section posited a belief in an 'anthropocentric heaven', such as 'bye for now Diana, see you later in heaven'. Such beliefs were most common among English messages, 10 per cent referring to a person-based reunion. Death is not the end, Diana and Dodi are the Romeo and Juliet of the modern world. Such messages offer to William and Harry the comfort that Diana is in heaven watching and waiting for them.

McDannell and Lang (1988) argue that during the twentieth century perceptions of heaven have become increasingly person-centred and less God-centred. Modern beliefs about life after death are sentimental and no longer integrated into a Christian theological system, and certainly the majority of paper messages that referred to Diana and Dodi fall into this category. Even the messages that referred to God still focus on the reunion of Dodi with Diana. Such beliefs can be traced to nineteenth-century romanticism, its obsession with death and the growth in sentimentality that surrounded death during this period (Morley 1971). Death then was characterized by hope that people were 'not lost, but gone before' (Wheeler 1990).

'Theocentric heaven' was more popular among Internet messages than the previously mentioned romantic beliefs, but still only 4 per cent of messages focused on such beliefs. In the messages that focused on God, Dodi was rarely mentioned and themes of reunion seemed unimportant. In total only 27 per cent of Internet messages contained reference to any form of life after death. The majority of messages on the Internet came from America which has a high percentage of Catholics and fundamentalist Christians. These messages interpret heaven as God's creation, and reflect more traditional Christian theological ideas. Heaven is conceived as being only for good people, therefore allowing the possibility of hell. Such ideas are not mentioned directly but are certainly not ruled out as the destiny of the paparazzi, compared with the English messages that make no such implications. The popularity of these different beliefs corresponds with previous research that reveals that the British are less likely to believe in hell compared with Americans (Ashford and Timms 1992).

Other themes raised in this section include the idea of 'heavenly sanctuary' for Diana. Heaven is a place of tranquillity and Diana's reward for the hurt caused by the press. Diana also deserves to go to heaven because of her good acts and deeds towards others when she was alive. This idea of heaven as 'God's reward' for Diana is much more popular among the Internet messages, as such messages tended to focus more upon her work. Some messages express the belief that Diana is an 'angel' and will go to heaven in order to carry on with her unfinished duties caring for the sick. Her children are again offered comfort through the belief that their mother will be their guardian angel. A similar theme but one that is more theological in content is the idea that God called Diana home because she is 'God's messenger'. Such ideas were more common on the Internet, 4 per cent of messages drawing upon such beliefs, with God conceived as a supremely powerful being who orders the world and is responsible for Diana's death. She is portrayed as an angel and messenger of God's love whom God called home after she performed His work on this earth. It is another way of explaining the tragic and untimely nature of her death, but only for those who believe that God is sovereign over the world.

Blame

Very few English messages apportion blame for the death of Diana, less than 1 per cent criticize the press or Royal Family, compared with 12 per cent of Internet messages. Very few of the messages in either books were critical of Diana herself, reflecting a culture where one should not speak ill of the dead. The process involved in writing a message in the books housed at the civic office may have fostered reserve which could explain why these books contained so many messages that were general in content. In America however high value is placed upon freedom of speech and the nature of electronic mail is more anonymous. English messages were written in a public social setting, hence there are more rules that need to be observed. Americans, inhabiting a culture of suing and more prone to conspiracy theories, are also more likely to blame someone.

Some messages blame the media for the death of Diana by drawing attention to their treatment of her when she was alive. Diana is portrayed as a weak animal that was hounded and hunted till it was dead because of their desire for financial gain. Diana is seen as saintly, attention being drawn to the tragedy that she had to die in order to be free. Nor are the Royal Family spared the blame apportioned by Internet messages, her death being very convenient for Charles and Camilla. Some authors blame themselves for her death, since they helped create the market for tabloids. At the time of her death several psychologists claimed that the outpouring of grief was a response to feelings of guilt. The process of writing such critical messages may provide the author with an opportunity to project blame and construct a positive moral identity (Seale 1995). There is a belief in these messages that the public has the power to take on the media and prevent another tragedy.

Diana's Work

Messages that referred to various aspects of Diana's work were common in both samples: 16 per cent of the civic office books and 29 per cent of Internet messages. The sentiments expressed in these messages tie in with previous research which shows how memories of the deceased play an active role in the ongoing life of survivors, the deceased becoming a role model and behavioural guide (Marwit and Klass 1995).

Eleven per cent of civic office and 12 per cent of Internet messages drew attention to all that Diana did for 'the needy'. She will be remembered first and foremost for all the good work that she did for those less fortunate than herself, indeed this legacy will make Diana immortal: 'dear Diana your memory will live on in the work you achieved during your life, you did so much to help so many. Thank you for all you did for the people with Aids. You did so much to raise the world's awareness'. These messages contrast her money and position with the selfless work that she did for those with nothing. Some messages also express hope that 'her boys' will carry on the good work started by her which otherwise would be left unfinished. This provides a degree of hope for the nation, and comfort for the children. Some of these messages positively plead that we carry on her good work and not return to the uncaring and distant way the Royal Family used to be.

Diana was also a 'role model' and an icon for others in our time: 'I admired your glamour and demeanour you perfected for the masses. I looked up to the woman you became. When my marriage fell apart and then yours crumbled I knew that it was okay. You represented the fact that I can go on after overwhelming troubles. Thank you for being my role model'. She accomplished so much despite her pain and this inspired others and gave them the courage also to deal with their troubles. People will now try to live by her example to ensure that all she stood for will continue. People see themselves as being responsible for keeping her unique spirit alive through taking the time to care for others and help them in a world that is generally seen as being cold. Ten per cent of Internet messages made reference to the fact that Diana was their role model, compared with just 3 per cent of paper book messages. Women who used the Internet often stated in their message that they too were single mothers or independent women like Diana. Paper book messages were more romantic than concerned with Diana's concrete achievements. Compared with the Reading books, the Internet women generally did not post messages on behalf of their families.

The Children

It was surprising when analyzing the messages how few of them directly addressed the children, Princes William and Harry. This was especially true of the civic office books where the majority of messages were addressed to Diana herself. Only 10 per cent of the Reading messages actually mentioned the children at all, and only 4 per cent were specifically addressed to them. It was common for authors to write their message to Diana and then simply acknowledge the children at the end, 'Diana you were so loved and were so beautiful, condolence to William and Harry'. Among Internet messages 47 per cent referred to the children; 21 per cent were addressed to William and Harry personally, and were primarily concerned with the children's loss of their mother. The majority of these Internet messages attempted to convey the author's love to Diana's sons. Also it was common to offer the children 'God for comfort'. This ties in with Levitt's (1996) analysis that while we do not attend church when we are adults, Christianity is seen as being inherently good for children. Perhaps it is this introduction to religion that then provides the basis for traditional ways of coping that were utilized by other authors in the Reading condolence books. This compares with the English messages that were overwhelmingly concerned with the author's personal loss. This is surprising because the paper books typically comprised messages written by women on behalf of their family. It might have been assumed that they would have been more concerned with the children's tragic situation because they have children of their own, but this empathy did not find its way into the content of their condolence.

Dodi

Among both samples of messages there were relatively few references to the other people that died in the crash with Diana. Only 11 per cent of the paper books and 6 per cent of the electronic messages refer to Dodi. The majority of messages that do mention Dodi simply include his name at the end of the message that was written specifically for Diana; they only mention Dodi in a very general and non-specific form. This reflects the media's dealing with the tragedy where the overwhelming focus was on the loss of Diana and the impact for her family. Very few of the Internet messages contained any reference to Diana and Dodi being reunited in some form of afterlife, such ideas being more popular among the paper messages.

Conclusion

It seems apparent from the different genres of messages which were popular among the civic office books compared with the Internet, that individuals may have perceived there were definite rules as to what themes were considered appropriate for the two different types of books because of their social setting. Internet messages tended to be more critical and explicit, with little of the reserve which characterized English forms of condolence. Garfinkel (1967) points to the local production of the social order by actors despite it being experienced as external. The social world is therefore perceived as constraining because it is based on shared common-sense knowledge from which actors develop typifications that enable them to understand and interpret the behaviour of others (Schutz 1972). Social situations come with responsibilities and obligations which are utilized to sustain cultural norms or enable social actors to adapt them through negotiation to fit current circumstances. This to some extent reveals how social order is produced and negotiated in unprecedented and traumatic circumstances such as the death of a prominent figure like Princess Diana. We interpret the world around us and adjust our behaviour in accordance with the expectation of others, and action is based on normative value commitments (Parsons 1937).

In the English books there was a definite sense of what was deemed an appropriate message because there were several instances where individuals had written messages highly critical of the Princess or Royal Family, and these were always followed by attacks directed at their author. Sometimes the entry was crossed out by a subsequent author, with a comment such as 'Have you no shame?' By contrast Internet messages were critical of the establishment, not of fellow authors expressing their opinions. Internet condolences have become increasingly popular over the last few years where special Internet sites are established after disasters such as the Dunblane shooting or the Oklahoma bombing, or for the death of movie stars and other prominent figures; and people may send their sympathy to other inhabitants of the 'global village' (Sofka 1997). Thus they provide an electronic template similar to the template of the written condolence card. Common culture is participant produced and social actors cope with the new and unfamiliar by reinterpreting the old. However, there appears to be more freedom in such types of condolence based on the sorts of messages posted on the Diana Internet memorial sites because it is a relatively new form of communication and involves a lone individual utilizing their technological knowledge rather than intimate social interaction and negotiation between mourners.

Bibliography

Ashford, S. and Timms, N. (1992) 'The Unchurching of Europe', in *What Europe Thinks*, Aldershot: Dartmouth Publishing House.

Bennett, G. (1987) *Traditions of Belief: Women and the Supernatural*, London: Penguin.

Bowker, J. (1991) *The Meanings of Death*, Cambridge: Cambridge University Press.

Brierley, P. (1989) *A Century of British Christianity: Historical Statistics 1900–1985 With Projections to 2000*, London: MARC Europe.

Bruce, S. (1995) *Religion in Modern Britain*, Oxford: Oxford University Press.

Bruce, S. (1996) 'Religion in Britain at the Close of the 20th Century: A Challenge to the Silver Lining Perspective', *Journal of Contemporary Religion*, 2(3): 261–75.

Davie, G. (1990) 'Believing Without Belonging: Is This the Future of Religion in Britain?', *Social Compass*, 37 (4): 455–69.

Davie, G. (1994) *Religion in Britain Since 1945*, Oxford: Blackwell.

Elias, N. (1985) *The Loneliness of Dying*, Oxford: Blackwell.

Finke, R. (1997) 'The Consequences of Religious Competition. Supply-Side Explanations for Religious Change', in L.A. Young (ed.), *Rational Choice Theory and Religion. Summary and Assessment*, London: Routledge.

Fowler, J.W. (1981) *Stages of Faith*, San Francisco: Harper and Row.

Freud, S. (1928) *The Future of an Illusion*, London: Hogarth Press.

Garfinkel, H. (1967) *Studies in Ethnomethodology*, NJ: Prentice Hall, Englewood Cliffs.

Gorer, G. (1965) *Death, Grief and Mourning in Contemporary Britain*, London: Cresset.

Houlbrooke, R. (ed.) (1989) *Death, Ritual and Bereavement*, London: Routledge.

Jalland, P. (1996) *Death in the Victorian Family*, Oxford: Oxford University Press.

Levitt, M. (1996) *'Nice When they are Young': Contemporary Christianity in Families and Schools*, Aldershot: Avebury.

Marris, P. (1974) *Loss and Change*, London: Routledge and Kegan Paul.

Marwit, S.J. and Klass, D. (1995) 'Grief and the Role of the Inner Representation of the Deceased', *Omega*, 30 (4): 283–97.

McDannell, C. and Lang, B. (1988) *Heaven: a History*, New Haven: Yale University Press.

Mellor, P. (1993) 'Death in High Modernity' in D. Clark (ed.), *The Sociology of Death*, Oxford: Blackwell.

Miller, A. and Hoffman, J. (1995) 'Risk and Religion: An Explanation of Gender Differences in Religiosity', *Journal for the Scientific Study of Religion*, 34 (1): 63–75.

Morley, J. (1971) *Death, Heaven and the Victorians*, London: Studio Vista.

Parsons, T. (1937) *The Structure of Social Action*, New York: Free Press.

Richards, A.T. and Folkman, S. (1997) 'Spiritual Aspects of Loss at the Time of a Partner's Death from AIDS', *Death Studies*, 21: 527–52.

Schutz, A. (1972) *The Phenomenology of the Social World*, London: Heinemann.

Seale, C.F. (1995) 'Dying Alone', *Sociology of Health and Illness*, 17 (3): 376–92.

Sofka, C.J. (1997) 'Social Support "Internetworks", Caskets for Sale, and More: Thanatology and the Information Superhighway', *Death Studies*, 21(6): 553–74.

Stark, R. and Iannaccone, L.R. (1994) 'A Supply-Side Reinterpretation of the "Secularization" of Europe', *Journal for the Scientific Study of Religion*, 33 (3): 230–52.

Stroebe, M. (1998) 'New Directions in Bereavement Research: Exploration of Gender Differences', *Palliative Medicine*, 12: 5–12.

Taylor, L. (1983) *Mourning Dress. A Costume and Social History*, London: Allen and Unwin.

Walter, T. (1997) 'Emotional Reserve and the English Way of Grief' in K. Charmaz, G. Howarth & A. Kellehear (eds), *The Unknown Country: Experiences of Death in Australia, Britain and the USA*, Basingstoke: Macmillan, pp. 127–38.

Whaley, J. (ed.) (1981) *Mirrors of Mortality*, London: Europa.

Wheeler, M. (1990) *Death and Future Life in Victorian Literature and Theology*, Cambridge: Cambridge University Press.

Winter, J. (1995) *Sites of Memory, Sites of Mourning: the Great War in European Cultural History*, Cambridge: Cambridge University Press.

14

A Provincial City Shows Respect: Shopping and Mourning in Bath

Marion Bowman

While the national and international media concentrated primarily on the extraordinary scenes in London, as a folklorist and scholar of contemporary religion, I felt it was important to provide a record of what was happening at the local level, on the basis that the great majority of people did not get to London and that there might be both regional variation and innovation. It seemed valuable to record some of the unreported reactions to events, and the personal and communal forms of expression that emerged, as this would give a more rounded picture of what was happening. This would also provide a snapshot of popular mores of 'appropriateness' and aesthetics in the face of death, and help to explain what changes (if any) it set in motion.

I selected Bath, a small historic city of 85,000 souls in the west of England, where I live, concentrating on the city centre and on one suburban shopping street. I also concentrated on the (Saturday) morning of the funeral, because one would expect that this was the day when showing respect would be at its height, yet also when most people would be indoors privately watching the funeral on television. So what would be happening in the city centre, and how would those who work there – chiefly shopkeepers and their staff – handle this liminal morning and signal their intentions? I therefore went into town that day from 11 a.m. to 2 p.m. with my camera and an open mind. Most striking were the shop window shrines to Diana – some had been created a few days back, others just for the day. Having photographed them, I returned a year later (just after the anniversary) to interview the staff who had created them.

A recurring theme to emerge from the media and from personal communication was that people felt the need to *do* something. In Bath, some of the activity was similar to, if on a smaller scale than, London. On the Friday evening before the funeral a memorial service at Bath Abbey was attended by 2,000 inside and a further 1,000 outside, to whom it was relayed. In the town centre, flowers were piled up outside the Abbey (Figure 14.1), and around the eighteenth-century obelisk at Orange Grove (Figure 14.2). The nearby village of Peasedown St John lit a beacon on the Saturday evening after the funeral, in the words of the local newspaper the *Bath Chronicle*, 'as a mark of respect to Princess Diana'.

Figure 14.1 Balloon and flowers left outside the Abbey, Bath. *Marion Bowman*

In the days between the announcement of Diana's death and the funeral, 'showing respect' became increasingly important. People seemed both to fall back on older, half-remembered traditions, and to seek innovative means of doing so. There was considerable touchiness about what was deemed appropriate or inappropriate. There were, for example, complaints when originally there was no picture of Diana beside the Book of Condolences in Bath's Guildhall, and when blue rather than black pens were provided.

The looped thin red ribbon used to commemorate AIDS deaths has become commonplace in the UK; Cancer Research uses a pink ribbon in similar fashion. In the week after Diana's death, a looped thin black ribbon was used as a modern symbol of mourning, although some in Bath wore more traditional black armbands, or a home-made inverted 'V' flash of black

Figure 14.2 Orange Grove, Bath. *Marion Bowman*

material. (It will be interesting to see whether the thin black ribbon worn in this way becomes common practice after other deaths, or becomes particularly associated with Diana.)

The Day of the Funeral

Clearly a particularly significant day for showing respect would be Saturday, 6 September, the day of the funeral. The streets were almost deserted, pavements in the centre of town and normally busy roads empty. The flag on the Guildhall flew at half mast, as, somewhat absurdly, did the five international flags on rather short poles over the doorway of a Bath hotel. An 'Out of Service' bus at the Bus Station had a picture of Diana against a black background displayed in the front window below the steering wheel.

By Saturday, the death of Mother Teresa had also been announced. One flower stall had a photocopied picture of Diana and Mother Teresa together, with a black ribbon bow underneath. I encountered only one 'dedicated' Mother Teresa memorial, in the form of a large piece of paper stuck on a wall, with a picture of Mother Teresa at the top centre, an artificial sunflower taped down the left side, and underneath the picture the handwritten words 'Mother Teresa RIP' with a Latin cross below.

One way of showing respect that occurred to and appealed to various people was to observe a period of silence. However, as there was no 'official' moment of silence, this was suggested and handled in a variety of ways. The local paper, the *Bath Chronicle*, urged people to join in a minute's silence at end of the funeral service at Westminster Abbey. At the Guildhall Market, there was a notice at the entrance, on a white word-processed sheet of paper, heavily edged in black: 'In Memoriam of Diana Princess of Wales the Guildhall Market will be observing a two minute silence at 11am on Saturday 5th [sic] September 1997.' Entering the market around 11.20 a.m. there were no other customers, and most stallholders were gathered round a television on the counter of the butcher's stall, watching the funeral. The bread stall had a number of night-light candles burning on its shelves.

On the door of a local hairdresser was a sign, handwritten in capital letters: DUE TO 'WEDDING BOOKINGS'! WE SHALL BE OPEN 'TODAY' A.M. – IN RESPECT OF DIANA 'PRINCESS OF WALES' – WE SHALL HAVE ONE MINUTE'S SILENCE @ 11.45! THE CLOSING SIGN WILL BE PUT UP AT THIS TIME. In the window there was a small formal flower arrangement, with a card indicating that the flowers had been paid for by the staff as a mark of respect for Diana.

A cartoon in the satirical magazine *Private Eye* (September 1997) bore two pictures of the same shop, the left-hand one with a sign in the window which read 'Closed out of respect for Princess Diana', the right-hand one bearing the sign 'Good Friday – Open as Usual'. That this should be satirized indicates an awareness that shop and business closure was one widespread means of showing respect in a society which generally has got out of the habit of doing so.

Many businesses and tourist attractions in Bath were closed until 2.00 p.m., although this was not absolutely standard. The snack shop opposite the railway station had a photocopied informal picture of Diana, and underneath a wordprocessed sign (Figure 14.3): THIS SHOP WILL BE CLOSED ON SATURDAY 6TH SEPTEMBER / IN RESPECT OF DIANA, PRINCESS OF WALES & DODI AL FAYED. While a number of the cards left with flowers in Bath had been addressed to 'Diana and Dodi', this was the only shop or business notice to pay respect to Dodi Al Fayed. A rather trendy bar and cafe had written on its blackboard in yellow, blue, pink and white chalk (Figure 14.4): 'As a Mark of Respect Bloomsbury's will not Open until 12 noon on Sat 6th when a % of our takings will be donated to Diana's Memorial Fund. May God Bless Her.' The *Big Issue* South-West office had a handwritten sign in the window, reading 'As a mark of respect for Diana Princess of Wales this office will not open until 1pm on Sat 6th Sept.' Most chainstores had photocopied, fairly standard signs informing customers that 'Out of

Figure 14.3 Sign in snack shop window, Bath. *Marion Bowman*

Figure 14.4 Blackboard outside bar, Bath. *Marion Bowman*

respect for Diana Princess of Wales, this store will not open until 2.00pm on Saturday 6 September'. The Laura Ashley sign was somewhat different. In a plain, light wooden frame, appeared a well-printed notice: 'The Directors and Staff of Laura Ashley offer their sincere condolences to the family of the late Diana, Princess of Wales. / As a mark of respect, our stores will remain closed until 2.00pm on Saturday 6th September. / Her support, generosity and kindness has enriched the lives of millions of people. She will be greatly missed by us all.' Of the chain stores, Laura Ashley had the most personalized notice.

Shop Window Shrines

What I found most interesting were what I came to think of as shop window 'shrines', that is window displays that included a picture of Diana, flowers, candles or any combination thereof. Here things had moved on from merely indicating that the shop was closed, to a more personal gesture of loss. Propped up in the window of a cafe was what appeared to be the cover of a 'Special Edition' of some magazine, featuring a very happy, informal picture of Diana with her hands clasped as if in prayer, alongside which was a large blue glass jug of white and pale yellow flowers on the right, and a flowering pot plant on the left. A small city-centre flower shop window had a photograph of Diana wearing a tiara, placed between two formal white flower arrangements.

The General Trading Company had, on a glass-topped coffee table, a large glass vase of white lilies in the centre, on the right in a tasteful frame a small informal photograph of Diana, and on the left, also in an elegant frame, a printed notice 'The General Trading Company will be closed until 2pm on Saturday September 6th as a mark of respect for Diana Princess of Wales.' The manager of this shop told me that the arrangement had been 'completely spontaneous', 'unprompted', a 'personal response to the situation' on the part of the staff. The General Trading Company did, of course, have close ties with Diana – 'she had her wedding list with us' – so there was an awareness of a commercial connection, but that had not been the motivating force. The staff 'identified with her, what she stood for', and from the Monday morning after her death had thought it 'appropriate' to have the display. When I asked why lilies had been chosen, the initial reply was that they are 'the standard thing for death', but this was elaborated upon: 'lilies are synonymous with a degree of elegance, very smart, very understated'.

Another department store had arranged a small table covered in a white cloth in its window in a shrine-like fashion (Figure 14.5). Raised up at the back of the table was a large frame containing a very informal photograph of Diana and below it printed in white on black the words from the Elton John song 'Candle in the Wind': 'It seems to me that you lived your life like a candle in the wind, never knowing who to cling to when the rain set in.' To the left and right in front of the frame were unlit white candles in elegant glass candlesticks with two tiny birds on the edge, and covering the table a large formal flower arrangement of white flowers and green foliage, white

Figure 14.5 Department store window, Bath. *Marion Bowman*

lilies predominating. The window dresser for this shop said that the display 'seemed like the right thing to do', and in addition to the shop closing for an hour on the Saturday, 'showed some sort of respect'. He did, however, comment that 'everyone was doing something', and that his display had gone up on the Thursday or Friday. When I asked about the elements of the display he commented that in a store like that 'there was a lot to choose from', citing their large candle department as an example.

Three local suburban, as opposed to city centre, shops had very different but striking displays. Probably the most subtle show of respect was made by a rather elegant clothes shop which had no flowers, notices, or pictures, but for the day of the funeral had changed its window display so that only black clothes were featured, in sharp contrast to the colourful, summery arrangement of the previous week. When I spoke to the proprietress, she explained that she always changes the window display on a Friday. On the day before the funeral, she felt it 'didn't seem right' to have bright colours in the window; 'Everyone seemed so sad.' She therefore felt it was 'more appropriate' to have dark colours. However, she insisted that she did not do it as a public statement, and was not aware that she had made any sort of impact until I approached her. The idea simply came to her as it 'felt appropriate' for the mood of that week.

A local newsagent and video shop had in its window a glass vase of white lilies, with a lighted white candle to its right, and further right on the window a word-processed poem to/ about Diana. The manageress of the shop set up the arrangement, and the poem was written by the assistant manageress. The manageress came into the shop at 5.00 a.m. on the day of the funeral to set up the display, and took it down after the shop closed at 11.00 p.m. The display had been a show of 'personal, private respect' from the staff in the shop who 'never had time to go off and say a prayer or sign a condolence book'. Nobody could afford it or had the opportunity to do it on their own, so they clubbed together to make 'a simple, basic display, a personal and private way of showing our feelings'. The manageress said 'We all wanted to do something. When someone dies, you want to show your sorrow in some way, don't you?' The manageress did also comment that the gesture was 'a reflection of the whole of the community of Great Britain' and there was also an element of 'respect for my public', but above all 'this was *genuine* respect from us'. She had been slightly anxious about the display but there had been only positive reaction; she added 'People didn't *dare* to have a negative reaction that day'.

The author of the poem that appeared in the window display claimed that it 'just came'; she cannot sit down to write something, but 'sometimes it just flows'. Thus, when the staff decided to buy some lilies for the window, she said 'Well, the poem's there if you want it.' People had come into the shop and commented favourably on the poem. When I asked the manageress why she had included the candle, she responded that everybody lights candles for someone who has died. She deliberately bought a huge candle, because she wanted it to be untouched once lit and wanted the flame to burn for the whole time the display was in the window. In response to the question about lilies, she said that as her mother is a florist she knew that lilies were 'the right flower', the purity of the flower and the whiteness of the flower representing death.[1] However, she added that lilies are simple and uncomplicated, and whatever people say about Diana 'she was a simple flower that blossomed into something fantastic.' Furthermore, a lily cannot be imitated and does not need enhancement.

Among the most artistic of all the shop window shrines was that of Jacaranda, a local flower shop. Soft white material was draped down and across the left side of the window and lined the base of the display. The centrepiece was a large glass vase of white lilies, and on the vase handwritten in capital letters, green ink on white A4 paper DIANA OUR THOUGHTS ARE WITH YOU. To the left of the central vase was a white urn with small white flowers, in front some green foliage, to the right a small pot with a spray of white flowers, and behind that a tall green foliage plant in a pot. There was also a candle. Considerable care and attention had gone into this display.

The owner of the shop came in and did the display on the Sunday that Diana's death was announced. It was 'my tribute to her in my taste'; he 'wanted to do some kind of tribute to her and her family' so the window was 'my way of showing my condolences'. He knew he wanted the arrangement to be white and simple, not fussy but eye-catching. He likes white flowers for funerals as they are not too ostentatious and he considered they would be fitting for that occasion. Watching the funeral procession on television, and realizing that all the flowers on the coffin were white, he thought it was nice to know that the family had also chosen them. He just thought of the candle 'like you go into a church and put a candle for someone, it was like that'. He had not thought of the window display in terms of showing respect, just 'a tribute' – 'It was just a creative reaction to a very sad occasion.' A lot of people had come into Jacaranda during the week to thank him for doing the window.

1. There seemed to be consensus about what flowers were most appropriate for such public display. One florist reported that several people had bought flowers to put in their shop windows: 'We've been selling a lot of white lilies,' said Kit Pace, of Pulteney Bridge Flowers. 'Traditionally, lilies are a mourning flower that is associated with church.' (*Bath Chronicle*, 6 September 1997, p.15)

As a florist, he is aware of different attitudes to flowers, particularly between generations. In his experience, older people tend to associate white lilies with death and funerals, to the extent that some will ask him to ensure there are none in bouquets as they are 'death flowers'. For gifts and pleasure, older people tend to like lots of colour. For younger people, he felt, 'less is more'; tastes are more minimalist and lilies are favoured for their architectural, elegant looks. Undoubtedly 'the language of flowers', though perhaps not frequently articulated and possibly in decline, still has a voice.

The shop window shrines were left for varying periods of time, the longest being one week. However, Bath charity fund-raiser Eli Collins turned part of his front basement garden (already a highly idiosyncratic and often nationalistic display of yard art) into a 'shrine for Diana' for twelve months, using pictures, royal wedding memorabilia, etc. He hopes that from coins thrown down into it from the street above, he will be able to raise money for charities with which she was connected.

Chapter 2 stated that the typical Diana mourner was a female aged between twenty and forty-five and of social class III or IV. Since this is also pretty close to the typical shop worker, it should be no surprise that many shop window shrines were motivated by the personal feelings of staff as much as by a sense of it being expected or it being commercially advantageous. A number of the people who had made displays and had stressed their personal motives and desire to 'do something' nevertheless felt that the mourning in some cases had 'become gratuitous', 'got a bit hysterical, over the top'. The newsagent and video shop manageress stressed that 'one day was enough'.

The shrines for the most part appeared in shops which were small and/or privately owned. Those involved were able to *do* something publicly to express respect through the medium of their shop windows. The aesthetics of appropriateness were also on display. The flowers taken to Kensington Gardens and other communal sites were usually coloured, as one person commented, 'like as if you were taking flowers as a gift for a friend'. The shop windows, in contrast, by being public displays seemed to be treated more formally as temporary shrines, with the mores of the church operating in terms of white flowers. The use of and comments upon candles also made this connection.

There is a further connection that needs to be made concerning shop window displays in the week Diana died. In an article on 'Folk Performance and Civil Religion at Royal Visits', Rowbottom (1998: 87) has pointed out that the floral and photographic pilgrimages made by Diana's mourners 'all reflect the ways in which the general public, and especially the "real royalists", greeted the living Princess and other members of the Royal Family'. One of the illustrations in Rowbottom's article (p. 79) shows an antique shop window decorated for a civic visit by the Queen, involving a large floral arrangement raised on an object covered with a Union Jack, in front of which is a framed picture of the Queen and Prince Philip – looking remarkably like some of the shop window shrines described here.

Afterword: the Ultimate Shop Window

While shop window shrines received virtually no media attention in the week following Diana's death, and while none of the Bath shops covered in this article commemorated the anniversary, on 31 August 1998 one shop window shrine grabbed the media's attention. This was the eight-foot-high shrine to Diana and Dodi which appeared in the window of Harrods, complete with photographs, white flowers and everlasting candles. Shortly afterwards, it was replaced by a smaller, permanent version inside the store at the base of the Egyptian stairwell. Harrods is, of course, owned by Dodi Al Fayed's father. At least one visitor (*Independent*, 1 September 1998) complimented Mr Al Fayed, still *persona non grata* to the British establishment and denied British citizenship, on being the only person yet to provide a permanent memorial to Diana open and free to the public every day. As this article shows, he is not the only one in this nation of shopkeepers who used their entrepreneurial creativity to transform sorrow into providing public shrines to Diana.

Bibliography

Rowbottom, A. (1998) 'The "Real Royalists": Folk Performance and Civil Religion at Royal Visits', *Folklore* 109: 77–88.

15

America Responds to Diana's Death: Spontaneous Memorials

C. Allen Haney and Dell Davis

Contemporary Western societies are the safest in human history, so when someone dies suddenly, violently or prematurely, it shatters the sense of safety and orderliness even for those who did not know the deceased well, often leading to spontaneous rituals over and beyond formal funeral ceremonies. Americans in particular have gained such a sense of control, if not mastery, over death that we expect death to come only in old age or as a result of voluntary choices or risky lifestyles. Only social marginals are expected to die unexpectedly, suddenly and violently at the hands of madmen or fools. We and our loved ones certainly will not. Neither will our idols, heroes and heroines.

Yet untimely death does sometimes come to those we revere and love, shaking our faith in an ordered world. The death of Princess Diana had such an effect on many Americans. Unlike reactions to the deaths of other notables such as Mother Teresa, whose death drew American sympathy of a more traditional sense, or John Lennon, whose death clearly shook the entertainment world and die-hard fans, the American response to the death of Princess Diana was not merely one specific expression of grief, but a response rich in ritual, individual melancholia and spontaneous mourning activity. In a country composed of many diverse cultures coupled with what some term a postmodern perspective, the Princess's death was met in America with some very creative and personal expressions of grief.

The data reported here derive from a systematic search of the Internet, examination of the nation's five major newspapers and three weekly news magazines. In addition, stories carried by the four leading electronic news outlets were examined for the ten days subsequent to the Princess's death. Participant observations were undertaken at two sites of spontaneous memorials as well as at the British Embassy in Houston. These sources were supplemented by extensive telephonic and face-to-face conversations with informants in New York, Chicago, Washington DC, San Francisco and St Louis. Analysis of this material was informed by comparative research into spontaneous memorialization after a number of other recent tragic deaths.

Formal Responses

Public and Governmental Statements. The news of Princess Diana's death astonished American political dignitaries. Initially, there was some question as to the proper political response from the White House. Confusion was somewhat alleviated by an announcement directly from British officials stating that 'Diana's family, and the royal family, wanted the guests at the funeral to be friends of the Princess or people she admired – not a collection of heads of state who barely knew her'(Hall 1997: 2). Although it was reported that President Bill Clinton considered himself to be eligible as a friend of the Princess, political protocol and recommendations from British Prime Minister Tony Blair suggested that First Lady Hillary Rodham Clinton attend in this capacity. Clinton did however address a letter of condolence to Prime Minister Blair.

Other American political figures expressed sentiment and paid respects to Diana's memory. Among these were Secretary of State Madeleine Albright who said Diana would be remembered for her 'tireless commitment to children and to the needy of the world' (Nando Times News 1997), while Ben Gilman, House of International Relations Committee Chairman, observed that 'the outpouring of emotion by the American people that we have witnessed is due to an identification with a woman who personified a fairy-tale Princess and who represented infinite possibilities. We are greatly diminished by this loss.' (Nando Times News 1997)

On 3 September 1997, the US Senate approved a resolution making 6 September, the day of the funeral, 'a National Day of Recognition for the humanitarian efforts of Diana, Princess of Wales.' The House resolution praised Diana for her work in such areas as AIDS, breast cancer, the homeless, and landmines (Slocum 1998). Through her humanitarian concerns, Diana also gained the respect of many prominent American organizations; the American Medical Association, the American Red Cross, women's organizations and special interest groups released public statements of condolence.

Although most statements were brimming with sorrow and respect, there were instances where interest groups took the opportunity to promote their organization's theme. Mothers Against Drunk Driving (MADD), a group whose goal is to stop drunk driving and support victims of this crime, immediately released an announcement stating, 'We've seen too many princesses die,' followed by a listing of over 100 girls and women killed by drunk drivers. Diana's name was on the list (Dallasnews.com 1997). The Libertarian Party also took a stand. National chairman Steve Dasbash was quoted in a press release as saying, 'Princess Diana is dead – don't let free speech be the next victim . . . the legacy of Princess Diana's death should not be new laws which infringe on the First Amendment.' (Getz 1997)

Condolence Books   In addition to the formal statements made by the nation's leaders and other notables, many Americans took advantage of the opportunity to pen brief messages in the 'Books of Condolence' made available at British embassies, consulates, and missions.

In Washington DC, thousands signed the books, some of them queuing for hours in stifling heat and humidity. In the end, fourteen books were filled with an estimated 22,000 signatures (Allen 1997: 3). In Dallas, Texas, and the other major US cities similar stories were reported. According to the British Information Service in New York, sixty-seven formal books of condolence containing over 97,000 signatures were received from British Consulate offices all over the United States. Several people interviewed by local media while waiting to sign condolence books had travelled from neighbouring cities to have this opportunity (Slocum 1998).

Ceremonies and Services   In New York City's Central Park, 14,000 mourners gathered to attend a formal service organized by the Episcopal Church's New York diocese and the Cathedral of St John the Divine. This service included speeches by New York Mayor Rudolph Giuliani, Dr Margaret Heagarty, director of pediatrics at Harlem Hospital Center and several ministers. The Washington National Cathedral also held a formal service. The Cathedral was filled to capacity and loudspeakers broadcast the service to those who had gathered on the lawn outside (Struck 1997). According to accounts in several national and community newspapers, regular church services held on the Sunday following Princess Diana's funeral made reference to her achievements and included prayers for her family and friends.

Semi-formal Responses

Websites   Those unable to make the trek to British diplomatic facilities could, if capable, avail themselves of various Internet sites to electronically send messages of condolence to the royals or other web pages dedicated to expressions of sympathy to the Royal Family and specifically to Diana's sons (see Chapter 13). During the week of the funeral, the popular Internet search engine *Yahoo!* reported two to three times its normal daily activity. 'Just on the Diana stuff alone, we've had over one to two million page-peeks a day,' according to *Yahoo!* co-founder David Filo (Thomas 1997). With the death of Diana, the world wide web was as close as it had ever come to an outpouring of sentimentality.

Broadcast Media   Ironically, the type of aggressive media coverage which allegedly led to Princess Diana's death was active with rivalry. Live broadcast coverage of the funeral competed for viewers and ratings. All eight major American networks provided coverage for an estimated 50 million viewers. Neilsen Media Research, which is an American broadcast ratings company, released figures confirming that 74 per cent of all television sets in use between 3 a.m. and 7 a.m. on the morning of the funeral were tuned to one of the major American networks.

To the surprise of many, America's national focus on Diana outdid even the wave of Camelot nostalgia which attended Jackie Onassis's death, and occupied more news time than the death of former President Richard Nixon and even approached in emotional intensity the reaction to President John Kennedy's assassination in 1963 (Nando Times News 1997).

Print Media   The print media also looked for ways to gain readership and increase sales. All major newspapers in the US ran front page coverage of Diana, beginning with the accident, continuing through the funeral and finally fading in intensity several weeks after the funeral (Slocum 1998). Approximately two weeks after the funeral, *People, Time, Newsweek* and *Entertainment Weekly* magazines ran Princess Diana's photo on the cover regardless of actual magazine content.

Celebrities/Personalities   Entertainers in the US felt a kinship with Diana and were devastated by the news of her death. They along with many Americans viewed her as a celebrity. Personalities such as actress and AIDS advocate Elizabeth Taylor, tennis player Andre Agassi, actors Arnold Schwarzenegger and George Clooney, and pop music star Michael Jackson spoke openly about the tragedy and recalled personal encounters with the paparazzi.

Several American musicians who had concerts or appearances scheduled around the time of her death, dedicated songs or entire concerts to her. In Ostend, Belgium, Michael Jackson cancelled his concert on Sunday and dedicated his 3 September concert to the Princess. During the MTV Video Music Awards show, entertainers such as Madonna, LL Cool J, and Elton John were among several who paid tribute to Princess Diana (Clerk 1997).

In an effort to raise money for Princess Diana's charitable concerns, the All-Star Charity Album was released in December 1997.

Informal Responses

Funeral tributes and memorial services were held all over the country in honour of Princess Diana, but the overwhelming response by Americans was participation in spontaneous memorials.

Shrines Spontaneous memorials in the form of shrines were erected in all US cities Princess Diana had visited, all US cities with British Consulate-General offices, sites associated with her humanitarian interests and many additional locations across the US that, on the surface, could not easily be associated with her or any of her special interests. Shortly after the announcement of Princess Diana's death, the steps of the British Embassy in northwest Washington DC became the site of a spontaneous shrine comprising hundreds of flowers, candles, cards and personal notes. This shrine included queen of hearts playing cards, an open 35 mm camera, a book advocating a ban on land mines addressed to 'a true humanitarian', and a quilt, possibly symbolizing Diana's work with AIDS victims. Other British Consulate-General offices in the US exhibited similar displays. In Houston, Texas the major spontaneous memorial was not located at the British Consulate, but evolved on the esplanade on Montrose Street (Figure 15.1). The 'Montrose' section is seen by most as the cultural and residential center of Houston's gay community. Similarly, San Francisco's largely gay Castro District was another site and the starting point of a candlelight procession to the British Consulate in San Francisco in which 14,000 people participated.

Spontaneous memorials in Diana's honour consisted of mementos symbolizing the relationship which mourners had established with her memory. As described elsewhere (Haney et al 1997), spontaneous memorialization is a public response to the unanticipated, violent deaths of individuals with whom the participants in the ritual share some common identification. Americans identified with Princess Diana for one or more of a number of reasons; her humanitarian efforts, her established independence from the Royal Family, her role as a woman of the 1990s (see Chapter 16) and her pop culture appeal.

Tributes Informal tributes and ceremonies were also heavily attended spontaneous activities. The San Francisco procession blossomed into an informal tribute with music, speeches and prayers. In Los Angeles, more than 2,500

Figure 15.1 Mourners gather to place flowers at a popular spontaneous memorial site in Houston, Texas. This particular memorial evolved on the esplanade in the heart of the gay community, and reappeared on the anniversary of her death.
Houston Chronicle

people assembled in a baseball field for a memorial held by an AIDS organization; participants spoke one word which, to them, described Diana. Words such as 'brave,' 'gracious,' 'beautiful,' 'giving,' and 'caring' were used (Russell 1998). The Gospel Mission Homeless Shelter in downtown Washington DC hosted a tribute to Diana's memory, with over a hundred people from the local Black community in attendance. The event organizer was quoted as saying that '. . . she [Diana] was worthy of a tribute by Blacks. The one thing that this woman did was to raise the level of concern about issues regarding the Black community. AIDS, homelessness, poverty are . . . issues that affect the Black community' (Wright 1997).

Community members and hospital staff at the Harlem Hospital Medical Center, located in a poverty-stricken, predominately Black community in New York remembered Diana with a display of mementos and photographs depicting her two visits to the Center. Another memorial was erected at Hale House, a neighbouring centre for children of addicted parents which she had also visited.

Entrepreneurial Responses

Novelty Item Sales   The 'Diana' business soon after her death was shamelessly booming with novelty, flower, book and music sales hitting all-time highs. Street vendors stationed near sites of memorial shrines and planned ceremonies sold Princess Diana T-shirts, mugs, key rings, and posters. Presumably their presence would be considered annoying or intrusive, but mourners seemed to welcome the convenience they offered to those wanting to purchase 'Diana' souvenirs. There has been no evidence that any profits from these vending operations were donated to charities in the Princess's name. Within a month, mail order Diana collectors' dolls were being advertised (Wood 1998).

Book and Music Sales   Many bookstores opened to small crowds of customers wanting to get their hands on any book with Diana's name in the title or her face on the cover. Bad reviews and questions of accuracy which at one time kept these titles on the shelf or caused them to go out-of-print were no longer issues. Sales rocketed as publishers and bookstores hustled to capitalize on this book-buying frenzy. One million of Andrew Morton's 1992 book, *Diana: Her True Story* and 400,000 copies of his 1994 publication, *Diana: Her New Life* were reprinted and distributed to book stores. Other books about the life of Princess Diana were also in great demand. Music stores were no different as people lined up before stores opened to purchase Elton John's

'Candle in the Wind' single. The Recording Industry Association of America certified the single as eight times platinum (Colton 1997). Music stores in the US reportedly sold out of copies during the morning of the day it was released.

Florists Florists were also unprepared as mourners purchased flowers to take to memorial sites, had flowers sent to Consulates and wired flowers to London. Popular florist FTD was forced to hire additional help to process the international orders. 'Even given the extraordinary tragedy of the Princess's recent death, we are taken aback by the sheer volume of calls and inquiries we are receiving,' said Bob Norton, President of FTD (Anonymous 1997a).

Although most businesses which pursued Diana's consumer market profited tremendously, some businesses reportedly lost money. A week prior to Princess Diana's death, Weight Watchers International had just launched a new $10 million advertising campaign. The print advertisement shows a smiling Sara 'Fergie' Ferguson, the Duchess of York, quipping about how hard it is to lose weight. How hard is it? 'It's harder than outrunning the paparazzi.' Weight Watchers public relations and advertising officials scrambled to pull those advertisements which had not yet been circulated (Dallasnews.com 1997). In a similar case, a cable TV channel had begun a promotion in malls across the nation which offered as a promotional prize a dress once worn by Princess Diana. The campaign slogan: 'a dress to Di for'. When news of the death was announced, the promotion was immediately cancelled (Dallasnews.com 1997).

An Interpretation of the American Response

> A few decades ago, we knew perfectly well what to make of the American way of death. It was overly sentimentalized, highly commercialized, and above all excessively expensive. We knew all this because our British friends, both visitors and expatriates, had told us so. (Gill 1996: 105)

Other writers, most notably, Philip Ariès (1974) said that Americans are a death-denying society; we are so fearful of death that we want little to do with it. Ernest Becker (1973) agreed. Jackson (1977) argued that Americans in the twentieth century have reduced the amount of time and the extent of resources which they devote to the dead. Gill suggests that this change has been evolving for centuries:

The important points for our purposes are two: (1) During the nineteenth century, there was a very strong increase in the ceremonies, expenses, and material attentions paid to the dead in the United States. (2) During our present century, at least from World War I on, though with some short-term and local variations, there was a decrease in the amount of attention paid to, and memorialization of, our dead. (Gill 1996: 110)

The more formal responses to death fit this trend. At the individual level, however, the evidence indicates that as the century draws to a close, ritual persists and indeed is evolving in new, more private and more personal forms.

One might also have anticipated that, on Diana's death, Americans might have experienced disenfranchised grief (Doka 1989), the grief of those whose attachment to the deceased is not recognized or validated. This was not so. The American response was intense and personal, not merely because so many Americans are Anglophiles and royal watchers but because she was a citizen of the world whose appeal spanned national boundaries and whose favourite causes resonated with the interest and concerns of countless Americans. 'Princess Diana was British by birthright but adopted and loved by the rest of the world for her beauty, charm and humanitarianism. She fought a valiant, public battle for the right to choose and define her own role in life, as opposed to having it designated for her.' (Anonymous 1997b: 12)

More Informal Responses

The following comments reflect the sentiments of mourners that are in keeping with the traditional ritualized purposes of mourning. Some of the sentiments expressed are not the type typically expressed at more formal, usually religious, funeral rituals, but reflect personal concerns.

'I came for the boys, I want to show them that we loved their mother and that they have our prayers.' (Middle class, female, three children)

'I just wanted to show my respect for the Princess and to show my gratitude for all she has done for us.' (African-American, female, secretary)

'I'm here to show the royal family that even if they did treat her [shabby], the world loved her.' (Working class, female, single mother of four)

'I came to pay my respect to a person who made a difference in the world.' (Self identified gay, male, professional)

'I want the English people to see that we share their loss and sorrow.' (Hispanic, male, clergyman)

Rando (1993) has argued that violent deaths complicate the mourning process for those whose life the death impacts (see also Chapter 6). We have stated elsewhere (Haney et al 1997) that they also heighten insecurity among people who can identify with the victim, the victim's family or the circumstances of the death; they erode cultural values and threaten the continued existence of society. Spontaneous memorialization is a public response to the unanticipated, violent deaths of people who do not fit into the categories of those we expect to die, who may be engaging in routine activities in which there is a reasonable expectation of safety, and with whom the participants in the ritual share some common identification. This process does not replace traditional funerary rites. Rather, it emerges as an adjunct ritual which extends the opportunity for mourning to individuals who would otherwise be disenfranchised and not conventionally included in traditional rites, and calls attention to the social and cultural threat raised by these deaths. Certainly, this was the case in the death of Princess Diana. The gruesome manner of the death was inconsistent with her fairy-tale glamour; moreover, road traffic accidents are an all too common cause of sudden bereavement in ordinary families. The death was ghastly, exotic, yet also a reminder of what could happen to any family, disturbing millions who had never met her.

By looking at a number of recent American examples, Haney et al (1997) identified spontaneous memorialization as being characterized by the following seven features:

1. It is a private, individualized act of mourning which is open for public display. It is difficult to know how these memorials get organized. In Houston the largest Diana memorial began with a single individual whose actions were relayed to others by word of mouth. Plans were subsequently broadcast by local radio stations. More recently, evidence indicates that Americans attending the World Cup soccer games in Paris made pilgrimages to the tunnel where the Princess died. Certain stylized elements which have appeared at various other spontaneous memorials – teddy bears, flags, etc. – were among the items also left at the memorials to Princess Diana. Unique to her memorials were the smashed cameras, destroyed photographic equipment and queen of hearts playing cards. Some items apparently had meaning only for those individuals leaving them there. While there may be little doubt regarding the meaning of the wedding bands left at memorials, much of the poetry and letters may have had significance only to the persons who wrote them.

2. Spontaneous memorialization often occurs at the site of the death, or some site which is associated with the death, rather than at a prescribed place of mourning such as a church, funeral home or cemetery. Many of the Diana memorials were at medical facilities and neighbourhood shelters for the abused and homeless. Apart from the more obvious locations such as

British Embassies, Consulates and churches, the sites selected tend to be associated with one of Princess Diana's charitable concerns.

3. No one is automatically included in or excluded from spontaneous memorialization. Participants are often not included in the culturally pre-scribed group of mourners – relatives, friends and associates. By participating in this ritual, individuals who may not even have known the deceased define themselves as mourners, thus creating a role for themselves which allows them to express their feelings occasioned by the death. Certainly this was the case with the death of Princess Diana as direct participation for the majority of American mourners was prohibited by distance. Very diverse groups came together in common memorials. Mothers receiving federal aid mourned with members of the gay and lesbian population and conservative 'royal watchers'. As in Britain (Chapter 2), Diana's death linked segments of American society which as a rule take little heed of each other.

4. As indicated earlier, spontaneous memorials are typically shrines com-prising an eclectic combination of traditional religious, secular, and highly personalized ritual objects. Those raised to Diana were no different. At her memorials were mementos and tokens left by the juxtaposition of various seemingly unrelated, and even contradictory objects such as crosses, teddy bears, bibles and prayer books resting beside smashed cameras, rolls of photographic film unwound and exposed and all manner of heart-shaped cards and displays. The mementos left at the Diana memorials were to a large extent cerebral/intellectual. A substantial portion of them were poems/quotations. Largely absent were more secular tokens with exception of the queen of hearts playing cards. In addition to these were the more traditional floral displays, particularly of roses and candles.

5. Mementos left at the site are often personally meaningful to the mourner and illustrate the meaning of the event for him or her. This was particularly the case with the Diana memorials, perhaps in part because her connection to her mourners covered so very many social issues. Some of the offerings reflected the mourner's desire that the social concerns championed by Diana should not fade from public view. Many notes made reference to contributions made to certain causes. Other tokens reflected the loss of her as a symbol of romance. Still other objects may have reflected emotions such as anger, as evidenced by the presence of photographic equipment and shredded tabloid newspapers.

6. Spontaneous memorialization is not constrained by culturally-based norms which prescribe the amount of time allotted for ritual action nor the appropriate amount of time for bereavement. Unlike traditional funeral rites, which occur at set times and continue for a set duration, spontaneous memor-ialization ebbs and flows as individual mourners make their pilgrimages and

contribute their offerings either immediately after the death, or during the weeks or months that follow. Focus upon the death of Diana and attention to her memorials has waxed and waned as each new bit of information about her private life or circumstances of her death are made public. Likewise, a predictable anniversary phenomenon has been observed, the date of her birth, the date of her marriage, and other significant occasions in her life have become opportunities for more tributes. The British Information Service in New York continues to receive items from mourners. On 1 July 1998, Diana's birthday, the Information Service reported a marked increase in the number of mementos received. They expected this also to be the case during the anniversary week of her death (Slocum 1998).

7. While these rituals do commemorate the deceased, they extend the focus beyond the victim and the private mourning of friends and family to the social and cultural implications of the death. Much attention has been given to the symbolic loss that Diana's death represents. Some have said it was the end of fairy-tale romances and little girls dreaming of becoming princesses. Violent deaths such as Diana's alter the existing social order and negate cultural values which bind us together. Spontaneous memorialization provides a method for grieving such personal, social and cultural losses. In this case the royals and the paparazzi were of central concern; but in addition divorce, child custody, scandal and other issues came to the fore.

Clearly, spontaneous memorialization does not replace traditional funeral rites. Instead, it is a more immediate, almost urgent, response soon after the announcement of the death. Formalized initiatives and memorials, such as the charitable funds to further the favourite cause of the deceased, often spring from spontaneous memorials.

Through spontaneous memorialization, participants can express emotions not typically addressed in traditional rituals but which are often part of bereavement, such as anger, revenge and guilt. The social dimension of spontaneous memorials is evident in some of the notes left at sites and items posted to various pages on the world wide web. They express feelings which imbue deaths such as Princess Diana's with meaning beyond the loss of an individual life, to the meaning of the death for closely held cultural values, and for the fate of our culture.

Bibliography

Allen, M. (1997) 'Products of Grief', *Washington Post*, 22 September, D: 3.
Anonymous (1997a) 'Media: Death of a Princess, Birth of a Thousand Press Releases', *Wall Street Journal*, 10 September 1997, B: 1.

Anonymous (1997b) 'Though British, Diana Belonged to the World', *USA Today*, 2 September, A: 12.

Ariès, P. (1975) 'The Reversal of Death: Changes in Attitudes Toward Death in Western Societies', in D.E. Stannard (ed.), *Death in America*, Philadelphia: University of Pennsylvania Press.

Becker, E. (1973) *The Denial of Death*, New York: Free Press.

Clerk, C. (1997) 'Award In Your Ear', *Melody Maker*, 13 September, 74: 6.

Colton, M. (1997) 'Elton John's Diana Tribute Breaks Record', *Washington Post*, 24 September, D: 1.

Dallasnews.com Web Site (1997) http://www.dallasnews.com/diana

Doka, K. J. (1989) 'Disenfranchised Grief', in K. J. Doka (ed.), *Disenfranchised Grief: Recognizing Hidden Sorrow*, Lexington, Mass: Lexington Books.

Getz, G. (1997) 'Don't Let Princess Diana's Crash Be Used As an Excuse to Restrict the First Amendment Libertarians Urge', The *Libertarian Party Home Page*, http://www.lp.org/rel/970904-paparazzi.html

Gill, R. T. (1996) 'What Ever Happened to the American Way of Death', *Public Interest*, Spring: 105–17.

Hall, M. (1997) 'Hillary to Attend Service First Lady Deemed Most Appropriate US Representative', *USA Today*, 3 September, A: 2.

Haney, C.A., Leimer, C., and J. Lowery (1997) 'Spontaneous Memorialization: Violent Death and Emerging Mourning Ritual'. *Omega*, 35: 159–71.

Jackson, C.O. (1977) *Passing: the Vision of Death in America*, Westport, Conn.: Greenwood Press.

Nando Times News Web Site (1997) http://www.nando.net/newsroom

Rando, T. A. (1993) *Treatment of Complicated Mourning*, Champaign, Illinois: Research Press.

Russell, B. (1998) personal interview, 23 June 1998.

Slocum, L. (1998) 'Personal interview with representative from the British Information Service in New York' 19 April 1998, 6 July 1998.

Struck, D. (1997) 'Princess Diana: 1961–1997 – At Cathedral and Embassy, Some Surprised at Sadness', Washington Post, A: 27.

Thomas, K. (1997) 'Cyberspace Clogged with Diana Condolences', *USA Today*, 4 September, 265: 1D.

Wood, J. (1998) 'Diana Memorabilia: Mail Order Values in Popular American Magazines', *Folklore*, 109: 109–10.

Wright, J. (1997), 'Princess Di's Death Saddens All', Washington Afro-American, 106: A1.

16

An American Paean* for Diana, an Unlikely Feminist Hero

Wendy Griffin

The American public has a notoriously short attention span. Nothing is older than yesterday's news. And yet, in 1997 alone, American network and syndicated television ran 696 stories on Princess Diana, the great majority of which appeared in the four months after her death. The programs ranged from examinations of the role the press might have played in causing the accident that killed her to the impact her death would have on hair design and fashion. One tabloid television program even featured a psychic who attempted to contact her from the 'other side.' Magazines as varied as *Car & Driver* and the *Ladies Home Journal* carried feature articles on Diana. Although the media coverage was largely supportive, it was not unanimously so. An editorial in the left-leaning newspaper the *Nation* (Hitchens 1997) accused the Princess of pursuing the rich and powerful and using the poor as accessories, and a right-wing radio talkshow host from Denver, Colorado, mused over the airwaves if God might have taken her when He did to curb some of the seemingly pagan worship of her (Hamblin 1997). But even if the coverage were not always positive, almost everyone in America was talking about her unexpected death. One industry report announced that stories about her would have a life far beyond the interest in her death, and be 'bigger than Elvis, bigger than Marilyn Monroe' (Press Telegram 1998). Eleven months later, that was echoed by nationally syndicated columnist Maureen Dowd (1998), who wrote that, 'The Princess of Wales is better box office in death than most superstars are in life.' Anti-monarchy for ourselves, we are

---

* 'Paean: an ancient Greek hymn in honor of Artemis (Diana) or Apollo; a war song before or after a battle; hence, a song of triumph generally; a song of joy or praise.' Grolier Webster International Dictionary.

a nation that makes others' royals into celebrities and our own celebrities into *pop royalty*. Yet the depth of the reaction on this side of the Atlantic to the death of Princess Diana was something no one could have foreseen.

It is trite to say it, but in America we face death every day. As I write, today's local newspaper informs me that a mother has been arrested for allegedly murdering her four children in a custody dispute, a six-year-old boy died in a fire, a man armed with a meat cleaver was shot and killed by police officers after attacking several people, and a young soldier is on life support after a training exercise went wrong. Today is nothing special. Tomorrow, there will be another list. Yet the death of Princess Diana was unique, and the response to it was far different than to any other fatality in this country's history. Americans, and American women in particular, were genuinely bereaved when Princess Diana was killed in the end of August 1997. In an attempt to understand why we responded with such profound grief at the death of this foreign woman that none of us knew, I began with primary sources – my own observations and a selection of newspapers and women's magazines from around the nation. In addition, I reviewed three discussion groups posted on the Net and a web site set up by Time Life, a media conglomerate. I chose to examine the media because one of the things that brought this death home to Americans was that it was a media event, and people around the world engaged in 'virtual mourning' (Grimes 1997).

America's Reactions

In Los Angeles, 5,000 miles away from Kensington Palace, hundreds of people lined up in front of the British Consulate for as long as four hours in the hot September sun just to sign a book of condolences. People wrote long paragraphs, some even taping letters they had brought with them to the pages in the black leather book. They left flowers, burning candles, teddy bears, poems, and hand-made cards. One young woman, suffering from multiple sclerosis and walking on forearm crutches brought flowers on Monday and returned the next day to wait in line for hours to sign the book. Late that afternoon, a 74-year-old woman who had waited three hours in line collapsed in the stifling heat and was taken to the hospital. The British Consulate in Los Angeles collected some 10,000 messages of condolence in twenty books. Interviews appearing in the local papers suggest this was a way people felt they could participate in the funeral (Hall 1997). There were book signings at British Consulates in every major city in America.

Though many homes in this country have at least one video recorder and people could have easily set their machines and slept through the live, televised ceremony, many chose to set their alarm clocks instead and rise in the dark hours before dawn to view the funeral while it was happening. Mothers woke their children so they could watch with them. Mourners gathered together in private homes, English-style pubs, all-night coffee shops and university dormitories. Freshmen at the University of California in Los Angeles, who got up at 2 a.m. to watch live coverage of the funeral, said Diana's death would mark their generation much as President John Kennedy's death had marked their parents'. St James Episcopal Church, part of the worldwide Anglican Communion, scheduled a special memorial service a week after the funeral, and in the Los Angeles Grand Prix, drivers of cars made in Britain drove them the wrong direction in a parade around the official route before the race, while the American chairman of the Grand Prix waved the Union Jack.

In San Francisco, 10,000 mourners held a candlelight procession to the British Consulate hours before the funeral began. A New Age journal reported that 'Thousands of floral tributes to Princess Diana were scattered in the Pacific Ocean, and witnesses said a school of dolphins frolicked through the water just as the blooms hit the ocean' (Walburger, 1997). Perhaps it isn't so surprising that the reaction on the West Coast was so strong, as British constitutional expert David Starkey argued from London that Diana represented 'the touchy-feely Californization of Britain.' (Montalbano 1997) Californians felt she was one of them.

But it was the same scene all over the country. In Washington DC and New York people gathered outside the British Embassies as well and created the now familiar sea of flowers. The mourners in New York came from all walks of life, and all five boroughs of the city: actors, housewives, doctors, students, runners from Wall Street. The card on one bouquet of flowers was signed by the housekeepers of the New York Palace Hotel. People interviewed said they came to the Consulate to be closer to Diana.

'She was a different breed to the other royals,' said a woman waiting in line to sign the condolence book outside the British Consulate in Chicago. 'Her children ate McDonald's hamburgers' (in Warnick 1997). Despite the chilly wind coming off Lake Michigan, there were 200 people in line at 10 p.m. Some of them had come from out of state, taking several hours to drive there after getting off work. Others simply came to the Consulate instead of going to work that day. Whole families were there, several of them spanning three generations. People who had never seen, let alone spoken to Princess Diana said they just wanted a chance to say good-bye. Consul officials estimated that as many as 5,000 people had visited in the four days of condolence signings. Seven hundred mourners packed a memorial service in

Saint James Episcopal Cathedral in the centre of the Windy City. Others stood outside on the street and listened to the service on loudspeakers.

It wasn't just in the large cities that people felt the need for public mourning. In the small Oregon community of Lake Oswego, south of Portland , where there is no British Consulate, people made a memorial site in the doorway of the Lady Di Country Store. Americans and a few British expatriates joined together in front of a large photograph of the Princess and a vase of red roses. Other flowers, bought from florists and picked from gardens, soon joined them. One card nestled among the bouquets read, 'I lost my mommy in a car accident' (Verzemnieks 1997). Other towns had their own small shrines.

The question that many journalists and social scientists struggled with was why so many Americans who didn't know Princess Diana, many of whom didn't particularly care about her during her lifetime, reacted with such profound grief at her death. Some of the answers came quickly.

Analysis in the Media

One of the popular reasons given was guilt. New Age columnist Kay Walburger echoed the thoughts of many tabloid readers when she wrote that the unexpected pain she felt when she learned of the accident in Paris was due to the disturbing feeling that her interest in celebrities may have helped to cause the press's behaviour (Walburger 1997). Far easier to become enraged at the tabloid press, the 'stalkarazzi,' than to deal with the disquieting knowledge that every person who read an article or watched a tabloid show on the Princess may have contributed to her death. The forces of capitalism were in the tunnel that night.

A more complex analysis came from scholars in the popular and professional press, who reminded us that a funeral is a rite of passage that has several functions. It says this period in our lives is over. It marks a time in a manner that tells us that, from this day on, our lives will never be exactly the same again. Funerals distract us, giving us something concrete to do for a set period of time, so that we don't drown in our grief, or so that we don't show too obviously that we don't feel the grief society might expect us to. But, as Grimes (1997) pointed out, funerals also teach us to grieve and to do so in an acceptable manner. As a media event, the funeral of Princess Diana was watched by approximately two-fifths of the world's human population. Not only did it teach us to mourn, but it *invoked* grief, and not just for a dead princess. Grimes (1997) argued, 'Diana wasn't the only object of our mourning but her funeral was its occasion . . . Funerals help us find our grief, even if the grief is left over from someone else's death.'

Perhaps this is the reason so many reporters, all male, compared the death of Diana to the death of Elvis Presley, whose power as an American cultural icon grows every year. 'His appeal in death has taken on a profundity that borders on the religious for thousands of people,' reported the Los Angeles Times (Jones 1997). Pilgrims come to Graceland, the entertainer's home that has been turned into a museum, tourist attraction and merchandising centre, as succour for their own pain, and they see Elvis as a hero who hurt in the same way that they hurt. It isn't the young, successful, virile superstar they seek, according to writer Ron Rosenbaum (in Jones 1997), but the older, heavier, lonelier man, the one who could have been their father, son, lover, or self. Elvis was one of them, just as Diana was one of us. What was profoundly different in the reactions of Americans to these two deaths is the gendered nature of the response to the death of Princess Diana.

Gendered Reactions

Male columnists, editors, men on the street and on the Net discussed whether or not the driver of the Princess's car was drunk, what his blood alcohol level was, and later, if the accident were the result of a conspiracy on the part of munitions manufacturers, conservative politicians, and even, some suggested, of the freemasons to silence her campaign against landmines. Women, on the other hand, discussed the Princess's compassion, her two boys, the tragedy of a death of one so young and so beautiful. From the deep south, columnist Maureen Downey wrote, 'men clucked sympathetically over Diana's death, but then went out to mow the lawn. Women appeared far more affected, frozen in front of televisions, tears streaming down their faces' (Downey 1997). In the Midwest, a headline announced 'Men Don't Get It, But Women Relate to Diana's Plight' (*St Louis Post-Dispatch* 1997: A, 6: 4). From the West Coast came agreement. Diana's 'hurt registered most with women, who tended to *get* Di's death long before men' (Jones 1997). This was confirmed from the East Coast, where one columnist reported that his wife was mourning for Princess Diana, while he was mourning for former star baseball player Richie Ashburn, who died the same week at the age of seventy (Vecsey 1997). Around the country reports came in that men seemed bewildered by the depth of women's grief, a fact picked up and discussed by the 15 September issue of newsmagazine *U.S. News & World Report*. A friend of mine, a Ph.D. in biology, confided that her husband was not only bewildered by her reaction to the death, but was beginning to get very impatient with it. The husband of a local reporter couldn't understand why she needed to watch the tape of the funeral over and over. She tried to explain to him that it was some sort of mystical event (Walburger 1997).

Some of this could be expected, of course. Gender role socialization would predict that women would be more comfortable than men showing certain emotions, especially public displays of grief and vulnerability. But this does not explain the gender differences that occurred. Some men were very sad. Some even shed tears. But American women reported feeling *devastated* by Diana's death, and many of them were caught by surprise at the intensity of their own feelings.

Several writers, almost all of them women, attempted to understand this by examining the mystical and mythical aspects of Diana's life and death. Some were inspired, perhaps, by Earl Spencer's funeral reminder of the Goddess Diana of the hunt. Others mentioned the fact that St Paul's, the Cathedral where she had been married, was built on the site of an ancient Roman temple to the Goddess Diana (Paxson 1998). The Princess was buried on an island and, for some, promised to become the new Lady of the Lake, restoring mythic vitality to the British throne. Religious Studies scholar Maureen Korp argued that we resonated so strongly to Diana's life and death because they were visual illustrations of Joseph Campbell's hero myth. 'No media coverage can invent ancient myths, encrusted with atavistic symbols. We suck in those stories with mother's milk' (Korp 1997). This may have explained part of what was happening. This and related themes were repeated over and over again in the press. From the nation's capital came the explanation that women mourned Diana because she '. . . embodied fairy tales they'd forgotten they believed in' (Britt 1997).

Some women said the death was so tragic because Diana finally had her chance at love. 'For the first time in my life I can say I am really happy' she had said earlier (in Oates 1997). 'She had finally met a man who seemed as smitten with her as she was with him' (Downey 1997). 'The minute Di seemed to have found her new prince, she was hounded to death' (Britt 1997). Whether or not a marriage with Dodi Fayed would have been a true 'happy ending' to their courtship, as Dodi's father Mohammed now insists in the tabloids, many women seemed to believe this hope added to the tragedy of the fatal accident. Yet, when asked directly if they thought that a marriage between the Princess and the playboy would have been a happy one, every single woman I asked replied in the negative. Female columnists were not so easily seduced by the promise of love. 'She was let down . . . by almost ever man she seems to have loved,' was a typical comment (Williams 1997: 29). And 'About the other men in her life . . . well, she wasn't the only woman in the world with bad taste and bad luck' (*Newsweek* 1997).

Despite the romanticism of the idea that American women were devastated at Diana's death because the Princess could now never find true love, the evidence suggests otherwise. And though there were mythic elements about her life, it wasn't the *mythic* hero for whom women mourned, but the heroic real-life woman who lived and died an ocean away at the end of the twentieth century. In spite of her money, her stunning beauty and her blood lines going back 600 years, Diana was indeed 'one of us.' It was this oft-repeated phrase in women's voices that sent me to examining what it was we had in common.

American Women in the Twentieth Century

Like the lives of women around the world, American women's lives have changed dramatically this century, especially in the latter half. Sociologists have historically defined the 'traditional nuclear family' as one where there is a fairly clear gendered division of labour, with the female as a stay-at-home housewife and mother and the male as the primary provider and decision-maker. Whether or not this was ever an accurate reflection of the American family is up for debate (for a discussion of this debate, see Coontz 1992). Nevertheless, it certainly was the stereotype that many of us were raised to believe was ideal, although race and social class played significant roles in determining to what extent we accepted and identified with it. The successful woman, as projected in dominant culture, was a female who filled the only legitimate adult roles available to her: wife and mother. In fact, a Gallup poll taken toward the end of America's Great Depression of the 1930s found that 82 per cent of those surveyed objected to married women working, and twenty-six states were considering legislation to keep them from holding paid employment (Kelly 1991).

World War II put an end to that way of thinking, as women were actively recruited to fill the jobs that men going to fight left vacant. After the war, many women were pushed out of the workplace, loosing the fleeting independence a wartime manufacturing economy had offered them. Their participation in the labour force dropped initially, before beginning to rise again approximately 10 per cent a decade (Goldin 1990). Young women went back to moving straight from their parents' home to their husband's. They took their husband's last name and learned to define themselves through him. They became Joe's wife and Billy's mom. The university, for those whose families could afford it, was a place to meet a future mate and 'earn a MRS,' not a place to prepare for a career, and if they grew as individuals or as scholars there, it was incidental.

But the old marriage bargain failed to hold. If it used to mean that being a virgin at marriage, keeping a home and raising children assured a woman that her partner would be faithful and provide for her and the children for the rest of their lives, it no longer meant that. The relative affluence of the 1950s gave way to the social unrest and sexual experimentation of the 1960s. Women's labour force participation, already on the increase, began to rise especially among married women, and by 1994, three out of four women between the ages of 25–54 were in paid employment (Herz and Wootton 1996). Many middle-class families began to be considered middle class only because of the wife's additional income (Stone and Dooley 1996). Effective birth control was developed and legalized, divorce laws became more liberal, and along the way, women began to change. And then the second Wave of American feminism hit.

Unlike English feminism with its strong roots in the political left, American feminism first grew out of the movement to end slavery. It was, and continues to be, largely a liberal movement, not a radical or socialist one, a fact which may make it more acceptable in American life and politics than it is in British. Although they may not define themselves as feminists, a Yankelovich Poll found that a large majority of American women show overwhelming support for the goals of feminism (*Time* 1989). Feminism and women's increased earnings are major contributions to the democratization of the family. One of the many things that feminism does is encourage women to explore their potential, to refuse to be limited by the social constrictions of gender. This theme became clear upon examining women's reactions to Diana.

An Unlikely Feminist Hero

Diana was young and uneducated when catapulted into fame, a pre-feminist Cinderella waiting the arrival of her prince. She had dropped out of school and worked in typically female jobs: cleaning woman, nanny, kindergarten teacher's aide. That she married royalty marks a difference between her and the women who mourned her. But like her, many of them married before they developed an independent sense of self and tended to identify themselves through their husbands. This condition of romantic dependence is one of the old themes of female socialization. Newsmagazine writer Marjorie Williams reminds us, '. . . it is the rare little girl who wants to grow up to be a queen. To wish to be a princess is not only to aspire upward, to royalty, but to aspire to endless daughterhood and perpetual shelter' (Williams 1997: 29). This was the role that the young Diana embraced. She was completely self-effacing. Although she changed with time, many of us have forgotten 'that during the first year of her marriage, she barely uttered a public word, too shy and nervous to make public speeches (Murphy and Hall 1997: 24).

Millions of us watched as she suffered, grew and rebelled. This was the Diana with whom American women identified. A woman lawyer from Washington DC said 'My fascination *began* when her marriage started to fall apart. She had so many expectations placed on her; she was struggling to find herself and present that reality to the world whether it liked it or not. And I think that's something any woman can relate to' (in Murphy & Hall 1997: 25).

A nurse from Chicago confided, 'At first I was just fascinated by her. Then as I watched her grow and mature, my admiration turned to respect. She went from being "Shy Di" to this courageous trailblazer, and you have to respect her for that' (in Stevens and Mills 1997). A feminist magazine put it this way:

> Diana emerged from being the insecure, put upon, and bewildered wife of a prince to becoming the outspoken, outraged divorcee – thanks to her considerable courage and the help of feminist therapy ... (which) helped Diana realize the fault was within the system, not herself ... Like many women, she could not believe what she was expected to put up with. Instead, she walked away and told the world exactly why she did. (Off Our Backs 1997).

We didn't identify with her just because Diana had an adulterous husband and in-laws who appeared to cast her out, as more than one male columnist suggested (for example, see Kass 1997). It wasn't the beautiful victim who was our hero. It was that she had *overcome* depression, bulimia, even suicide attempts and was finally beginning to taste 'the pleasure of independence' (*Newsweek* 1997). She was defining herself on her own terms; with her compassion, willingness to embrace and champion AIDS sufferers, and her moral outrage at landmines, she was even redefining what it meant to be a princess. Feminist psychologist Carol Gilligan (1997) wrote that Diana

> failed publicly and, in doing that, shattered an icon that imprisons all women ... And then she broke the spell. She aired in the full public eye of the media humiliations that for centuries have silenced women because women feel that they reflect failures on their part and because speaking out carries the risk of further rejection and shame ... she began to model for other women a way out of what often is seen as a failure but in fact may be a release ... she was resisting shame and refusing to hide.

She was crucially unashamed of insisting on being a whole person, not just the mother of 'an heir and a spare'. As she struggled with the realities of divorce and joint custody, she was also searching for a life with meaning and where her needs might finally be met. 'In her ordeals, in the courage, stubbornness and idealism of her attempt to reinvent herself as an independent woman, women have found a model for themselves. It was this Diana, stronger for her own suffering, heroic for all she was vulnerable, with whom women will continue to identify' (Oates 1997).

Though race and social class may shape our understandings of gender, this search for identity crosses racial and class lines. A Black woman from Washington DC who had joined friends at a 'houseparty' to watch the televised funeral as it was happening said,

I can't explain it, but I found myself crying and unable to leave the television until 3:30 in the morning. I never idolized Diana as a fairy princess or even saw her as a white female. She was just a woman living publicly what many of us were experiencing privately: divorce, the battle with weight, the quest for respect. (in Milloy 1997)

Princess Diana's life was as unexpected as her death. No longer the 'Prisoner of Wales' as she once had called herself, she fought a battle for identity, respect and integrity of self. It was a battle many American women believed she won. And that gave us hope for ourselves.

Bibliography

Britt, Donna (1997) 'An unexpected lament for a princess', *The Washington Post*, 5 September, B1.

Coontz, Stephanie (1992) *The Way We Never Were*, New York: Basic Books.

Dowd, Maureen (1998) 'Di in death', *Press-Telegram*, 7 July: A7.

Downey, Maureen (1997) 'She said humanity gave Diana her place in our hearts', *Atlanta Journal*, 2 September: C1.

Gilligan, Carol (1997) 'For many women, gazing at Diana was gazing within', *New York Times*, 9 September, C4: 1.

Goldin, Claudia (1990) *Understanding the Gender Gap: An Economic History of American Women*, New York: Oxford University Press.

Grimes, Ronald L. (1997) 'Diana's funeral: a ceremonial distraction?' *Religious Studies Newsletter*, American Association of Religion, November: 21.

Hall, Carla (1997) 'Bereft in L.A.', *Los Angeles Times*, 3 September: A9.

Hamblin, Ken (1997) 'Worshipping the wrong icons', *Denver Post*, 9 September: B9: 4.

Herz, Diana E. and Wootton, Barbara H. (1996) 'Women in the workforce: an overview', in Costelle, C., Wootton, B. and Krimgold, K. (eds), *The American Woman 1996–97*, New York: W. W. Norton, pp. 23–33.

Hitchens, Christopher (1997) 'Throne and altar', *Nation*, 29 September: 29.

Jones, Robert (1997) 'The enigma of the Di pilgrims', *Los Angeles Times*, 7 September: B1.

Kass, John (1997) 'On cue for the camera, let's shed a tear for dear departed virtue', *Chicago Tribune*, 8 September, Sec. 1,3: 1.

Kelly, Rita Mae (1991) *The Gendered Economy*, Newbury Park, CA: Sage.

Korp, Maureen (1997) 'Teaching from the headlines: myth and the media coverage of Diana's death', *Religious Studies Newsletter*, American Association of Religion, November: 20.

Mannies, Jo (1997) 'Men don't get it, but women relate to Diana's plight', *Saint Louis Post Dispatch*, 3 September, A, 6: 4.

Milloy, Courtland (1997) 'Tragedy of many colors', *Washington Post*, 7 September: B1.

Montalbano, William (1997) 'A royal farewell to Diana, tradition', *Los Angeles Times*, 25 September: A1.

Murphy, Dean E. and Hall, Carla (1997) *Los Angeles Times*, 1 September: A1, 24–5.

Newsweek (1997), 22 December, 24–7, 52–3, 60–3.

Oates, Joyce Carol (1997) 'The love she searched for', 15 September. URL http://mouth.pathfinder.com/time/magazine/1997/dom/970915/princess.the_love_she_.html

Off Our Backs (1997) 'In memoriam', V. 27, #9, October: 7.

Paxon, Diana (1998) 'Myth, lore, history and ritual', *PanGaia*, 15, Spring: 55–60.

Press Telegram (1998), 3 February: A1.

Stevens, Darlene Gavron, and Mills, Steve (1997) 'Some begin day, others end night with funeral', *Chicago Tribune,* 7 September: C20.

Stone, Anne J. and Dooley, Betty (1996) 'A perspective on America's working women', in Costelle, C., Wootton, B. and Krimgold, K. (eds), *The American Woman 1996–97*, New York: W. W. Norton, pp. 23–33.

Time(1989) 4 December: 85.

U. S. News and World Report (1997) v. 123, 15 September: 22–40.

Vecsey, George (1997) 'Guy heroes, female heroines', *New York Times*, 12 September, B, 9: 1.

Verzemnieks, Inara (1997) 'Mourners carry sorrows to a little patch of Britain', *Oregonian Sunrise*, 3 September: E3.

Walburger, Kay (1997) 'A living legacy of love', *Awareness Magazine*, November: 14.

Warnick, Mark S. (1997) 'Hundreds line up to pay their respects', *Chicago Tribune*, 5 September: N12.

Williams, Marjorie C. (1997) 'The princess puzzle', *U.S. News & World Report*, v. 123, 15 September: 28–30.

17

Jokes on the Death of Diana

Christie Davies

Within forty-eight hours of Princess Diana's death in a car crash I knew of two jokes about it. Soon there were many more and literally hundreds have been invented. At first they spread by word of mouth and then via the Internet which acted as a medium for the circulation of jokes from America, Australia, the Netherlands and Denmark as well as Britain. The general pattern was similar to that of other earlier joke-cycles that have followed a well-publicized accident or shocking event. In earlier major joke-cycles such as that which followed the explosion of the NASA space shuttle in 1986, the jokes, which began minutes after the event, grew rapidly in numbers, peaked after a few months and then gradually faded away. The jokes never really disappeared, for individuals store them in their memories, notebooks and computers and they lingered as graffiti and got published, sometimes in academic studies (Dundes 1987a, b, Oring 1992, Simons 1986, Smyth 1986), sometimes in popular collections of 'sick', 'gross', 'tasteless' and 'offensive' jokes (Alvin 1983, 1983a, 1984; Knott 1982–4; Thickett 1983–4; Wilde 1979).

The Diana jokes are in this sense no different from previous jokes about accidents, disasters or shocking crimes as can be seen by alternating post-Diana jokes with examples from other joke-cycles.

Not only was the driver drunk, so was Di. She'd got three pints of Carling inside her. (Oral circulation, England 1998. Also on the Internet. It was alleged that Diana had had an affair with Will Carling, the England rugby captain.)

What's the coldest place in Scotland?
Dunblane. It's minus sixteen. (Oral circulation, England 1998. A suspected paedophile murdered fifteen children and their teacher in a primary school in Dunblane.)

What would Diana be doing if she was still alive today?
Trying to claw her way out of her coffin. (Oral circulation, England 1998. Also on the Internet.)

What is the national anthem of Monaco?
'She'll be coming round the mountain'. (Bronner 1985: 75, collected Los Angeles 1983; Smyth 1986: 246) (Grace Kelly, Princess of Monaco, also died in a car crash.)

What was the cause of Diana's crash?
Fitting a BMW with parts from a 1961 Princess. (Oral circulation, 1998)

What's worse than glass in baby food?
Astronauts in tuna. (Oring 1992: 32)

What were Diana's last words to the driver?
Have you ever seen a Princess's tits? (Internet, DER Thoroweb 1997–8)

What was the last thing to go through Christa McAuliffe's (the female civilian schoolteacher sent up in the space shuttle) mind?
A piece of fuselage. (Alternately: her ass.) (Oring 1992: 33. See also Smyth 1986.)

What did the mortuary attendant say as he unzipped the body bag?
Zippady Dodi, Zippady Di. (Internet 1997)

These jokes constitute a remarkable tribute to the power of spontaneous popular humour. They are a truly people's humour, for they owe nothing to the mass media, to script-writers or to published joke-books. They are invented in large numbers by ordinary people and circulate by word of mouth, a process accelerated by the ease of long-distance telephoning, the use of e-mail and the setting up of joke-sites on the Internet. Such jokes never appear on radio or television or in established newspapers, for media executives stringently censor out any such material lest an influential or vociferous segment of their audience or readership feel offended (Davies 1996). Mass media humour is bland, impoverished and timid by comparison with the creations of the ordinary folk who create their very own cycles of highly shocking, riddle-type jokes. These begin as 'proto-jokes', as witticisms that occur spontaneously in conversation in a particular context. Either the author or some other person then polishes and adapts the original remark so that it can be told and understood away from its original context; it becomes a free-standing joke. Further polishing by yet more people makes the structure snappier and the aptly named punchline punchier. Through these endeavours a people's joke is born (Davies 1992: 433–4), something that is more genuinely a *popular creation* than the most heavily watched of sitcoms or the most purchased of blaring tabloids, for these only have audiences and depend on a mere handful of writers, who are set apart from the people for whom they write. Nonetheless the flourishing of jokes about *specific shocking events* in the last thirty years or so *is a product* of the rise of the mass media and in particular of television and of the direct, dogmatic and yet ambiguous and paradoxical way in which accidents and disasters are presented to the public by the media. Such jokes did not exist in their present form in the past; so far as is known, there were no cycles of *contemporary* riddle jokes about the Tay Bridge disaster of 1879 so memorably recorded by William McGonagall, or the sinking of the *Titanic* in 1912, or the death of the dancer Isadora Duncan in the 1920s strangled when her scarf got caught in the wheels of her car, or the eating of the Vicar of Stiffkey by a lion in the 1930s or the crashing of a Comet airliner in the 1950s. There easily could have been jokes on these subjects but there weren't, for there was no television and the mass media had not established their current position of cultural dominance.

Sick humour had, of course, existed from a much earlier time and in the twentieth century there have been the Little Willie joke cycle, possibly stemming from the earlier turn of the century *Ruthless Rhymes* of Harry Graham, followed by the dead baby joke cycle, and the quadriplegic joke cycle (Dundes 1987: 3–18). These jokes display a similar humour of 'playing with the shocking' but they were not focussed on specific events. Humour about specific horrific incidents was at that time more characteristic of the occupational humour of those who experienced risk, danger, accident and disaster as part of their everyday lives, such as high-iron workers in the US construction industry for whom a false step twenty storeys up could mean instant death (Haas 1977). From this latter phenomenon and studies of natural disasters such as earthquakes has arisen the thesis that humour was and is a way of coping with disaster, at least in some cultures (Abe and Ritz 1996). For those who have regularly to experience danger, perhaps it is a way of coping (Obrdlik 1942), much as the savage comic songs of the soldiers of the First World War such as 'The Bells of Hell go ting-a-ling-a-ling for you but not for me' or 'He's hanging on the old barbed wire' may have been a way of dealing with the stress, fear and pain of life in the trenches. It is, however, nonsense to apply this theory to recent jokes about disasters which have only been experienced *indirectly* by means of sanitized television pictures in the safety and comfort of the viewers' own home.

I am not denying that some people feel genuinely moved at distant mass media reported events, just as others get genuinely upset when their favourite soap-opera character is killed off. I am merely saying that these negative emotions are not the source of the telling of disaster jokes. No coping is required by those whose sole link with the world of disaster is through broadcasting. There is nothing for them to need to cope with – no personal stress, no loneliness, no sudden adjustments to make, no void in intimacy caused by the loss of a loved one, no fear, no hardship. All they have to do is to change television channels.

In any case, those who keen at the events of the television set and those who enjoy disaster jokes could be two different (though admittedly over-lapping) sets of people. Why should hard-nosed jokers need humour to cope with the sentimental anguish experienced by a quite different group of people who wouldn't have found the jokes funny anyway?

There is, though, no evidence that the hard-nosed jokers are in everyday life callous people who would feel unmoved in the presence of a real disaster or who in the face of misfortune would pass by on the other side of the road. It is relevant to quote here the splutterings of a Californian media person uttered at the time of the jokes about the death of Christa McAuliffe and the astronauts in the exploding space-shuttle:

> If you have never heard these jokes, count yourself lucky . . . A colleague here at the paper has a whole list of the jokes. They had upset him greatly . . . How could people joke about a thing like this? he asked . . . The McAuliffe jokes are different . . . In them the targets and the tragedy are only too real . . . maybe we joke . . . to satisfy some deep dark urge within us to speak the unspeakable, to push against the limits of decency . . . I am not sure who makes these jokes up . . . I am not sure how they get the jokes spread around the country so fast. I am only really sure of one thing. They are not doing it to be funny. (Oring 1992: 33–4)

He is wrong. They are, and what is more the inventors of the jokes have succeeded, for otherwise the jokes would not be so immensely popular.

The mediaman is, of course, a believer in his own propaganda and unable to see that those who don't take his messages as seriously as he would like and laugh at jokes on the same themes are not callous but simply keenly aware of the incongruities of media-mediated disaster – and incongruity is the source of most humour. The first incongruity is between the mediaperson's urging of viewers, listeners and readers to feel strong emotions that are congruent neither with their physical absence from the scene of the tragedy (Smyth 1986: 236) nor with the sanitized, stylized pictures presented on television, the medium that originally set off modern disaster jokes. The second incongruity is that televised disaster reporting is a rubbish sandwich in which solemn announcements about the disaster and garment-rending calls for grief alternate with trivial quiz shows, banal soap operas, football players hugging and smooching ecstatic at a goal, advertising jingles in a commercial break, a party political broadcast or an appeal for money by an adulterous televangelist.

Modern television cannot be solemn for long; a trivial cheerfulness keeps breaking through. If there is a transport crash in the real world, comedy programmes involving crashes are postponed but that is about the extent of the rescheduling. After Diana's funeral was over, the trivia soon resumed. To some extent the same problem existed in the newspaper era but in newspapers the serious, the solemn and the tragic can be spatially segregated from the trivial, the irreverent and the salacious, and readers can choose to read them separately. In television there is no segregation, merely a temporal sequence of the serious and the trivial such that the two categories merge and viewers have incongruity thrust upon them. It is this incongruity that accounts for the rise of the cycles of disaster jokes *since and only since* television became a dominant medium.

The essential incongruity of television has been well illustrated by Elliott Oring (1992: 38) in relation to the interplay between American disaster jokes and television advertisements:

> a number of the shuttle (as well as other disaster jokes) incongruously employ the names of familiar and amiable commercial products from television advertising: Coke, Seven-Up, Tang, Head and Shoulders, Ocean Spray, Bud Light. 'What were the last words said on the Challenger? . . . I want a light . . . No, a Bud Light.' The juxtaposition of commercial products with images of disaster seems a particularly appropriate commentary on the television medium and images it presents to viewers at home. Television news programs regularly conjoin images and stories of death, disease and destruction with images of commercial products. Virtually every television report of a news disaster is preceded and followed by a commercial message (or each and every commercial message is preceded and followed by the report of a disaster). Thus the concatenation of brand name products and images of disaster achieved in the jokes is really no more incongruous than that achieved several times each evening by national and local television news programs.

It has long been known that humour is often, perhaps usually, rooted in incongruity. The level of incongruity provided by the media and particularly television was perhaps especially high following the death of Diana because of the extraordinarily strong media coverage of her death and funeral. Hence the enormous volume of jokes that followed.

The Diana jokes also invite comparison with another very large genre of jokes, the political jokes of totalitarian countries such as the former Soviet Union and the formerly socialist countries of Eastern Europe. In those countries there was only one ruling political party, one hegemonic ideology and one owner and controller of all newspapers and radio and television broadcasting stations. There was literally a party line and no public deviation from it. In practice most people felt alienated from this monolith and indeed it eventually collapsed in a spectacular fashion, something which was predicted in advance by observers of the jokes (Davies 1989). While communism prevailed there was no freedom of speech but there was freedom of conversation. People used this private freedom to invent jokes that played with the forbidden (Davies 1998a and 1998b), that put into joke form ideas and sentiments that were the very antithesis of those propagated by the apparatchiks who controlled the official media.

> Question to Radio Armenia: Would it be possible to introduce socialism in the Netherlands?
> Answer: In principle, yes, but what have the Dutch ever done to you? (Polish 1980s)

> Under capitalism man exploits man. Under socialism it is exactly the other way round. (East European 1970s)

> Stalin, Khruschev and Brezhnev were travelling in a train when it ground to a halt and refused to go. Stalin said, 'Leave this to me' and left the compartment. Five minutes later he came back and said, 'now it will be alright, I have shot the engine driver.' The train still refused to move. Khruschev now got up and left the compartment. When he came back, he said, 'I have rehabilitated the engine driver, the train will start soon.' The train remained stationary. Next Brezhnev reached across and pulled down the blind plunging the compartment into darkness. 'There you are,' he said, 'now the train is moving.' (Polish 1980s)

> Lenin's widow Krupskaya visited a school to give a talk about Lenin. 'Lenin was a very kind man,' she told the children. 'One day he was shaving outside his dacha in the country, when a little boy came and stared at him. "What are you doing?" asked the little boy. "I am shaving, little boy," replied Lenin.'
> 'Why does that make Lenin a kind man?' asked one of the schoolchildren.
> 'Can't you see?' said Krupskaya. 'Lenin had a razor in his hand and could have cut the little boy's throat, but he didn't.' (Russian 1980s.)

Some of the enthusiastic joke-tellers were enemies of the regime but others among this group occupied privileged positions within it (Deriabin and Gibney 1960: 173-5) and stood to lose if the regime were overthrown or democratized. It was possible for powerful people and supporters of the regime to laugh at the jokes, even though they agreed with the party line and abhorred the thrust of the jokes, for the jokes were time off, a welcome relief from a life of compulsory agreement with the authorities. They took delight in playing with the forbidden, much as American students revel in jokes that defy the earnest political correctness preached at them and forced on them by their college authorities or Roman Catholics delight in jokes about the illicit and often perverse and paedophile sexual practices of the clergy and the members of religious orders and orders of lay brothers.

By the same token, the Diana jokes are also a rebellion against monopoly, against the torrent of sentimentality that poured out of the media's treacle well after her death, against the abrupt canonization of a well-meaning but rather ordinary person whom the press had previously derided, mocked, hounded and harassed. In fairness it must be admitted that Diana had always courted media sensation, manipulated the media with great skill and cunning and warmed and tanned herself in the light of its glowing lime (see e.g. O'Hear 1998: 184–5) but she did not deserve to be chased by paparazzi any more than she deserved to be made a plaster saint. What has also made Diana's death the subject of far more jokes than even the tragic death of Christa McAuliffe (who was also in her thirties and the mother of two even younger children) has been its intense and sentimental celebration by a very large public. Those who tried with high seriousness to point out the excess, the sentimentality, the unseemliness of inappropriate displays of emotion and loss of self-control, the disloyal misuse of the events after her death by closet republicans as a means of attacking the Royal Family and the neglect of the deaths of other worthier people that occurred in the same period of time were put down, pushed out and shut up. After a decent interval the disting-uished philosopher, Professor Anthony O'Hear, noted in a justly celebrated article:

> It is, though, in Diana's role as Queen of Hearts that her and our sentimentality presents herself in its purest form . . . If so Diana and what she stood for and what came through on September 6th were decadent. Feeling was elevated above reason, caring above principle, personal gratification above commitment and propriety . . . the Queen herself had been taunted by the tabloids for staying in seclusion in Balmoral, not showing grief for Diana publicly. Unless the Queen shows some emotion, we'll soon have a republic, we were told . . . A non-stop encounter group took over the area around Kensington Palace. The culture of caring, of niceness, of the people was triumphant. (O'Hear 1998: 188–90)

O'Hear's sensible, measured and insightful comments were received with angry abuse by an outraged press and even the socialist Prime Minister Tony Blair, then in Saudi Arabia, uttered a suitably well-spun rebuke on behalf of caring, niceness and the people (Sylvester 1998). There was very little room for dissent, for on this particular issue, the atmosphere if not the institutions of the old Eastern Europe had temporarily taken over – sentimental central-ism. This emotional monopoly (*Nation Spoke as One*, 1997), only broken by the outrageous satirical journal *Private Eye*, was an obvious invitation to popular humorists to start inventing jokes. Humour is the only area of social life where dialectical relationships prevail, so that the strong assertion of a thesis calls into play a humorous antithesis. The more insistent and emotional the thesis, the more numerous the antithetical jokes. The Diana jokes are a series of reversals of the hegemonic sentimentality, for they are the only way in which independence and opposition can be asserted.

One common theme raised in opposition is the obvious one that all the world's other tragedies were being neglected by those who wallowed in this one:

> A ferryboat leaving Haiti capsized and drowned 300 people. But a tragedy was avoided when they discovered that none of those on board was a princess. (Oral circulation England 1998)

> Why is Jesus different from Diana?

> 1. You don't have to apologize for not believing in Jesus.
> 2. No one ever postponed a Port Vale game for Jesus.
> 3. Schoolchildren can opt out of the compulsory act of worship for Jesus.
> (Internet 1998, Steve Platt)

It is a telling comparison. England, the country that wailed over Diana, fails to celebrate Easter and has forgotten its meaning. The events that followed Diana's death were a display of thoroughly secular and irreligious emotions substituting for a faith that has been lost.

One much repeated theme in the jokes was the mockery of Diana as the glamorous high status 'victim'; this also may well have been the basis of the sense of identification with her of other people who felt themselves to be victims of life in a similar way. In Britain in the 1990s there is a great deal of divorce and a great deal of social mobility and both experiences can bring anomie, uncertainty and unhappiness. Diana Spencer, though already an aristocrat, had been upwardly mobile at the very top of the social scale by marrying royalty and becoming Princess of Wales and had found it difficult to adjust to life at the pinnacle. She had been forced out, going through a distressing divorce and lost her royal title as HRH. Women lower down the social scale from working-class backgrounds, unable to adjust to the mores of the lower-middle class, or lower-middle class women finding it difficult to adapt to the ways of the upper-middle class, could all identify with Diana as could divorcees and bulimics. The Princess of Wales built further on this victim image by systematically visiting, smiling at, hugging and cuddling other categories of victims such as those suffering from AIDS (which endeared her to male homosexuals and to show business people) or people blown up by landmines (which led her to meddle unwisely and unconstitutionally in political matters). It was Diana's 'high-status victim' and 'lover of victims' image that was a crucial generator of grief when she died. The oppositional jokes pick on and mock exactly the categories of victims with which she sought to associate herself:

Tonight we could all memorialize the sainted Mother Teresa and the beloved Princess Diana by eating curry and then sticking our fingers down our throats. (Oral circulation, England 1998)

Did you know Diana has AIDS?
Automobile Impacted Diana Spencer.
Another Idiot Driver Smashed. (Internet 1998)

How did the Royal Family stop the paparazzi from visiting Diana's grave?
By placing landmines around it. (Internet 1998)

Why is Jesus different from Diana?
Jesus only healed the lame. He never got his picture taken with them. (Internet 1998, Steve Platt)

Diana, Queen of Hearts?
More like, off with her head. (Internet 1998)

Why did Elton John take his boyfriend to the funeral?
So at least one old queen would be seen to cry in public. (Internet 1998)

As the last joke suggests, the jokers were willing to comment in a detached and cynical way on the rift between Diana and the Royal Family. Where the Diana fans, including her brother, had taken sides and attacked the Royal Family for their alleged indifference and supposed preference for protocol over mass feeling, the jokers took it for granted in a totally unjudgemental way that Diana had been a nuisance to the Royal Family and that they may well have been glad to see the last of her. The jokes do not comment on this, they merely state it.

What did Prince Charles say when he heard the news?
Shall I garage your bike, mum? (Internet 1997)

When Prince Charles was told of Diana's death he was all ears. (Internet, ThoroWeb 1997–8)

What is the Queen giving Fergie for Christmas?
Two tickets for Paris and a chauffeur driven Mercedes. (Oral circulation, England 1998)

In these several different ways the jokers have creatively and inventively defied the ruling sentiments of the time and inverted the assumptions of a media-dominated culture about the death of Diana. They show that the popular judgement about Diana is not unanimous. The jokes taken as a whole, and there are very many of them, are oppositional in the same sense that political jokes were in the old Eastern Europe, involving a deliberate pleasure in breaking a taboo and defiance of a suffocating hegemonic set of attitudes. They are the people's jokes in a more profound sense than she was the people's princess for they really are the jokes of 'us' against 'them', the them who try to tell us what we ought to think and feel. It may well be that many of us would think and feel in the prescribed way anyway but the compulsion is still likely to be resented. The jokes with their suggestion of conflict and of resistance to control are more true to the nature of not just Britain but of all modern industrial societies than the false cosy-Blairie myth of the unity of the people. In a Britain where an unfortunate Japanese businessman can be universally abused in the press because it was revealed that he said in private 'Princess Diana has a long nose' (Warden and Gysin 1998), a traditional Japanese appellation for Westerners, the jokes are a necessary form of resistance.

The Diana jokes, like the image of Diana herself and like the over-reaction to her death, are very much a product of the dominant position now held in society by the mass media and especially television. This works at two levels and in two opposed ways. The first is that many individuals are sucked into direct involvement with distant or even fictitious persons with whom they have no direct contact, such as the question of whether Deirdre from the Northern soap 'Coronation Street' should go to jail. The second is that viewers, listeners and readers have come to laugh in defiance of the media, when they are over-preached at following a disaster, in this case the death of a princess. Because the media class has so much manipulative power over viewers, listeners and readers, its members have come falsely to assume that they are the legitimate social leaders of a community, of a *Gemeinschaft*. They are horrified when from time to time disaster jokes and other popular cynical humour remind them that there is no global village, only a mass of alienated individuals trapped in dysfunctional, urban settlements where 'Neighbours' has replaced neighbours. Television cannot put together what it has clearly destroyed.

My analysis of the Diana jokes in terms of the incongruity of television and the mass media and of resistance to cultural hegemony will not please those who are offended by the jokes and want a moral put-down of jokes apparently hostile to Diana, not an explanation. But as Willie Smyth noted after the Challenger jokes:

> It is unlikely that hostility is directed either at NASA or the disaster victims in any personal sense. The fact that the same jokes with altered names and places appear

after many disasters is evidence that the hostility is not usually directed towards the victims and topical references but to some psychically significant theme underlying the jokes. What is regularly depicted in these jokes is death, deformation, disease and illness. Decapitation, decomposition, bodies washing ashore, being eaten by fish or blown to bits recur as themes in the disaster jokes, often despite the fact that the graphic portrayal is an inaccurate representation of what actually happened to the victims. (Smyth 1986: 252–3)

Diana's heart was in the right place, if you consider the glove compartment to be the right place. (Oral circulation, England 1997. Also on Internet. Danish 1998)

Did you hear that Princess Di was on the radio a couple of weeks ago?
Yep, and on the dashboard and on the window and on the hood. (Internet, American 1998)

Just as jokes about sex or racial groups or in the old Eastern Europe about the political system play with the shocking, with the unmentionable, with the forbidden, with the politically incorrect, so too do jokes about death. There is no need to invoke unconscious forces such as repression or guilt in explaining the joy people take in playing with the forbidden in jokes. In Eastern Europe it might have been imprudent to tell jokes against the regime but very few people felt guilty about telling such jokes, since they had no internalized sense of loyalty to their illegitimate rulers; the same is true of those who tell jokes breaking the rules of political correctness which are perceived as external and coercively imposed. Ask any 'good old boy'.

Death and its concomitants, decay and dissolution, are a taboo area in a modern society and are either denied or hidden away. The delusion is maintained that through diet and jogging and being protected from saccharine, beef on the bone and passive smoking (Neal and Davies 1998) we can all remain young, ageless and physically perfect for ever, perhaps with a little help from the embalmer (Davies 1996). When alive, Diana epitomized this fantasy despite a few problems with bulimia and cellulite, and, in the view of the Japanese, an excessively long nose. She was the fairy-tale princess, forever moderately young, glamorous and radiant with a glistening smile and thighs gripped in tight shorts for her latest gym conveyor-belt workout. Hence, the tremendous shock when she proved to be mortal and breakable like everyone else; in this way a delusion that many people share was exploded. It is this delusion and its temporary violent shattering that provided one of the bases for the Diana jokes. The jokes play with the shocking shattering of simulated youth by sudden accidental death, a fate that can happen to anyone and now and again does. The mass distress at Diana's death was thus profoundly irreligious for it was based on the idea that a this-worldly immortality can be attained by purely secular means. If Diana's nose had been a lot longer, Cyrano longer, they wouldn't have grieved. This same widespread, almost unchallenged, ideology of safety and youth and perfection for ever underlies many of the jokes.

What do you give the princess who has everything?
A seat-belt and an airbag. (Internet 1998)

What's Di getting for Xmas?
The Queen Mother. (Internet 1998)

It seems likely that many of those who have told and enjoyed the Diana jokes had themselves been shocked at the time of her death or had watched her obsequies. The observations about human ambivalence made by Smyth in relation to the American shuttle disaster apply in the case of the Diana jokes too:

> Herein lies the paradox that underlies most of the jokes about public tragedies . . . the media made (the disaster) appear as if it happened to people we really knew but for most Americans this was not a private tragedy as in the death of friends or loved ones but a public tragedy which victimised people who could not be grieved for with the same intensity . . . The great sense of personal loss accompanying a personal tragedy generally keeps people from readily making jokes about the events . . . Unlike personal tragedies which leave haunting memories such as childhood days spent together or regrets for all the emotional debts which can never be repaid, the losses people feel when those whom they do not know are victimized by tragedy tend to be less heart-felt and more replaceable. (Smyth 1986: 256–7)

Smyth goes on to suggest on the basis of his own observations that 'many of the people who tell disaster jokes react to the news of the incident with horror and sadness' (Smyth 1986: 257). An essentially similar sequence probably took place with the Diana jokes, with more and more people being drawn into the joking as their initial sense of shock and horror subsided (Gunnell 1998).

Seen overall, the Diana and disaster jokes are not really shocking at all for they indicate a sense of proportion, a recognition that this was not the same thing as a personal bereavement and a statement that grief beyond a certain time and intensity is inappropriate; the jokes suggest that in the case of the death of Diana many people failed to respect and observe these limits. The most shocking of these is the case 'of the man who said Diana's death meant more to him than that of his parents' (O'Hear 1998: 183).

Many will find this claim far more upsetting than any of the jokes about the death of Diana. For anyone who has experienced the searing and continuing sense of loss felt after the death of a parent, child or other close relative, the idea that it could even be compared with the feelings following the death of a media-image stranger, however worthy, is grossly offensive. It indicates that for many people their more hysterical, emotional and inappropriate impulses have broken the old framework that put the private and the familial first and that they have gone to live in a false world of electronic images. It is a bad omen, a sign of future social collapse.

By contrast the jokes about Diana's death are essentially harmless. No one is any the worse off for their existence (unless someone foolishly tells them to her surviving close relatives, but that would be the fault of the immediate teller) but large numbers of jokers have exercised a great deal of creativity in producing them and obtained a great deal of fun from them. As Alan Dundes (1987: 80) has put it: 'Jokes themselves are neither good nor evil . . . It is, therefore, futile to protest against the existence of sick humour. As long as natural and human-made disasters occur, jokes about these disasters are probably inevitable.'

But is it true? A Methodological Postscript.

There are many ways in which the numerous jokes told after the death of Diana could have been collected and analysed. How is it possible for me to claim that there is more truth in my version of events than in possible rival accounts? In essence I am using a comparative method, as against the approach of those who know little about responses to Diana's death because that is all that they do know. By contrast, I have systematically sought out other circumstances in the past that have produced similar cycles of jokes, notably other disasters, and looked for common elements in the genesis and content of both sets of jokes; from this, some kind of causality can be inferred. The argument is strengthened by bringing into play another more distant but similar genre of jokes – the political jokes of the former socialist countries of Eastern Europe and the Soviet Union. From this comparison emerges a broader factor, namely that all the jokes involve a playing with the forbidden and a defiance of a hegemonic ideology or hegemonic sentimentality.

It is also important to apply a second methodological principle – the identification of joke cycles that could exist or could have existed but which in fact do not or did not exist. Prior to our modern cultural dominance by television there were no large cycles of disaster jokes and it is therefore reasonable to postulate that the uniquely incongruous way in which television presents disasters, including the death of Diana, is the source of the jokes.

The comparative method thus tries to locate the truth by means of empirical triangulation based on the author's experience of tens of thousands of jokes from many cultures and circumstances. Without comparison (the nearest thing sociologists and historians have to an experiment) all attempts to read off the meaning of a joke become mere expressions of the observer's own framework for viewing them. To compare and to compare and to compare is the only true method.

Bibliography

Abe, G. and Ritz S. (1996) Survivor Humor in Disasters, Research Institute for Comparative Culture, Tokushima Bunri University, *Annual Report,* 12: 20–8.

Alvin, J. (1983) *Gross Jokes*, New York: Zebra.

—— (1983a) *Totally Gross Jokes*, New York: Zebra.

—— (1984) *Utterly Gross Jokes*, New York: Zebra.

Bronner, S. J. (1985) 'What's Grosser than Gross: New Sick Joke Cycles', *Midwestern Journal of Language and Lore*, 11: 72-81.

Davies, C. (1989) 'Humor for the Future and a Future for Humor' in A. Shtromas and M. A. Kaplan (eds), *The Soviet Union and the Challenge of The Future, vol 3 Ideology Culture and Nationality*, New York: Paragon, pp. 299–319.

—— (1990) 'Nasty Legends, Sick Humor and Ethnic Jokes about Stupidity' in G. Bennett and P. Smith (eds), *A Nest of Vipers*, Sheffield: Sheffield Academic Press: 49–68.

—— (1992) Review of 'In Stitches', *Humor the International Journal of Humor Research*, 4–5: 431–5.

—— (1996) 'Dirt, Death, Decay and Dissolution: American Denial and British Avoidance', in G. Howarth and P. Jupp (eds), *Contemporary Issues in the Sociology of Death, Dying and Disposal*, Basingstoke: Macmillan, pp. 60–71.

—— (1996) 'Puritanical and Politically Correct, a Critical, Historical Account of Changes in the Censorship of Comedy by the BBC' in C. Powell, G. Paton and S. Wagg (eds), *The Social Faces of Humour: Practices and Issues*, Aldershot: Ashgate, pp. 29–61.

—— (1998a) 'The Dog that Didn't Bark in the Night: a Sociological Approach to the Cross-Cultural Study of Humour' in W. Ruch (ed.), *The Sense of Humor, Explorations of a Personality Characteristic*, Berlin and New York: Mouton de Gruyter, pp 293–306.

—— (1998b) *Jokes and their Relation to Society*, Berlin and New York: Mouton de Gruyter.

Deriabin, P. and Gibney, F. (1960) *The Secret World*, London: Arthur Barker.

Dundes, A. (1987a) *Cracking Jokes*, Berkeley: Ten Speed Press.

—— (1987b) 'At Ease, Disease – AIDS Jokes as Sick Humor', *American Behavioural Scientist*, 30: 72–81.

Gunnell, B. (1998) 'If mourning Diana isn't your cup of tea, is it at last all right to tell those tacky jokes', *The Observer*, 22 March.

Haas, J. (1977) 'Learning Real Feelings, a study of high-steel ironworkers reaction to fear and danger', *Sociology of Work and Occupation*, 4(2): 147–70.

Kaufman, G. (ed) (1991) *In Stitches*, Bloomington: Indiana University Press.

Knott, B. (1982-4) *Truly Tasteless Jokes: Vols 1–4*, New York: Ballantine.

Macintyre, B. (1997) 'French angry at "scandalous" size of Diana inquiry', *The Times*, 7 November: 11.

'Nation Spoke as One After Death' (1997) *South Wales Echo*, 30 December: 6–7.

Neal, M. and Davies, C. (1998) *The Corporation under Siege, Exposing the Devices used by Activists and Regulators in the Non-Risk Society*, London: Social Affairs Unit.

Obrdlik, A.J. (1942) 'Gallows Humor, A Sociological Phenomenon', *American Journal of Sociology*, 47: 709-16.

O'Hear, A. (1998) 'Diana Queen of Hearts, Sentimentality Personified and Canonised', in D. Anderson and P. Mullen (eds) (1998), *Faking It, The sentimentalisation of modern society*, London: SAU: 181–90.

Oring, E. (1992) *Jokes and their Relations*, Lexington: University Press of Kentucky.

Simons, E.R. (1986) 'The NASA Joke-Cycle: The Astronauts and the Teacher', *Western Folklore*, 45: 261–77.

Smith, P. (1989) 'Aids, don't die of ignorance: exploring the cultural complex' in G. Bennett and P. Smith (eds), *A Nest of Vipers*, Sheffield: Sheffield Academic Press: 113–41.

Smyth, W. (1986) 'Challenger Jokes and the Humor of Disaster', *Western Folklore*, 55: 243–60.

Sylvester, R. (1998) 'Diana critics are snobs says Blair', *Daily Telegraph*, 20 April.

Thickett, M (1983) *Outrageously Offensive Jokes: vols 1&2*, New York: Pocket.

Warden, B. and Gysin, C. (1998) 'Princess Diana has a big nose and the women here are fat pigs', *Daily Mail*, 24 April.

Wilde, L. (1979) *The Official Book of Sick Jokes*, Los Angeles: Pinnacle.

Wilson, A.N. (1998) 'The Danger of Charles playing up to the Hype', *Evening Standard*, 10 February: 11.

Internet Web-Sites containing Diana Jokes
(Most of the Internet jokes occur on more than one site.)

1. Http://www.herald.com/tropic/docs/008947.htm
2. Http://www.hjem.get2net.dk/nonline/home5/dijoke.2.htm
3. Http://www.msnbc.com/news/108086.asp
4. Http://www.ricardis.tudelft.nl/blokkendoos/misc/Diana-jokes.htm
5. Http://www.tip.net.av/~bpalmer/diana.htm

Acknowledgements

Many people have helped me in the compilation of the jokes and other materials cited above. My thanks to Goh Abe, Elliott Oring, Eugene Trivizas, Tony Walter, Roy Wolfe and the students who took my course Sociology of Morality in 1997–8 and did the practical work in the section Sociology of Humour.

Part 5

Conclusion

18

And The Consequence Was . . .

Tony Walter

In reading the history of nations, we find that, like individuals, they have their whims and their peculiarities; their seasons of excitement and recklessness, when they care not what they do. We find that whole communities suddenly fix their minds upon one object, and go mad in its pursuit; that millions of people become simultaneously impressed with one delusion, and run after it, till their attention is caught by some new folly more captivating than the first . . .

These words from the introduction to MacKay's *Extraordinary Popular Delusions and the Madness of Crowds* (1852, vol. 1: vii) might have been written a century and a half later by any of those who criticized the mourning for Diana as mass hysteria. MacKay continues however:

. . . We see one nation suddenly seized, from its highest to its lowest members, with a fierce desire of military glory; another as suddenly becoming crazed upon a religious scruple; and neither of them recovering its senses until it has shed rivers of blood and sowed a harvest of groans and tears, to be reaped by posterity.

Mackay's two-volume work includes case studies of the Crusades, the South Sea Bubble, witch-hunting and duelling, all of which clearly had serious and (in the light of hindsight) terrible consequences. Compared to these, the 'floral fascism' of Diana's mourners seems distinctly innocuous in its consequences. In this brief and inevitably tentative concluding chapter, written in November 1998, I will discuss some of the actual and possible consequences of the mourning for Diana.

It is clear from the preceding chapters that there is very little in the mourning that was utterly new, and therefore little that could possibly start an entirely new trend. Even the clapping from the crowd as the cortège passed on the day of the funeral, remarked by some as an innovation ('people don't clap at funerals'), is not: video footage reveals precisely the same wave of modest clapping as the cortège of King Baudouin passed the Belgian crowds four years earlier. A British funeral that concluded with clapping had been screened a decade earlier as part of a BBC television documentary (*Remember Terry*) about the death of a man from AIDS. Drivers stopping their cars on the southbound M1 motorway to watch the cortège as it drove north, along with crowds of pedestrians standing on the northbound carriageway, was surely unprecedented, but has (thankfully!) not started a trend in motorway behaviour. But Diana's mourning, if not in itself constituting a cultural revolution, did have consequences.

The Next Twelve Months

If the world was shocked to hear on 31 August 1997 that Diana was dead, the ensuing months revealed that, for most people, she had not died at all. Though thousands had met her or knew people who had, millions more never had and knew her only as a media image. Her image was as present in the ensuing as in the preceding year, and in that sense after 31 August she remained as socially alive (Mulkay 1993) as she had been before, as socially alive as she was physically dead. Several popular biographies emerged in the ensuing months, foremost among them being the reissue in October 1997 of Andrew Morton's 1992 *Diana – Her True Story* as *Diana – Her True Story in Her Own Words*. It transpired that the book was based on taped interviews with Diana, and is as much autobiography as biography. Interest in the 'real' Diana continued at an all-time high, prompting considerable controversy. Some argued that people needed to know the truth, others that it was too soon after the death, and did two grieving young boys really need to know how unhappy their mother had been, or how unfaithful their father? The need of mourners to discuss endlessly who exactly it is they are mourning (Walter 1996) was played out to the great profit of certain publishers and virtually all the national newspapers. The early calls for stronger laws restraining journalists and photographers from invading individuals' privacy came to nothing. Politically, the most obvious consequence was the British government's willingness to push through the treaty banning landmines.

Donations continued to pour into the Diana memorial fund, which itself became a frequent topic for news stories. By May 1998, the fund was receiving two hundred applications a week to use Diana's name or image (chiefly for advertising purposes), in addition to which there were many unlicensed uses. A controversy over whether Flora margarine should have been re-branded as Flora Diana margarine was but the tip of an iceberg of commercial and charitable exploitation of her name and image. (Flora sponsored the April 1998 London Marathon, in which Diana's butler ran.)

By the end of 1997, the messy divorce of Earl Spencer had squandered most of the credibility he had gained from his funeral oration. His opening of a Diana museum at Althorp, the family estate, to be open each summer for a couple of months received mixed reviews but was, predictably, sold out. Meanwhile, the Windsors began a long and to date successful rehabilitation, aided by a press that faithfully printed pictures of a more touch-feely Monarch and Prince of Wales doing their best to imitate something of Diana's highly popular informality. In November 1997, the Queen and Prince Philip invited a wide range of 'ordinary people' to their fiftieth wedding anniversary banquet. The Queen visited a pub and a McDonalds hamburger restaurant and made sure the press were there to photograph these visits.

'Men . . . go mad in herds, while they only recover their senses slowly, and one by one.' (MacKay 1852: viii) Most people's grief was short-lived, and a proportion of mourners came to wonder why they had behaved as they had, though polls in the *Mail* (23 August 1998) and the *Mirror* (24 August 1998) did not agree as to the percentages who felt that they or others had over-reacted. The press portrayed the continuing interest in Diana as a continuation of grief – I was regularly asked by journalists in the first half of 1998 when the mourning was going to end? My reply was that it already had done, way back in early autumn 1997, and that continuing interest need not equate with continuing grief. Journalists (American as well as British) geared up to cover the anniversary. A number rang me, confessing after a while 'I'm really bored with the whole thing and want to take the bank-holiday weekend off with my family, but my editor wants me in London to provide copy on what people are doing for the anniversary.' In the event, very little happened at the anniversary. That said, when in October 1998 a biography of Prince Charles was published that portrayed Diana in less than flattering terms (Junor 1998), its hostile reception revealed that it was still too soon to go into print criticizing the Princess. Though grief was for the majority of people long over, the requirement to idealize that so often accompanies mourning was by no means over.

Long-term Effects

Mourning   A society's culture of mourning is never static. Though Western society in the twentieth century has been described as one in which death is taboo or hidden (Ariès 1974), there have been clear signs of death and its representations becoming more visible in the last third of the century (Walter 1991a, 1994). More public forms of mourning seem to be coming back into fashion. One is the ribbon, worn originally in support of those with AIDS, subsequently expanding through a range of colours for a range of causes.

After Diana's death, a number of personalities and other mourners were seen sporting black ribbons. Does this herald the return of mourning wear?

Another revived ritual is the minute's silence, observed at 3.06 p.m. in the city centres of Liverpool, Nottingham and Sheffield the week after the Hillsborough disaster on 15 April 1989, and nationwide in churches and other gathering places on the Sunday after the Dunblane shooting in Spring 1996. Since 1995, many supermarkets now stand silent for two minutes at 11 a.m. on 11 November, and are exploring other ways of becoming cathedrals of the post-Christian era. Their provision of books of condolence for Diana and the shutdown of virtually all shops on the morning of her funeral (Chapter 14) indicate that for deaths that capture the public's attention, gestures of public mourning are once again possible. Whether the mourning for Diana will further this ritual development is still an open question. Given the criticisms subsequently levelled at her mourning as excessive, not least by those who themselves engaged in it, it may be that in future institutions will be more cautious in leaping to provide time and space for public gestures of grief.

Spontaneous memorialization at the scene of accidents and other tragic deaths has evolved rapidly over the past fifteen years. Leaving flowers at the scene of an accident is a tradition going back much further (Monger 1997), but recently the numbers engaging in such practices have escalated – probably because of television and tabloid coverage of disasters such as Hillsborough and the Oklahoma City bombing. Curiously (Haney et al 1997, see also Chapter 15), this escalation has occurred simultaneously in both Britain and the USA. It seems unlikely that British behaviour has been affected significantly by news coverage of American folk responses to disaster, or vice versa, so we are not talking about a simple media-amplification effect. There is clear evidence that, within hours of both the Hillsborough disaster (Walter 1991b) and the death of Diana, large numbers of people responded by going with flowers and messages to what they individually intuited as the symbolic place of pilgrimage – *before* they had seen any television coverage of others engaging in this behaviour. Recent royal deaths in Belgium and (Aagedal 1994) Norway provide interesting national variations. The interaction between folk custom, grief and the mass media requires more research before we can say exactly how this kind of mourning behaviour has evolved and how, if at all, the mourning for Diana created any mutation in its evolution.

Reacting against charges of impersonality and hypocrisy, the 1990s have seen a substantial proportion of British funerals become more personal and less bound by traditional religious requirements. Still, though, a number of Anglican clergy refuse requests from families to play pop music or to abandon the funeral sermon in favour of a personal eulogy. It seems hard to know how clergy can refuse such requests in future when the family's response is likely to be 'But Princess Diana had a pop song/eulogy at her funeral, in Westminster Abbey and with the Archbishop of Canterbury in attendance!' Diana's wedding did not create white weddings but certainly boosted the fashion for them; so too her funeral did not create the personalized funeral but will inevitably boost its fortunes.

Nation and politics   It has been commented that Diana's death did for Tony Blair what the Falklands War did for Margaret Thatcher: turned them from Prime Ministers into Presidents, giving them the authority to dominate their own parties and thus the national polity. Blair promised that her legacy will be a 'more compassionate Britain' (*Daily Telegraph*, 8 September 1997, p.1). A few weeks after Diana's death, the Conservative Party annual conference concluded that the party had lost the May 1997 election because – unlike Blair – it had not been like Diana, it had not been touchy-feely. Two of the hardest men of John Major's deposed government appeared as penitents on the conference stage: 'Our reputation has suffered because we failed to wear our hearts on our sleeves' (Michael Portillo). 'It's to do with language . . . After eighteen years the people got fed up with our language' (Michael Howard) (*Daily Telegraph*, 10 October 1997). The new party leader, William Hague, concurred: 'Hague seeks the party that cares' announced *The Times* in its front page headline the same day. Whatever else the week of mourning was, it was a liminal celebration of mother love and human compassion over 'the dominant values of greed, territoriality and war that make up so much of the usual international news' (Sofoulis 1997: 18). Consequently, a generation of political leaders now has to present a caring image, however tough their actual policies.

Fears that the mourning for Diana revealed, or encouraged, a worrying form of fascism in which the will of 'the people' (actually a minority of the population) triumphed over the silent majority were, I argued in Chapter 2, misplaced. After no death is anyone allowed to object to the mourning until the deceased is properly buried. More worrying was the story that, a month or so later, temporarily pushed Diana off the headlines: the mindless support for another English rose, the nineteen year-old nanny Louise Woodward, tried by a Massachusetts court for murdering the baby in her charge. While countless studies have shown that grief entails a certain madness and that mourning reverses normal social structure, to proclaim a defendant as innocent simply on the basis that she belongs to one's own village or nation and is being tried by a foreign court – that is truly worrying.

Diana herself was no narrow English nationalist. Nava (1997) has argued that Diana's friendships with outsiders, foreigners and especially Muslims was the basis of her appeal to an ethnically diverse Britain. She connected with ethnic minorities, and also with the homeless, without losing touch with *Hello!*-reading middle England, an achievement not matched by the otherwise remarkable new Labour government. She celebrated a glamorous, ethnically diverse Britain in touch with the non-Western world, not as the mother of a Commonwealth of nations but as a woman who identified with the 'other'. She redefined what it means to be British (or was it English?). Whether her life and death will actually help bring ethnic minorities in the from the cold, as her holding the hand of a man dying from AIDS did for the gay community, remains to be seen.

Monarchy   If there will be any significant long-term effect of the mourning for Diana, it is likely to be on the evolving style of the monarchy. Diana's 'people' are not calling for any European-style bicycling monarchy, but they do want a hugging monarchy. That millions were clearly attracted by her warmer, more vulnerable style and mourned her in precisely this style got through to the Windsors what Diana had failed to get through to them in life: that they were cold, stuffy and out of touch, and had better shape up if the monarchy was to retain popular legitimacy. The speech that the Queen made from Buckingham Palace toward the end of the week of mourning pledged that there were 'lessons to be drawn from (Diana's) life and from the extraordinary and moving reaction to her death'. Clearly, the Windsors were doing their best in the ensuing twelve months to restyle their image, and to this extent Diana's death – undoubtedly aided by a prime minister in tune with her emotional, populist style – may have saved the monarchy. Not from immediate extinction, but from a long lingering illness. If the Monarch is the representative Briton, then the youthful and beautiful Elizabeth's family had mastered representing themselves as the 1950s family gathered around the bakelite radio (Williamson 1986), but subsequently struggled to represent a more recent generation brought up on glitz, chat shows and emotional disclosure. Diana's death forced the Windsors into attempting this, to them doubtless uncongenial, transformation.

But Diana's death left them with a conundrum, namely the routinization of charisma. Royals have to be special yet ordinary (Billig 1992, ch.4), indeed they are in reality the most ordinary of famous people, having done nothing (unlike presidents, pop-musicians, movie or sports stars) to achieve their position. Their position is ascribed entirely by birth, and requires no personal talent of any kind, which is precisely why they can represent their subjects (Williamson 1986). Those such as the Queen Mother and King Baudouin who perfect this combination of being special yet ordinary, royal yet 'one of us', evoke from their subjects not just respect, but love. As her mourners' messages bore witness (Figure 10.5), Diana evoked more love than any other royal in living memory, in any country, indeed it became her trademark. More than this, she was beautiful, glamorous and charmed everyone she met. Elizabeth had once been beautiful, but Diana will always be beautiful. All this makes hers a particularly difficult act to follow – the more so because, for Diana, much of it was not an act. Somehow, the royals have to learn how to cultivate more personal charisma, while acknowledging that they will never be as beautiful or as glamorous or as loved as Diana. Combining vulnerability and regality as did Diana is easier for a woman than for a man; whether, as Davies suggested in Chapter 1, King William V will in the eyes of his subjects inherit his mother's charisma remains to be seen.

Walter Bagehot's *The English Constitution* (1867) was read by both George V and George VI in preparing for kingship. Bagehot advised the Monarch that his duties were 'grave, formal, important, but never exciting'. This worked up until the last quarter of the twentieth century, but then social changes and failing royal marriages undermined this dull but worthy image. By the 1980s, the Windsors came to be seen as 'cold-hearted, aloof, and miserably dull in contrast to Diana. The mourning for her had a strong element of yearning for excitement in national life, for something that would bring Britain glamour and glory' (Bennett and Rowbottom 1998). The Queen's subjects, living in a glossy global televisual age yet also inhabiting an increasingly dreary and not-so-great Britain, preferred Diana to Elizabeth (or Charles) as their representative figure. In inviting television cameras into their palaces years before Diana's wedding, the Windsors had initiated a slow process of change that was catalysed by her death into a wholly unstoppable force. Post-Diana, the traditional authority of the Monarch must be supplemented both by personal charisma and by the vulnerability of the modern celebrity whose private life is laid open to public gaze, and that is a terrible burden for the ordinary person that the Monarch is, and must be.

Bibliography

Aagedal, O. (1994) 'The Grief for a King and the Grief over a War' in O. Aagedal *Doden pa Norsk (Death in Norway)*, Oslo: Ad Notam Gyldendal.

Ariès, P. (1974) *Western Attitudes toward Death: From the Middle Ages to the Present*, Baltimore: Johns Hopkins University Press.

Bagehot, W. (1867/1965) *The English Constitution*, Glasgow: Fontana.

Bennett, G. and Rowbottom, A. (1998) 'Born a Lady, Married a Prince, Died a Saint: the Reification of Diana in the Press and Popular Opinion in Britain', unpublished paper.

Billig, M. (1992) *Talking of the Royal Family*, London: Routledge.

Haney, C.A., Leimer, C., and Lowery, J. (1997) 'Spontaneous Memorialization: Violent Death and Emerging Mourning Ritual', *Omega*, 35: 159–71.

Junor, P. (1998) *Charles: victim or villain?*, London: HarperCollins.

Mackay, C. (1852) *Extraordinary Popular Delusions and the Madness of Crowds*, Vols 1 & 2, London: Office of the National Illustrated Library.

Monger, G. (1997) 'Modern Wayside Shrines', *Folklore*, 108: 113–14.

Morton, A. (1992) *Diana – Her Own True Story*, London: Michael O'Mara Books.

—— (1997) *Diana – Her Own True Story in Her Own Words*, London: Michael O'Mara Books.

Mulkay, M. (1993) Social Death in Britain' in D. Clark (ed.), *The Sociology of Death*, Oxford: Blackwell.

Nava, M. (1997) 'Diana, Princess of Others: the Politics and Romance of "Race"', pp. 19–26 in Re:Public (ed.), *Planet Diana: Cultural Studies and Global Mourning*, Kingswood, NSW: Research Centre in Intercommunal Studies, University of Western Sydney.

Sofoulis, Z. (1997) 'Icon, Referent, Trajectory, World', pp. 13–18 in Re:Public (ed.), *Planet Diana: Cultural Studies and Global Mourning*, Kingswood, NSW: Research Centre in Intercommunal Studies, University of Western Sydney.

Walter, T. (1991a) 'Modern Death: Taboo or Not Taboo?' *Sociology*, 25(2): 293–310.

—— (1991b) 'The Mourning after Hillsborough', *Sociological Review*, 39(3): 599–625.

—— (1994) *The Revival of Death*, London and New York: Routledge.

—— (1996) 'A New Model of Grief: Bereavement and Biography', *Mortality*, 1(1): 7–25.

Williamson, J. (1986) 'Royalty and Representation', pp. 75–89 in *Consuming Passions*, London: Marion Boyars.

Index